■

And so, prepared for coping with dreams by discussion, and equipped for sweet dreaming by protective figures, may our children cross the border to sleep. May they feel loved and protected while they dream and return, when they awake, bearing treasures from the night.

— Patricia Garfield (1985)

DREAMWORKING

How To Use Your Dreams
For Creative Problem-Solving

By

Stanley Krippner, Ph.D.
Joseph Dillard, Ph.D.

Illustrated by

Fariba Bogzaran

bearly limited

Copyright © 1988

Bearly Limited
149 York Street
Buffalo, New York 14213

Printed in the United States of America
ISBN 0-943456-25-8

Copyrights & Permissions

For Montague Ullman, M.D., who has taught so many of us how to work wisely with our dreams.

ERRATA:

p. 157

Morris Stein (1974) once prepared a list of precepts to reflect the ways that industrial researchers may have to behave in order to adequately fulfill their roles while obtaining the opportunity to pursue their creative interests. Noting that these precepts should not be taken too literally, and presenting them in a humorous vein, Stein observed that:

1. "The industrial researcher is to be assertive without being hostile or aggressive.

2. He is to be aware of his superiors, colleagues, and subordinates as persons but is nevertheless not to become too personally involved with them.

3. He may be a lone wolf on the job, but he is not to be isolated, withdrawn, or uncommunicative. If he is any of these he had best be particularly creative so that his work speaks for itself.

4. On the job he is expected to be congenial but not sociable.

5. Off the job he is expected to be sociable but not intimate.

6. With superiors he is expected to 'know his place' without being timid, obsequious, submissive, or acquiescent.

7. But he is also expected to 'speak his mind' without being domineering.

8. As he tries to gain a point, more funds, or more personnel, he can be subtle but not cunning.

9. In all relationships he is expected to be sincere, honest, purposeful, and diplomatic, but never unwilling to accept 'shortcuts,' be flexible, or Machiavellian.

10. Finally, in the intellectual area he is expected to be broad without spreading himself thin, deep without becoming pedantic, and 'sharp' without being overcritical" (pp. 260-261).

Stein points out that role analyses such as these are not yet available for creative persons working in a variety of fields but that, "If they were, we could possibly understand better the role conflicts that all creative persons endure and possibly develop ways of coping with them. In this manner not only would creative persons have more time and energy available for creativity but there would also be less confusion in the communication between creative persons and others" (p. 261). We agree with Stein in recognizing the complexity of the situation confronting the creative individual in the organization. No one is suggesting that creative persons do anything unethical, even though — for some people — ethical questions may arise.

Contents

The authors would like to thank David Feinstein, Karen Hagerman-Muller, Steve Hart, Cael Kendall, Lelie Krippner, Patrick Scott, David Sweet, and Larissa Vilenskaya for their helpful contributions and suggestions.

Introduction

It's a pleasure and an honor to provide an introduction to this impressive work. Drs. Krippner and Dillard are to be congratulated for having produced an extremely readable, broad-ranging book on the potential of dreams for helping each of us to become a more fully aware and awake human being.

The authors trace the cultural role of dreams from antiquity to the present and provide succinct summaries of the many theories which have been advanced for our nocturnal imagery, ranging from visits by deities to models of cognitive processing based upon computer technology. The facts which have emerged from laboratory studies of EEG-monitored sleeping individuals about the frequency and duration of dreaming and the physiological changes accompanying them are presented in a very comprehensible manner. The authors bring together considerable material related to creativity and problem-solving and make several suggestions about how these principles could be applied in practical ways in an educational or business setting. However, marketplace applications are kept in an appropriate perspective and the possible enhancement of spiritual growth through attention to dreams is also considered.

Recognizing that we still know little about the parameters of the mind, Krippner, who has had an illustrious career as a parapsychological researcher as well as an academician, and Dillard, who has been increasingly recognized in the wholistic health field, escort the reader on a guided tour of the possible psychic realms with which dreams may be involved. They provide provocative data to support the hypothesis that dreams may reveal previously undiagnosed medical conditions, foretell events before their occurrence, and provide a means of telepathic exchange between dreamers. The authors are careful, however, not to over-generalize these data and they provide the necessary cautions and caveats to remember when considering these possibilities.

Numerous examples of dream reports from historical accounts as well as from contemporary people are interspersed and commented upon. One of the strongly appealing features of this book is that each chapter contains useful and easily understandable exercises which allow the reader to test the principal concepts about dream appreciation developed in that chapter. This enables their book to be used as both a text and as a workbook. It would be an excellent choice, therefore, for the individual who wishes to understand better his or her dreams on one's own or for a classroom instructor to employ in a course on dreams. The authors provide a fine bibliography of source material for those who may wish further illumination on the many intriguing ideas about dreams spotlighted throughout this book.

Robert L. Van de Castle
Professor, Department of
Behavioral Medicine and Psychiatry
University of Virginia Medical School;
President, Association for the
Study of Dreams 1985-86

Such Stuff As Dreams

Dreams are the true interpreters of our inclinations, but art is required to sort and understand them.

— **Michel Eyquem,** Seigneur de Montaigne.

Are you aware of your full creative capacity? If you had a tool allowing you to tap hidden reservoirs of creativity for practical purposes, how would you use it? Our intention is to help you discover and use your dreams, a powerful problem-solving tool you already possess. We believe your night-time adventures can teach you methods of creative problem-solving that may dramatically improve your personal and professional life.

Montague Ullman (1965), a psychiatrist internationally known for his work with dreams, once listed four reasons why every dream partakes in the creative process. All dreams are original. They join various elements to form new patterns. Like

Figure 1.

Dreams are . . .

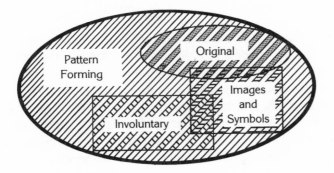

many other creative processes, dreams are involuntary experiences. Dreams contain images and symbols; humankind's capacity to produce them spontaneously demonstrates their creative potential.

The word "creativity" has several possible meanings. To most observers, it denotes the ability to bring something new into existence. For others it is not an ability but the psychological process by which novel and valuable products are fashioned. For still others, creativity is not the process but the product. Definitions of creativity range from the notion that it can be simple problem-solving to conceptualizing it as the full realization and expression of an individual's unique potentialities. Thus, there are at least four aspects of creativity: the creative process, the creative product, the creative person, and the creative situation (MacKinnon, 1978, p. 46).

The psychologist E. P. Torrance (1962) provided a definition of creativity congruent with what seems to happen in dreams. Torrance holds that creativity is a process of being sensitive to problems, deficiencies, gaps in knowledge, missing elements, and disharmonies. The process identifies problems, searches for solutions, makes guesses and formulates hypotheses about these problems. It then tests and retests the hypotheses, possibly modifying and again testing them, and finally communicates the results. Dreams are similar to Torrance's concept of creativity because they also identify problems, search for solutions, and test hypotheses before communicating the results to the dreamer.

Images and Symbols

In *The Tempest,* William Shakespeare wrote about "such stuff as dreams are made on." Many of the images appearing in dreams can be symbols. Although the boundaries between images and symbols may overlap at times, some distinctions do exist. Images are mental representations of objects or persons not physically present. While an image directly represents the object it pictures, a symbol is an object (or an image) standing for something else. For example, if you dreamed about your

Uncle Carlos after spending an evening with him, it is likely that the image of Carlos simply represents the person with whom you had contact before retiring. However, if you dreamed about Uncle Carlos after a period of little or no contact, his image might represent some activity, idea, or trait you associate with him. In this case, Carlos appears in your dream as an image with symbolic meaning.

Sometimes the images in your dreams make no sense if you presume that they refer to the people or objects they depict. In those instances, they are probably symbols referring to something other than themselves. Sigmund Freud complicated the issue by asserting that the symbols occurring in dreams differ radically from other symbols because dreams express, in disguised form, wishes the dreamer has repressed. However, this assertion implies a discontinuity in nature. Most current dreamworkers believe the symbol-making process in dreams exhibits more commonalities than differences with the symbol-making process in other fields of human endeavor such as the arts (Rycroft, 1979, pp. 73-74).

This continuous, "cognitive-psychological" position is taken by David Foulkes (1985), a psychologist who sees dreams as meaningful and symbolic but not as preplanned, encoded messages that need to be "translated" the way a linguist would work with a foreign language. According to Foulkes, the dream is "knowledge-based" and "bound to reflect some of the ways in which the dreamer mentally represents his or her world" (pp. 46-47). Indeed, almost all people awakened after a dream are able "to identify *some* events as having rough parallels in her or his waking experience" (p. 200).

Yet some differences between waking cognition and dreaming cognition do exist. Charles Rycroft (1979), a psychoanalyst, notes that if dreams are poetry, they are in an incomplete form. They need to cast their meaning in symbols that are a part of the shared legacy of one's culture. In most cases, dream imagery is too dependent on the dreamer's personal experiences to be convertible into works of art with wide appeal (p. 165). There are a few exceptions; a study has been reported of a woman who composed poetry while asleep and related it to her roommate while talking in her sleep. Her roommate transcribed it and read it to her the following morning. In this woman's case, her early childhood conditioning caused her to repress any type of creative behavior. It was not known if the poetry came to her in dreams or while awakening as she had no memory for the experience (Krippner & Stoller, 1973).

Some dream theorists urge the dreamer to accept dream images and dream experiences in their own right and on their own terms. Medard Boss and Brian Kenny (1978), for example, deny that a hidden, symbolizing agent lies within the dreamer. They work with dreams by having clients attempt to determine the emotional connections between the dreamer and the dream. The therapist might ask:

> *Does it not strike you that you found yourself, in your dreaming state, standing high up on a shaky iron scaffolding, clinging in terror to its iron shafts lest you fall down to your death? Do you perhaps have an inkling now, in your waking state, of an analogous position?* (p. 161)

At this point, the client may relate a feeling of anxiety to the dream images. Some would claim that Boss and Kenny *are* using symbolism in their approach. Nevertheless, they are a welcome counterbalance to those therapists whose extremely intellectual approach to dream symbolism in a dream, ignores the *feeling quality* of the dream itself (Boss, 1958).

R. W. Weisberg (1986) states that creative problem-solving has occurred when a person produces a novel response that solves the problem at hand (p. 4). Creative problem-solving in dreams can take place either by focusing on the images as realistic representations or by considering them as symbols. It has been reported that the naturalist Louis Agassiz succeeded in locating a fossil through a dream. The dream contained specific directions about how he should break open a stone with a chisel to reveal the fossil (Krippner & Hughes, 1977, p. 118). In this dream, the stone, the chisel, and the fossil were realistic images.

Sir Frederick Grant Banting is said to have discovered a procedure for the mass production of insulin through a dream. Like the images in Agassiz' dream, Banting's were realistic (Talamonte, 1975).

On the other hand, Elias Howe reportedly had a symbolic dream in 1844 which assisted his development of the lockstitch sewing machine. For several years, Howe constructed needles with holes in the middle of the shank. None suited his purpose, so his attempt at practical entrepreneurship came to a halt. One night he dreamed that he had been captured by a tribe of savages. Their king roared, "Elias Howe, I command you on pain of death to finish this machine at once." Try as he would, the inventor could not solve the problem. Frustrated, he cried aloud. This did not move the monarch who ordered his warriors to take Howe to a place of execution.

Although overcome with fear, Howe observed eye-shaped holes near the heads of the spears his guards were carrying. Then he realized what he needed was a needle with an eye-shaped hole near the point to make his sewing machine work. Awakening, Howe leaped from his bed and whittled a model of the needle he saw in his dream, thus bringing his efforts to successful completion (Kaempffert, 1924). In this case, the spears represented the needles required to bring the lockstitch sewing machine into being.

Sometimes historical accounts of dreams tend to differ. Another somewhat dubious version of Howe's dream holds that the savages forced Howe into a cauldron of water to boil him alive. As the water began to bubble, Howe's bonds loosened and he was able to free his hands. Each time he tried to climb out, the savages poked him back into the cauldron with their sharp spears. Howe noticed holes near the spearheads and awakened with the solution to his problem (Taylor, 1983, pp. 7-8). Both versions of the dream end with Howe's noticing the pierced spears of his captors, who may represent the inner creative forces that found the solution before his rational, waking mind did.

The lockstitch has been the basic design of all sewing machines ever since Howe's invention. Howe's dream, and his creative use of it, changed society by spurring the Industrial Revolution, which had stalled because only skilled manual labor could transform raw cloth into salable goods still dependent on skilled hand-labor.

Writers, as well as inventors, vary in how dreams facilitate their creative problem-solving. William Burroughs, author of *Naked Lunch* and *The Place of Dead Roads,* once stated: "A good part of my material comes from dreams. A lot of it is just straight transcription of dreams with some amplification, of course" (Howell, 1985, p. 36). In 1954, Steve Allen remembered portions of a dream which led to his popular song, "This Could Be the Start of Something Big" (Morris, 1985, p. 126). John Sayles, a screenwriter, discarded two dreams containing ideas for a film before he found one he turned into "The Brother from Another Planet":

> *First I dreamt I had a terrible job rewriting a script about used car salesmen from another planet. Then I dreamt about shooting a film noir Big Foot movie. I liked that, but it was too esoteric. When I dreamt about a black alien lost in New York, it all started to come together.* (Springer, 1983, p. 13)

However, the poets William Morris and John Squire are on record as dreaming verses so inferior to their usual output that they could not be published (Megroz, 1939). A. C. Benson dreamed an entire poem but was unable to fathom its esoteric symbolism (Brook, 1983, p. 140). Simply because a novel idea, lyric, or song appears in a dream does not guarantee its creative value. Waking thought can be trivial, and so can dream imagery.

The Creative Process

The varied experiences of inventors, artists, and scientists illustrate the role dreams can play in creativity. Gardner Murphy (1958), the eminent personality theorist, constructed one of the most useful frameworks for understanding the creative process. First, before the creative process can begin, the sensitive mind prepares for a long immersion in a specific medium such as color, tone, movement, space, time, language, or social relationships. For dreamers, this period of preparation typically occurs before sleep as they gather relevant information, narrow the focus on a problem, and may even use pre-sleep suggestions to evoke an appropriate dream.

The second phase in the creative process occurs with the consolidation of "storehouses" full of experiences and information organized into structured patterns outside conscious awareness. These "storehouses" may hold color combinations as well as linear combinations of the world in pencil, crayon, and brush. They may reserve organized patterns of temporary and spatial relationships involved in mechanics and technology. There may be social interactions, organizations, and leadership. Like data banks, these living "storehouses" of data cannot be retrieved at a single moment so they are organized outside of conscious awareness into systems upon which people may draw when needed. In problem-solving dreams, these data are incubated, remain adaptable and flexible, and can be evoked in a dream by pre-sleep stimulation or a need for expression.

Figure 2. Murphy's Components of Creativity.

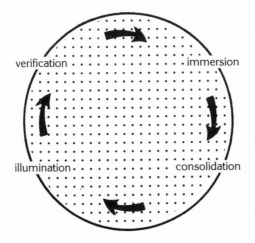

According to Murphy, illumination is the third phase in the creative process. Archimedes experienced illumination when he jumped from his bathtub shouting "Eureka!" ("I have found it!") after finding that gold displaced less water than an equal amount of silver. Murphy observes that illumination need not occur unconsciously. The "storehouses" of experience he describes can also be drawn upon consciously. But when illumination does occur in a dream, it often follows a long period of immersion in a particular problem or area of work.

The Russian chemist, Dmitri Mendeleev once went to bed exhausted, following another unsuccessful attempt to categorize the chemical elements. He later reported, "I saw in a dream a table where all the elements fell into place as required. Awakening, I immediately wrote it down on a piece of paper. Only in one place did a correction later seem necessary" (Kedrov, 1957). This is how Mendeleev created the Periodic Table of the Elements. In another (and less highly-regarded) version of this dream, the chemical elements appeared in the form of chamber music (Taylor, 1983, p. 7); both accounts demonstrate creativity's illumination phase at work.

In 1893, Herman Hilprecht, an anthropologist, had been attempting to decipher the inscription on two small fragments of agate believed to belong to the finger rings of a Babylonian nobleman. The fragments bore cuneiform writing of the Cassite period in Babylonian history. After midnight, weary and exhausted, Hilprecht went to sleep and dreamed that a Babylonian priest appeared to him, explaining how to put the fragments together to show that they once belonged to the same prayer cylinder. Upon awakening, Hilprecht followed the instructions in his dream, verified the suggestion, and made the necessary translation (Van de Castle, 1971). Hilprecht's experience also teaches us how a dream can produce characters who convey a living presence that assists the creative process.

Many people feel that creativity ends with insight or illumination. However, verification, the fourth phase, is equally important. Does an idea actually work? Does it result in greater productivity, efficiency, or beauty? Does it lead to greater satisfaction with oneself or one's work? Can it be effectively communicated to others so they can enjoy it, use it, or reproduce it? There is nothing magical about dreams which assist creativity; they can facilitate the middle two phases of the creative process but cannot substitute for the essential careful preparation and the rigorous verification. When preparation, consolidation, illumination, and verification are used in tandem the largely logical, objective, and verbal skills of stages one and four are balanced with the principally emotional, subjective, and visual processes of stages two and three. Together, they increase the likelihood of finding solutions to both professional and personal problems.

Figure 3. Dream Creativity.

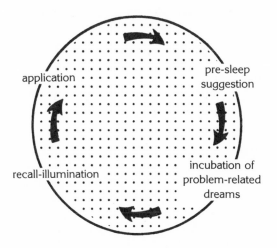

One of the most assiduous investigators of human cognition, Edward de Bono (1969), has defined a problem as the difference between what one has and what one wants (p. 228). For de Bono, there are three basic types of problems: those that require processing available information or gathering more information; those that are solved by restructuring the pattern into which information has been formed; and those in which the existence of a problem is denied.

De Bono observes that the first type of problem can be approached by logical thinking and/or the collecting of more information. Logical, or "vertical" thinking is limited because it cannot generate new ideas easily. The other two types require "lateral" thinking which uses existing information in new ways rather than gathering additional data. Lateral thinking rearranges available data so they form a new and more effective pattern. This rearrangement has the same effect as insight.

With vertical thinking, an approach to a problem is selected in one of two ways. With lateral thinking, as many alternatives as possible are generated. In the case of vertical thinking, one moves only if there is a direction in which to move. With lateral thinking, one moves to generate a direction; one may not know what one is looking for until after it has been found. Creative problem-solving in dreams is an example of lateral thinking.

Skeptical Viewpoints

Over the years, some observers have taken skeptical points of view regarding the importance of de Bono's lateral thinking and Murphy's second and third stages of creativity (incubation and illumination) claiming that systematic thought is a more dependable way to solve problems (Altshuller, 1984).

These critics often cite research data to support their position. Catherine Patrick (1935) interviewed artists and poets about their creative processes, finding that they reported thinking about their projects when they supposedly were "incubating" the problem unconsciously. She deduced that unconscious processes may have added little to the conscious awareness that contributed to the final product. Patrick (1937) later showed poets a picture of a landscape and asked them to write poems about it. Most of her subjects produced works of high quality, demonstrating no need for an "incubation" period. The typical sequence began with general impressions and recalling of relevant memories in response to the picture. This was followed by a few lines of poetry or the blocking out of a format; these products were subsequently revised and elaborated. The stages were not completely separate, however, and a replication study with artists found it was difficult to separate the proposed four stages because of their overlap (Eindhoven & Vinacke, 1952). Weisberg (1986) claims that data of this nature do not support the concept that unconscious processes are important in creative thinking, and expresses doubt about the accuracy of first person accounts that argue to the contrary (pp. 24-27).

Weisberg also takes a skeptical position on the importance of lateral thinking in creativity. He claims that his examination of the journals describing great discoveries gave no evidence of lateral thought, citing as evidence those of Charles Darwin (on evolution by natural selection) and James Watson (on the structure of the DNA molecule). Weisberg summarized a number of studies examining the performance of scientists on tests measuring lateral thinking; highly creative scientists did not use lateral thinking more often than less creative scientists on these tests (p. 67). The point Weisberg seems to be making is that a person may solve a problem from what someone else considers an unusual perspective, but from his or her point of view the perspective follows naturally from what had preceded it. Creative thinking is judged to be extraordinary because of what the thinker produces, not because of the way in which it was produced (p. 69). These skeptical viewpoints should stimulate researchers to focus more precisely on individual differences in cognitive styles and can serve as correctives to writers who place too much emphasis on unconscious aspects of creativity.

Dreams and the Zeitgeist

Everyone lives in a unique historical time with its own resources and limitations. How people approach problems and make the assumptions they hold about what is possible is influenced by their worldview. In German, the word *Zeitgeist,* or "spirit of the times," is used to express this important concept (Boring, 1950). Because the Zeitgeist inevitably colors and distorts one's vision, it is not surprising that people often lack the objectivity to rise to their creative potential. They are unable to see beyond the boundaries of the house and garden in which they live. Everything outside the garden wall is foreign territory—unwelcome, foreboding, and threatening. Like the Roman Catholic prelates who persecuted Galileo, it is easy to limit one's view of the world or oneself.

Visionaries, however, refuse to be threatened by the world outside their garden. They climb the walls surrounding their house, look around, and sometimes venture into the world beyond the walls. Most people lack the brashness, curiosity, or persistence that climbing and looking around require. When these innovators report what they see, their community often dismisses them as dreamers, radicals, or lunatics. It takes courage to look over the walls in the face of such potential criticism, but the alternative is a slowly enveloping mental paralysis. Rather than accept a life of complacency, innovators call into question their culture's Zeitgeist or anticipate a future Zeitgeist long before their neighbors know it is about to arrive.

The concept of the Zeitgeist also helps explain what occurs when a highly creative work, once ignored, suddenly wins acceptance. When Johann Sebastian Bach died in 1750, public performance of his works essentially died with him and his music was ignored for nearly 75 years. Vincent Van Gogh only sold one painting while he was alive. Gregor Mendel's work on genetics was overlooked while he was alive but attained great importance after his death. The definition of artistic or scientific creativity depends on the response of an audience; the cultural Zeitgeist may change radically over the years, and a creative person's reputation may fluctuate accordingly (Weisberg, 1986, p. 85).

The importance of the Zeitgeist is also apparent as one takes a historical perspective on dreams. The Babylonians and Assyrians believed that devils and spirits of the dead influenced dreams negatively. Clay tablets have been found, dating to about 3000 B.C., which contain interpretive material about various types of dreams (Van de Castle, 1971). Flying dreams usually indicated disaster; imbibing wine in a dream forecast a short life but drinking water foretold a long one. This "dictionary" approach to dream content always gave the same meaning for everyone regardless

Figure 4.

of the dreams and their circumstances. It was a stereotyped method common among people living in those times.

The Egyptians were less concerned with demonology and interpreted dreams as messages from the gods. The Egyptian papyrus of Deral-Madineh dates between 2000 and 1790 B.C. and gives instructions on how to obtain a dream message from a god (Webb, 1979). This is probably the oldest dream manual in existence. Serapis was the Egyptian god of dreams and several dream temples or *serapims* were located throughout the land. Incubation, the deliberate effort to induce dreams through sleeping in these temples, was widely practiced. "Stand-in" dreamers were even sent to the serapims to have a dream for someone who could not make the journey (Van de Castle, 1971, pp. 3-4).

The dreams of royalty were given special attention; a dream of Thutmose IV is recorded on a stela in front of the Sphinx.

The earliest Chinese work on dreams is the *Meng Shu*, dating to about A.D. 640. The Chinese classified dreams according to their source. The source of a dream was important because it revealed physical and mental changes taking place in the dreamers—changes which, if better understood, could enable the dreamers better to cope with their personal problems through self-knowledge. The Chinese believed dreams usually came from an internal source, the dreamer's "soul," but that external physical stimuli could also be important. Sleeping on a belt, for example, could induce a dream about snakes. To the Chinese, proper dream interpretation depended on the context; positions of the sun, moon, and stars, as well as the season of the year, were taken into account in working with the dream. Images from the *I Ching* or *Book of Changes* were applied to dream imagery as well as to other patterns in human experience (O'Neil, 1976, p. 33).

The sacred *Veda* of India contain lists of favorable and unfavorable dreams. This literature, probably written sometime between 1500 and 1000 B.C., contains specific interpretations for dream symbols (O'Neil, 1976, p. 32). Dreams from different periods of the night were given different interpretations and the dreamer's temperament was also considered before an interpretation was made. Furthermore, early philosophers in India conjectured that there are four states of the "soul," waking, dreaming, dreamless sleep, and mystical unity (de Becker, 1968, p. 212).

The Chinese and Indian approaches to dreams took more variables into account than most other ancient traditions, thus encouraging innovation. We might say it is impossible to look seriously at your dreams without questioning your Zeitgeist and peering over your garden wall. By committing yourself to dreamwork, you implicitly agree to rise above the limits of your current worldview and to partake in potentially creative experience. Albert Rothenberg (1979) defines creativity as a series of thoughts and actions which result in a new product of positive value (p. 3). E.

Paul Torrance (1979) observes that creative thought transcends logical and ordinary rational modes (p. 5).

For Rollo May (1959), creativity is the process of bringing something new into birth; it typically begins with an encounter. Frank Barron (1969) also conceives creativity as the ability to bring something new into existence. Psychologist Carl Rogers (1970) saw the creative process as the emergence in action of a novel relational product growing from the uniqueness of the individual and the materials, events, people, or circumstances of his or her life (p. 139). Another psychologist, A. H. Maslow (1971) pointed out that society requires innovative thinkers who are flexible and creative. Maslow held that executives and administrators in business and industry must be capable of dealing with the inevitably rapid obsolescence of any new product or service. Therefore, they must anticipate change rather than resist it (pp. 98-99). Dreaming is humankind's hidden link to creativity. When people dream, they often catch a glimpse of their future and its potentials. When they act in their dreams, they can begin to bring that future into reality.

Voltaire once commented that he knew lawyers who pleaded cases in their dreams, mathematicians who had sought to solve problems, and poets who composed poems. The French philosopher observed that he had written verses in dreams himself, and that some were "very passable." He concluded that ideas can come "in spite of us" during sleep (Fromm, 1951, p. 138). Even so, it must be remembered that dreams and creativity do not share exactly the same functions. Scientific and artistic processes serve many purposes other than impulse expression and reviewing the day's events. Dreams are usually intensively private and idiosyncratic affairs. But, the exceptions generally pertain to creative individuals who conceive of themselves as part of the greater social matrix and lack the conflict between their inner needs and the world-at-large which may render other people resistive to their own imaginative capacities. Creative dreamwork can demonstrate the commitment of the whole person to problem-solving (Gruber, 1974, p. 246). Therefore, highly creative individuals such as Mendeleev can allow themselves to evoke dream imagery which may ultimately have both private and universal meanings (Rycroft, 1979, p. 167).

In Summary

- Dreamwork can be a powerful tool for creative problem-solving.
- Dream images can symbolize the dreamer's ongoing, real-life concerns.
- Dream images have played an important historical role in certain aspects of creative development.
- Gardner Murphy has described four phases in the creative process: preparation, consolidation, illumination, and verification.
- While some types of problems are best solved by logical, or vertical thinking, other require rearrangement, or lateral thinking.
- Some writers are skeptical about Murphy's stages and the concept of lateral thinking, noting that creativity becomes extraordinary because of what the thinker produces rather than how the problem's solution was conceived.
- Throughout history, the worldview prevailing in a particular place and time has determined attitudes about dreams.
- Creative people typically have been able to rise above the worldviews of their time.
- While one's assumptions about the usefulness of dreams are influenced by one's worldview, dreamers can challenge cultural assumptions and use their dreams in new, creative ways.

Exercises

1. *Starting Your Dream Notebook.* If you wish to commit yourself to using your dreams for creative problem-solving, obtain a notebook which will be used for no other purpose. Some people prefer a loose-leaf notebook so they can rearrange the pages from time to time. Some purchase workbooks which have been commercially prepared for dreamwork (e.g., Black, 1977; Garfield, 1976). Others store their dreams in their computer and print them out on their word processor when necessary. Decide

which approach you would prefer to use as you begin your inner exploration.

2. *Recalling Your Dreams.* Some people have difficulty remembering dreams in the morning. It helps to have a pad of paper and a pencil at your bedside to jot down a dream if you awaken in the middle of the night. The notebook is intended to record your dreams in greater detail. Some people use a tape recorder. Others use a penlight so they can see what they are writing. Whatever you decide, the very preparation of making notes about your dreams will give your unconscious a message that you will honor it as you attempt night-time creativity. This message may suffice for ensuring dream recall.

3. *Self-Suggestion.* Remembering one dream per week is sufficient to attempt the exercises in this book. But if you cannot meet this quota, you might try self-suggestion. Before going to sleep, simply tell yourself (silently or aloud), "I will remember a dream when I wake up. I will remember a dream when I wake up." You may adapt the words to your purposes, then repeat the message 20 or 30 times. After a few nights, this technique should begin to yield results.

4. *Looking for Creative Elements.* Do not get discouraged if your dreams do not resemble those of Mendeleev or Hilprecht. Highly creative dreams such as these are rare even among professional scientists and artists. Your first step is simply to remember some of your dreams. However, you might begin to inspect them for the signs of creativity cited by Ullman. Do you see two or more life experiences joined in a dream? Are there original elements in your dreams that you would never have thought of during waking hours? Are you surprised at how complex some dreams are, even though their creation is involuntary? Are there puzzling, humorous, or provocative images in the dreams? If so, what life event or creative process could they symbolize? Whatever it is, these images confirm your creative potential and will provide raw material for the exercises in the next chapters.

2

Of Dreams And Destiny

That which the dream shows is the shadow of such wisdom as exists in man, even if during his waking state he may know nothing about it.

— Paracelsus

Sigmund Freud used the term *dream work* to describe the process in which unacceptable dream content is transformed into acceptable material. We use a similar term, *dreamwork,* to refer to any process in which people attend to their night-time dreams, appreciating them, examining them, or interpreting them.

Dreamworking has always been part of the human potential, hidden beneath the surface like a mother lode of gold. Shamans, those men and women who were the first to alter their consciousness voluntarily, obtaining information they claimed was not available to other people in their society, listened patiently to the dreams of tribal members and explained them in terms of the culture's myths. Somewhat later in social evolution, diviners and prophets searched their dreams to solve their societies' problems, as well as to predict the future. Priests and priestesses viewed dreams through the lens of religious dogmas. Sorcerers and witches claimed to find omens in dreams to assist their clients in locating lost objects or winning romantic favors. In each case, ordinary people had little confidence that they could offer any insight into their own dream content; they assigned that power to specialized practitioners and usually believed what they were told about their dreams and their inner lives (Winkelman, 1984).

Dreams and Military Decisions

Dreams were taken seriously in most ancient cultures because they appeared to yield practical benefits. Alexander the Great recorded his dreams and even announced some of them publicly. Virtually everyone in his day, particularly soldiers, believed that dreams could foreshadow the future and reveal the will of the gods. They also felt the dreams of kings and commanders had special validity. Alexander's principal tutor was Aristotle, the Greek philosopher whose works included three books on sleep and dreams. During his campaign through the Persian Empire, Alexander took with him a seer named Aristander of Telmessos, who inspected everything from the flight of birds to the markings on organs of animals sacrificed for omens. Artemidorus of Daldis, who wrote the oldest surviving "dream dictionary," *The Interpretation of Dreams,* noted that Aristander also wrote on dream interpretation (White, 1975). Artemidorus' book was quite profound for its time, categorizing dreams into nightmares, daydreams, divine revelations, those expressing wishes, and those containing symbols (Rycroft, 1979, p. 145).

During the siege of Tyre in 332 B.C., Alexander dreamed that the Greek god Hercules stretched out his right hand to him from the wall and called him. Hercules was an appropriate figure because Alexander, upon arriving in Tyre, insisted on his right to worship this god in one of the Phoenician temples. Alexander believed he was related to Hercules and served as his representative on earth. Aristander interpreted the dream to mean that Alexander would capture Tyre, but only after a great deal of effort, just as Hercules' achievements had required effort.

In another dream, Alexander saw a satyr, a demigod who typically lived in wooded areas. The satyr mocked Alexander from a distance and eluded his grasp until Alexander captured him, after considerable coaxing and chasing. Aristander divided the Greek word *satyros* into *sa* and *Tyros.* The news that "Tyre is yours" encouraged Alexander to wage the war more zealously and win (Hughes, 1984). Aristander's method predated Freud's examination of dreams for puns which could assist in dream interpretation.

Even before Alexander, dreams were sometimes used in military decision-making. Xerxes, the leader of Persia, had been deliberating whether or not to invade the Greek peninsula. One night he reportedly was visited, in a dream, by an imposing figure who criticized him for not carrying through his invasion plans. On successive nights, the dream visitor reappeared, warning Xerxes that if he did not invade Greece, he would lose his power. Xerxes consulted his uncle who had been advising against the invasion. The uncle dressed himself in Xerxes' robes and slept in the king's bed. The dream visitor was not fooled; he told Xerxes' uncle that if he continued to oppose the invasion his eyes would be gouged out. Xerxes was convinced that the orders were a divine mandate and, in 480 B.C., invaded the Greek city states. Xerxes was soundly defeated in the naval battle of Salamis and lost the war (Woods & Greenhouse, 1974, p. 41).

In other words, military dreams do not always reflect *strategic* reality accurately. De Becker (1968, pp. 66-67) conjectures that this dream series represented *interpersonal* reality–a struggle between a young, brash ruler and an old, wise, advisor and father-figure. Xerxes' rebelliousness assumed the dream image which asked him why he submitted to the dictates of an old man. The uncle, realizing his tenuous political situation, used the dream to resolve the interpersonal conflict. At one level, he probably was aware of the violence of which Xerxes was capable if his wishes were opposed. Wearing his nephew's robes to bed reinforced this insight and stimulated a dream that would resolve the conflict between them. Adroit discrimination is often needed to choose wisely between conflicting interpretations of a dream. Both Xerxes and his uncle believed the dreams were divine messages and did not consider alternative approaches.

Hannibal, the Carthagenian general who crossed the Alps and invaded Italy, had a dream in which a huge serpent moved along, destroying everything in its path. The sky filled with smoking clouds and became illuminated by piercing flashes of lightning. A young man appeared in the dream, telling Hannibal he was to follow the instructions given in the dream, the snake symbolizing Hannibal's army. Upon awakening, Hannibal gave orders to march, beginning a campaign that very nearly led to the conquest of Rome.

A century or so later, Julius Caesar, at that time a Roman general, reported a dream in which he slept with his mother. The dream was interpreted as representing the "Mother City" of Rome. Thus bolstered, Caesar continued his insurrection against the government, crossed the Rubicon, and captured Rome without spilling a drop of blood (de Becker, 1968).

Genghis Khan, the Mongol conquerer, is reported to have recalled two dreams which directed his life. The first dream told him he was destined to reign over the Mongols; the second instructed him to expand his domain by conquest. Following both dreams, Genghis Khan embarked on one military campaign after another, extending his empire to the Dnieper River in Eastern Europe before he was stopped.

The Moslem leader Tariq Ibn-Ziyad recalled a dream in which he saw Mohammed and his companions armed with swords and lances. Mohammed instructed them to advance into Andalusia; the next morning, Tariq began to make plans to invade Spain (Van de Castle, 1971, p. 2).

In 1863, Prussia confronted considerable opposition to its expansionist plans, so much so that even Otto von Bismarck, well known for his determination to unite the German states, was beginning to lose self-confidence. He recalled a dream he had one night:

> *I dreamt that I was riding on a narrow Alpine path, precipice on the right, rocks on the left. The path grew narrower, so that the horse refused to proceed and it was impossible to turn round or dismount, owing to lack of space. Then, with my whip in my left hand, I struck the smooth rock and called on God. The whip grew to an endless length, the rocky wall dropped like a piece of stage scenery and opened out in a broad path, with a view over hills and forests, like a landscape in Bohemia; there were Prussian troops with banners . . . I woke up rejoiced and strengthened.* (Evans, 1985, pp. 222-223)

Bismarck's singleness of purpose was confirmed; he united Germany and became its first chancellor.

The accuracy of these dream reports is uncertain because so many of them occurred centuries ago and were not reported by the dreamers themselves. However, in cases like Alexander the Great's, several historical accounts give virtually the same report of a dream so we can be more confident about its accuracy. In other cases dreams may be fabricated for political purposes. In a speech delivered in the Iranian Parliament in May, 1951, Mohammed Mossadegh revealed, "I dreamed one night of a personage shining with a bright light who said to me: 'This is not the time to rest; arise and break the chains of the people of Iran.' Responding to this call, I resumed my work with the Oil Commission, and two months later, when this Commission adopted the principle of nationalization, I had to admit that the apparition in my dream had inspired me successfully" (de Becker, 1968, p. 80). Whether the wily Iranian political leader actually had such a dream or whether he used the dream as a sign of divine inspiration is unknown.

Mossadegh was deposed by forces loyal to Iran's Shah, but the Shah lost his power several years later during a period in which another dream attracted attention. In late 1978, word spread through Iran's Shi'ite community that Ayatullah Qumi of Mashad had dreamed he had been visited by Imam Reza, an ancient sage. In the dream, the Imam accused Ayatullah Khomeini of turning Muslim against Muslim and that his teachings were running counter to Islamic law. Among the faithful, many were stunned, yet others dismissed the report as a government trick which attempted to use the Islamic veneration of dreams for its own purposes (Anon., 1978).

Perhaps the most striking example of a dream associated with conquest was one purportedly experienced by Adolf Hitler. In 1917, as a corporal in the front lines of the First World War, Hitler dreamed about being buried beneath an avalanche of earth and molten iron. While warm blood flowed down his chest, he experienced the sensation of choking. Hitler awakened from the dream alarmed, and left the shelter to walk openly on the nearby fields. He reproached himself for this action because it placed him in danger of being killed or wounded by exploding shrapnel.

Indeed, artillery began firing and Hitler heard a nearby explosion. After throwing himself on the ground, he looked about and noticed that the area he just left was directly hit. Returning to investigate, he discovered a mass of fallen earth across the trench burying his comrades alive, just as his dream depicted. From then on, Hitler felt he had been entrusted with a divine mission (de Becker, 1968).

This report is placed in a different setting by George Ward Price (1937, p. 41) who claimed that Hitler was eating dinner in a trench with several soldiers when a voice told him to switch his position. Hitler obeyed, carrying his dinner with him. Hardly had he moved when a shell hit the trench, killing every member of the group he had just left. Hitler did not mention either version of this account in *Mein Kampf*, his autobiography.

Not as well known is the case of D. B. Parkinson, an engineer with Bell Laboratories. In the spring of 1940, he was working with a group of technicians who were trying to develop an improved automatic level recorder. This recorder was to be used to improve the accuracy of measurements in telephone transmission. At this time, Hitler's forces were marching through Western Europe. One night Parkinson had the following dream:

> *I found myself in a gun pit . . . with an anti-aircraft gun crew . . . There was a gun there which . . . was firing occasionally, and the impressive thing was that every shot brought down an airplane! After three or four shots one of the men in the crew smiled at me and beckoned me to come closer to the gun. When I drew near he pointed to the exposed end . . . Mounted there was the control potentiometer of my level recorder! There was no mistaking it—it was the identical item.* (Delaney, 1979, p. 135)

In his dream, Parkinson, who had no knowledge of the technology of fire control, had dreamed the key to the development of extremely effective gun directors. The first all-electric gun director which evolved from research based on Parkinson's dream became known as the M-9 electrical analog computer. The M-9 was the precursor of guidance systems for the antiaircraft and antiballistic missiles developed later (Fagen, 1978).

In contrast to the dreams of militarists are those of Harriet Tubman, the escaped slave who led hundreds of her people to freedom in the northern United States in the years preceding the Civil War. Her "Underground Railroad" was a system of way stations controlled by anti-slavery advocates; Tubman never lost a "passenger" on her 19 rescue forays into the south. She led the escaped slaves on foot through all kinds of weather, evading slave-hunting patrols who had been promised a large reward for her capture. In addition, Tubman led members of her own family to freedom only days before they were scheduled to be tried for aiding a fugitive. She claimed God guided her actions and that dreams helped her find the pathways to freedom on the Underground Railroad (Bradford, 1869/1981).

Mahatma Gandhi used his dreams to deal with the United Kingdom's Rowlett Act which harshly suppressed any agitation aimed toward India's independence. Gandhi meditated for weeks to devise a non-violent, yet effective, expression of the populace's refusal to submit to the Rowlett Act. Finally, he claimed to find the solution in a dream which suggested that for 24 hours the people of India should stop working. These mass strikes of 1919 were major events in initiating India's successful struggle for self-determination (Gandhi, 1957, pp. 459-460). Dreams, therefore, have played a critical role in the lives of both the heroic and the horrible, the noble and the notorious.

Dreams and Synthesis

Laboratory research about dreaming indicates that the psychophysiological state in which most dreams occur appears to be as different from non-dream sleep as non-dream sleep differs from wakefulness. Because dreaming sleep is marked by rapid eye movements (REMs), this stage of one's night-time activity is often referred to as REM sleep, Stage REM, or as "a third basic form of human existence" (Jones, 1970, p. 24).

Figure 5. Dreaming: A Third Basic Form of Human Existence.

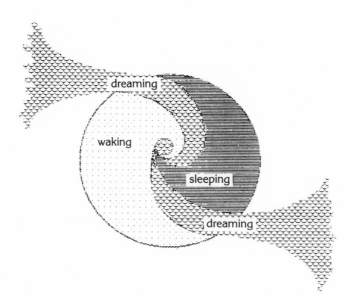

REM sleep is found in almost all human sleep patterns; only a handful of people who rarely dream have been identified. For example, a lawyer in Israel was referred to a sleep laboratory because he occasionally shouted in his sleep. In studying his sleep patterns, the physicians discovered that the lawyer engaged in Stage REM no more than five minutes per night, less than any documented sleeping subject. In search of an explanation, the physicians found that a piece of shrapnel had pierced their patient's skull during a 1970 battle and destroyed a group of cells deep in the brain stem. This area had been associated with the REM sleep of animals in some studies and its impairment was the likely cause of the lawyer's anomalous sleep patterns (Lawren, 1986).

Some writers have speculated on which portion of the brain is responsible for dreaming. Current neurophysiological research indicates that there is a vertical synthesis between the "old" and "new" brains in dreaming, as well as a horizontal synthesis between the left and right cerebral hemispheres (Stevens, 1983). The brain waves characterizing Stage REM originate in the brain stem and spread upward through the midbrain to the cortex, or "new brain." Studies with rats indicate that REM sleep is important to the integration of instinctual programs for attachment and territorial behavior with the higher learning and planning processes of the rats' cerebral hemispheres (Smith, Kitahama, Valtax, & Jouvet, 1974). Anthony Stevens (1983), a psychiatrist, suggests that investigations of such themes as falling, being chased, being attacked, and repeatedly attempting to perform a task provide evidence that "old brain" structures play an important part in the dreams of contemporary human beings (p. 268).

It has been proposed by Paul Bakan (1977-1978) and others that the predominance of imagery in dreaming indicates it is a "right hemisphere" function. However, neurophysiological studies have not given clear support to this proposal. Indeed, a review of animal studies indicated that both the left and right hemispheres are active during REM sleep (Hobson & McCarley, 1977). In addition, human patients were studied who had undergone removal of large sections of the corpus callosum, a neurological structure connecting the two hemispheres. No evidence was found for selective visual dream mediation by the dominant hemisphere, as one would suspect had the right hemisphere been more important (Greenwood, Wilson, & Gazzaniga, 1977).

Neurophysiologists J. Allan Hobson and Robert W. McCarley (McCarley & Hobson, 1979) hypothesized that the elements in dreams derive from a synthesis of information produced by activation of motor pattern generators and sensory systems. This internal information is linked and compared with information about the organism's past experiences. They conclude that "dreams are not a result of an attempt to disguise but are a direct expression of this synthetic effort" (p. 125). In other words, the brain is first internally activated and then synthesizes this information to form the physiological concomitants of the dream experience. One's memories are scanned for images that will match these internally generated patterns.

Hobson and McCarley attribute the shift between REM and non-REM sleep to the interaction of "multiple, anatomically distributed sets of neurons" (Hobson, Lydic, & Baghdoyan, 1986, p. 371). Waking and REM sleep are seen to be opposites of a continuum with non-REM sleep as an intermediate stage (Hobson, 1983). During REM sleep, brain stem neurons activate the brain and generate rapid eye movements as well as various sensory-motor activities and aspects of the affective (emotion-producing) system. The brain uses its stored information to synthesize dream imagery and construct plots to fit this autostimulatory process (Porte & Hobson, 1986).

This "activation-synthesis" theory of dreaming holds that stimuli are generated within the central nervous system, which then are processed as if they came from the outside world. The waking function of these neurons is sensory-motor integration; their expression during sleep provides the "signals" from which dreaming takes its form (Hobson, 1983, p. 126). For example, most dreams occur during Stage REM when the eyes move rapidly back and forth as well as up and down. Hobson and McCarley propose that the internal commands for eye movements produce internal stimuli which are the basis for visual imagery in dreams. Just as they shape perception when someone is awake, eye movements generate portions of the dream story while one is asleep (p. 102). Although there seems to be a relationship between the intensity of REMs and the intensity of the dream, the eye movements appear to influence dream content rather than to watch the dream, as was once thought to occur. Dream intensity is also associated with respiratory rates, heart rate, and fluctuations of skin potential (Hauri & Van de Castle, 1973).

Hobson and McCarley also note that external stimuli can be incorporated into one's dream content. External fluctuations in light, heat, and sound can influence dreams, even though the laboratory attempts to measure this phenomenon have produced capricious results (Moss, 1967, chap. 3). Sometimes a dreamer will hear a doorbell ring but awaken to an alarm clock. An increase in room temperature may shift the setting of a dream to a hot, sandy desert. The fact that dreams can synthesize so many elements from internal stimuli, external stimuli, and one's memory bank demonstrates their remarkably creative potential.

Many orthodox psychoanalysts and other psychotherapists insist there are psychodynamic determinants for every bit of dream content. However, this dogmatic position was never taken by Freud, who admitted that external sensory and internal somatic stimuli could initiate dreaming. Freud (1933) simply assigned a more critical role to psychodynamic factors, concluding that "the objective sensory stimulus encroaching upon sleep plays only a modest role as a dream source, . . . other factors determine the choice of the memory-image to be evoked" (p. 29). Hobson and McCarley have given the key role to internal stimulation. One's memories, no matter how pressing at the time, may not appear in the dream at all if they do not match the internally-generated patterns of light and other sensations (McCarley & Hobson, 1977).

The difference between Freud, who attached importance to one's psychodynamics, and Hobson and McCarley, who assign primary emphasis to internal stimulation, might be regarded as one of degree. On the other hand, it also could be stated that one's neurophysiology determines the state in which dreams typically occur, but not the content of these dreams; content is determined by life events and their specific connections to the past, not by random neuronal discharges. However, both points of view hold that some dreams are more worthy of the dreamer's attention than others. Further, if Hobson and McCarley are even partially correct, one should not expect all elements of the dream to make equal sense as some items may reflect internal or external stimuli one's memory bank can not easily match.

As might be expected, Hobson and McCarley's point of view is extremely controversial. Jerome Rothenberg (1979), a psychoanalyst, asserts that Hobson and McCarley's theory does not adequately explain the postulated interaction between neurophysiological and psychological effects. He states that by insisting that patterns of neuronal generation are responsible for dreams, Hobson and McCarley do not explain why such mechanisms as symbol formation occur at all (p. 387). Gordon Globus (1986), a psychologist, credits Hobson and McCarley with

Figure 6.

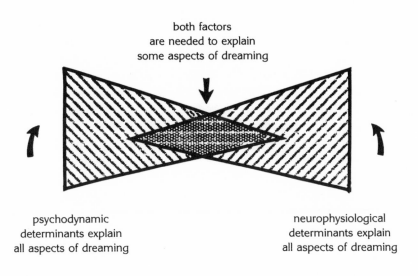

both factors
are needed to explain
some aspects of dreaming

psychodynamic
determinants explain
all aspects of dreaming

neurophysiological
determinants explain
all aspects of dreaming

disproving Freud's contention that dreams are instigated by unconscious wishes, but finds their theory overly mechanistic and unable to explain the "extraordinary creative capacity" of dreamers (p. 62).

Harry Fiss (1984) holds that the validity of Hobson and McCarley's theory depends on the proposition that dreaming occurs solely during REM sleep—which it does not. He contends that their theory states that formal characteristics of dreaming are neurophysiologically determined but, given this, they do not explain why dreams over the course of an entire night can be closely related in content. Fiss points out that, Hobson and McCarley to the contrary, "brains do not dream; only dreamers dream" (p. 10). It can be seen that Hobson and McCarley have many questions to answer and many research studies to conduct before countering these objections.

On one level or another, it can be claimed that dreams reflect a process of creative synthesis at work. Dreams synthesize the activity of various parts of the brain and many sources of dream content. However, it is important to stress that dreams are private experiences which can contribute to personally or socially useful creative behavior. The psychiatrist Silvano Arieti (1976) went so far as to call dreams "original" but not "creative." Arieti claimed that dreams can be of value once they are interpreted, but "then they are no longer dreams; they are translations of dreams" (p. 10). This was certainly true in the case of Alexander the Great; his military dreams led to the capture of Tyre but only after dreamwork revealed their message. Again we are reminded of Gardner Murphy's four stages of creativity. Dreams may assist problem-solving in the illumination stage but verification is needed before the creative product can be completed.

The Dream Generator

If Hobson and McCarley are correct, then dreams result from attempts by higher brain centers to "make sense" of cortical stimulation by lower brain "dream generators." Dreams take the stimuli produced by these dream generators and use the images

Figure 7.

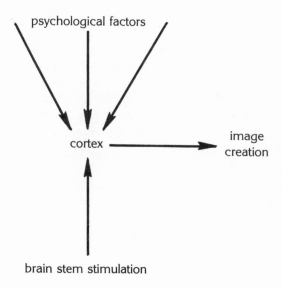

as story material. As a result any number of psychological functions can be superimposed upon the basic biological process, e.g., integrating daytime experiences with memories already stored away; providing a safety valve so the dreamer can deal with upsetting issues and events; addressing one's unsolved problems and coming up with tentative solutions. A few writers (e.g., Crick & Mitchison, 1983) would claim that dreams function only to purge unnecessary brain cell connections produced during wakefulness and that dream content is best forgotten. But even if this neurological function occurs, the advice to forget one's dreams is not necessarily logical because divergent thought may contain creative ideas.

An early attempt to study dreams and creative problem-solving was initiated by M. E. Maillet who obtained 80 replies from mathematicians to whom he had sent questionnaires. Four of them cited mathematical dreams in which they actually found a solution to a problem. Eight mentioned that the beginnings of solutions occurred in dreams. Fifteen mathematicians claimed they awakened with complete or partial answers to mathematical questions, even though they did not recall dreams about them. Another 22 said they recognized the importance of mathematical intuition, even if they did not recall specific dreams about their problems (de Becker, 1968, p. 85).

Robert Davé (1979) attempted to determine if dreams could facilitate creative problem-solving on behalf of 24 people who were at an impasse in solving a creative problem. One group of eight subjects was hypnotized, a "hypnotic dream" was evoked, and the subjects were told they would have night-time dreams offering solutions to its problems. Another group was given instructions about how to solve its problems through activities emphasizing rational, cognitive thought exercises. Eight other participants simply were interviewed about their problems, and served as a "control" group.

Davé judged the treatment a success for six of the eight members in the hypnotic dream group, for one member of the rational-cognitive group, and for nobody in the interview group. An example was a writer who had completed extensive research for an article about an art store but was unable to develop a format for the piece. His hypnotic dream image consisted of three piles of material, indicating the article could be divided into three parts. In a subsequent dream, he found himself floating into an art store and observing activities constituting the subject of his proposed article. Upon awakening, he composed a draft in the ensuing hour. It used a format consisting of taking the reader on a walking tour of the store. Another subject was blocked in her efforts to complete a poem; she had only been able to write one stanza before treatment. On the third night after her hypnotic session, she awoke from a vivid dream which motivated her to immediately compose three stanzas.

Michael V. Barrios and Jerome L. Singer (1982) queried 48 volunteer subjects about their creative impasses, finding that most had been blocked for over three months. Their reported difficulties involved completing literary or artistic works, professional or vocational projects, or scientific or technical tasks. The subjects were administered a battery of psychological tests, divided into four groups of 12 subjects each, and randomly assigned to one of four conditions.

The subjects in the "waking imagery" group engaged in ten directed imagination exercises and subsequently generated three waking fantasies related to their creative projects. Those in the "hypnotic dream" group were exposed to a hypnotic induction procedure and subsequently produced three hypnotic dreams associated with their creative projects. Subjects in the "rational discussion" group were led through a highly focused and logical collaborative examination of their creative projects in which distractions and task-irrelevant thoughts were avoided. The "control" group was simply encouraged, in a non-directive fashion, to discuss their projects.

Results of the treatments indicated that the waking imagery and hypnotic dream conditions were most effective in promoting the resolution of creative blocks. When the psychological test data were examined, it was found that subjects able to regulate their attention with a low level of negative daydreaming (involving guilty or hostile fantasies) were most likely to demonstrate positive changes. For example, a writer in the hypnotic dream condition had published poetry and non-fiction but was having difficulty writing fictional material. With each successive hypnotic dream, however, the action and dialogue of her proposed short story became more elaborate. Elements of conflict between characters, which initially had been notably absent, began to emerge and enliven the plot. In retrospect, the writer reported a high level of satisfaction in relation to the story and also reported enhanced productivity in writing poetry.

In other words, the two treatment techniques involving imagery appeared to be the most successful. And images typically lead to creative breakthroughs in dreams. Ingmar Bergman used dream imagery as the inspiration for some of his films and William Styron had the idea for *Sophie's Choice* in a dream. It is often claimed that Niels Bohr visualized the model of an atom in a dream (Cherry, 1981, p. 65). William Dement, the sleep researcher, wrote him to confirm this, and Bohr replied that the claim was spurious and that Lord Rutherford had first conceived that particular model (Delaney, 1987).

Sir Francis Galton established, in 19th century inquiries into imagery, that the formation of abstract theoretical concepts is sometimes accompanied by color associations or spatial arrangements. Psychologist Rudolph Arnheim (1969) observed that theoretical concepts usually are not handled in empty space but may be associated with a visual setting (p. 111). Albert Einstein (1952) said "The words or the language, as they are written or spoken, do not seem to play any role in my mechanism of thought." For him, the entities that seemed to be important were visual or kinesthetic images that could be voluntarily reproduced and combined (p. 43).

How frequently are problems solved in dreams? William Dement (1974) studied one type of problem with 500 volunteer students in his sleep laboratory at Stanford University. Each was given one of three possible problems, a questionnaire, and instructions not to look at the problem until 15 minutes before retiring, then the subject was to spend that 15 minutes trying to solve it before going to sleep. The next morning the subject was to record any dreams remembered from the previous night; if the problem was still unsolved, 15 additional minutes were provided that morning for its solution.

The first problem stated: "The letters O, T, T, F, and F form the start of an infinite sequence. What is the rule for determining any or all successive letters? According to your rule, what are the next two letters of the sequence?" (The rule is that the letters are the first letters of the words one, two, three, four, and five; so the next two letters are S from six, and S from seven.)

The second problem stated: "Consider these letters: H, I, J, K, L, M, N, O. The solution to this problem is one word. Find that word." (The solution is water, "H to O," or as a chemical formula, H_2O—because water consists of two parts hydrogen to one part oxygen.)

The third problem stated: "Observe the sequence 8, 5, 4, 9, 1, 7, 6, 3, 2. What is the rule governing their order?" (The rule is that the numbers are arranged alphabetically when spelled out.)

The subjects' questionnaires recorded 1,148 attempts to solve the problems, of which 87 appeared to be linked to relevant dreams, 53 directly and 34 indirectly. The correct solutions, however, appeared only nine times; in two of these, the subjects determined the right answer before retiring. Dement admitted some shortcomings in his study: The students had no strong motivation to solve the puzzles, and the problems did not reflect high level creativity.

Nevertheless, some of the responses demonstrate how dreams attempt to solve problems. One student solved the first problem after this dream: "I was standing in an art gallery looking at the paintings. As I walked down the hall, I began to count the paintings—one, two, three, four, five. But as I came to the sixth and seventh, the paintings had been ripped from their frames! I stared at the empty frames with a peculiar feeling that some mystery was about to be solved. Suddenly I realized that the sixth and seventh spaces were the solution to the problem." In this case, the student arrived at the answer by the sort of mental process which is difficult to deliberately apply but which is common in dreams.

Figure 8.

Another student believed he solved the second problem before falling asleep by stating "alphabet," an incorrect answer. However, he reported: "I had several dreams, all of which had *water* in them somewhere. In one dream I was hunting for sharks.

In another I was riding waves at the ocean. In another I was confronted by a barracuda while skin diving. In another dream it was raining quite heavily. In another I was sailing in the wind." In other words, the student's problem-solving processes were still at work, even though he thought he had set aside the puzzle before falling asleep.

On the basis of the Dement experiment, Christopher Evans (1985) concluded that analysis of key features of a dream experienced during a period in which one is working on a problem may yield a solution. To benefit from such a dream, however, one needs to exert a certain amount of effort; the solution "may leap at you in a sudden flash of insight but more likely you may need to work at it to tease it out" (p. 234). In other words, dreams are no panacea. Dreams do not solve problems for everyone. However, the track record of dreams is encouraging enough to warrant the dreamer's attention. They have assisted in solving problems for *some* celebrated people as well as for *some* laboratory subjects. Dreamwork will probably result in self-knowledge and growth in some area of your psyche, even though the specific path, like so many of life's adventures, is difficult to predict.

In Summary

- Dreams have been an important source of information for some politicians and military leaders throughout recorded history.
- Dreaming involves both cerebral hemispheres, and both the "older" and "newer" parts of the brain.
- Both internal physical states and external environmental stimuli can influence dream content, although the role played by the latter is minor in comparison to the former.
- Some researchers believe that dreaming is a process of random "unlearning" and that dream content is psychologically irrelevant. Most research data, however, support the view that dreams express a process of synthesis at work.
- The dream's potential meaning depends upon the dreamer's taking the time to look for it.

Exercises

1. *Recalling Stimuli.* Examine your dream notebook, paying special attention to nights when there may have been a noticeable internal or external stimulus (e.g., a meal of hot, spicy food; dogs barking outside). Did your dreams demonstrate any discernible reflection of those stimuli? Can you recall any dream that clearly was influenced by an easily identifiable internal or external stimulus? How did your dream transform that stimulus? Did that transformation provide useful information about your behavior or your inner life?

2. *Searching for Synthesis.* Review the dreams you have recorded. Do any reflect a process of creative synthesis to you? If so, how? In what ways? It is useful to review your dreams in series whenever possible because the synthesis reflected in dreams becomes more apparent over several nights.

3. *Having Fun with Puns.* Study your dreams to determine if any contain puns or plays on words. The British psychologist Ann Faraday (1974) categorized several types of puns commonly found in dreams. In "verbal puns," one word represents another of similar pronunciation but different spelling. Being dressed in "gilt" might mean experiencing "guilt." In "reversal puns," the word or words must be reversed to understand their meaning; a dream of "filling full" a jar might express a sense of being "fulfilled." "Visual puns" produce a picture based on one sense of a word to express an idea involving a different sense of the same word. A dream of a "baseball game" may reflect a feeling of being involved in a "base" and underhanded "game," or activity. "Slang puns" involve a colloquial or slang metaphor; being "shot down" may express one's fear of being verbally attacked. "Body puns" contain some type of body language. For example, the need to "get something off one's chest" may lead to a dream about a bare chest. "Name puns" give clues as to someone's name. Faraday dreamed of a man in long johns shooting her down with a machine gun. The next day she appeared on Long

John Nebel's radio program where a psychoanalyst tried to "shoot her down" for criticizing some of Freud's ideas.

4. *Bias Control.* It is said that Xerxes' dreams led to his defeat at the Battle of Salamis. How do you know when your dream is expressing an implausible wish or desire and when it is expressing a realistic solution to a problem or question? Eugene Gendlin (1986) suggested several ways people can control their biases when working with their dreams. For example, if the decision is an important one, do not settle for one interpretation. Look at your dream again and find a different, or opposite, interpretation. Take each interpretation into your body and determine how you *feel* about it. Which interpretation *feels* more plausible to you? Now examine how you behaved in the dream. Imagine behaving in an opposite manner. How would the interpretation of the dream differ if you behaved differently? Find the part of the dream, or dream character most objectionable to you. *If* that were an aspect of yourself, how would the interpretation change? Take these new interpretations into your body and see if one *feels* correct to you. What was the most imaginative part of the dream? Did you use this part in your interpretation? If not, you may have left out the most valuable part of the dream. Re-interpret your dream, giving special notice to the most imaginative, unusual, uncharacteristic, bizarre portion of the dream. How do you *feel* about that interpretation, from a bodily perspective? Or by learning how to utilize bias control, you can use these techniques, especially when the dream interpretation stimulates potential decisions on major life issues.

5. *Evoking Dream Recall.* Perhaps some members of your family or some of your friends claim they never dream. Obtain their permission to conduct an experiment. While they are asleep, observe their eyelids. When you see their eyes moving beneath their eyelids, wait a few minutes and then gently awaken them, asking "What was going through your mind?" Two or three attempts should be enough to evoke dream recall and to convince most people that they do, indeed, dream.

3

The Symbol That Expresses

Those things that have occupied a man's thoughts and affections while awake recur to his imagination while asleep.

— St. Thomas Aquinas

We have invited you to explore your dream life and to consider it a potential wellspring of creativity. You may find buried treasure or you may discover that the well seems dry. If the latter is true, you simply need to plumb deeper into your psyche to locate the source of your wellspring. In either event, you will have learned something about yourself.

In the meantime, there is evidence that dreams are an integral part of your life. They are probably affecting your health, attitudes, and your decisions whether you attend to them or not. Dreams play no favorites. They have influenced saints and sinners, idealists and pragmatists, Marxists and capitalists, the young and the old, the loved and the lonely. Yet, dreams have had a bad press in Western intellectual circles for many centuries. St. Ambrose composed prayers to be spared from dreaming and medieval literature sometimes referred to the dream as a "nocturnal terror." During the Reformation, John Calvin had a low regard for dreams (Evans, 1985, pp. 35-36). Since the advent of the Enlightenment in the 17th century with its emphasis upon reason and empirical science, educated people have tended to regard dreams as unimportant and meaningless. To do otherwise, they insisted, would represent a regression into superstition and the occult. However, this attitude began to shift at the turn of the century, and more positive views have continued to gather momentum.

Freud, Adler, and Jung

Dreamwork began to become respectable as a result of two scientific undertakings: the psychoanalytic exploration of the unconscious and the electrophysiological study of sleep. In 1895, Sigmund Freud's *Project for a Scientific Psychology* was published, followed, a few years later, by *The Interpretation of Dreams,* a book with the same title as the epic by Artemidorus written 1,700 years earlier. Freud's publisher was quite excited by the second book. Even though it was published in 1899, he advanced the date on the title page to 1900 to herald the new century. However, only 351 copies were sold in the first six years after its publication, and the importance of Freud's work was not initially recognized.

It was clear to Freud (1900/1965) that he was making a distinct break from the prevailing Zeitgeist by assuming dreams could be interpreted. Pointing out that philosophers and psychiatrists of his day considered dreams as "fanciful," Freud stated, "I must affirm that dreams really have a meaning and that a scientific procedure for interpreting them is possible" (p. 132). For Freud, dreams served the function of "wish fulfillment." The raw materials used in dream construction included recent experiences, such as events from the day preceding the dream. Freud termed these elements "day residues" which were "worked over," yielding the ultimate dream product, a complex and bizarre patterning of the original material. Although these residues typically represented rather inconsequential daily occurrences, Freud felt they could serve as screens for disguising socially unacceptable impulses and wishes which were being discharged in the dream. Hence, the dream helped maintain a psychological equilibrium by allowing an outlet for disturbing thoughts and feelings, especially when the dreamer was asleep and more vulnerable to incursions of unconscious material. In addition, Freud differentiated between the "manifest" and "latent" levels of dream content, the former being the disguised content as the dreamer reports it and the latter referring to the actual meaning as it emerges during the psychoanalytic session.

Figure 9. Freud's Model.

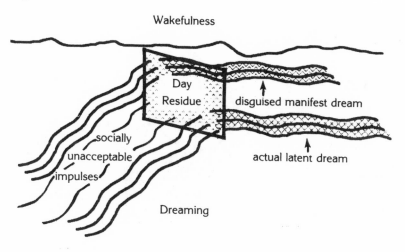

Wakefulness

Day
Residue

disguised manifest dream

socially
unacceptable
impulses

actual latent dream

Dreaming

A one-time follower of Freud, Alfred Adler, took issue with his former mentor. Adler (1938) felt day residues were important in and of themselves because they represented waking concerns. The function of the dream, therefore, is to work through unresolved problems from waking life rather than discharge unconscious and repressed problems. Both Adler and Freud thought day residue served as raw material for dreams. However, Adler proposed that the individual's concerns were openly revealed in the dream while Freud held that these concerns were disguised. Adler also argued for a continuity between sleep and wakefulness; for him, the dream expressed one's life-style, serving as an integral part of the individual's mental functioning. The dream, being the creation of the dreamer, must reflect his or her basic personality. Hence, Adler considered the dream to be purposive in nature, seeking to solve problems in a manner consistent with the dreamer's typical daily behavior. However, both Adler and Freud erroneously concluded that people who function well in their daily lives rarely dream because they deal adequately with their problems while awake (Ansbacher & Ansbacher, 1956, p. 359).

Figure 10. Adler's Model.

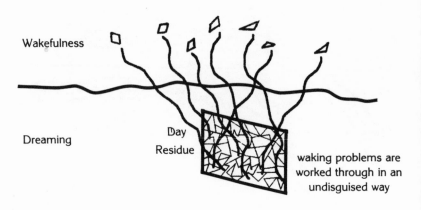

For Adler, dream symbols were a type of language which expressed the individual's current life situation. His emphasis on the symbol which expresses rather than the one that disguises is consistent with his emphasis on the continuity between waking-style and dream-style. For Carl Jung, another of Freud's early associates who broke with him, the dream symbol also revealed the inner life rather than concealed it. Jung (1974), however, held that one's dream-style often contradicted one's waking-style; the dream may represent a suppressed or poorly developed function, or a pattern of behavior to be expressed in the future.

Jung also believed that dream images frequently represent emerging forces in a person's life rather than the repressed sexual wishes and past experiences stressed by Freudians. In contrast to Freud, Jung found it valuable to have his clients write down both their dreams and waking fantasies, and to take an active role in interpreting their dreams. He often used the technique of "amplification" in which both cultural myths and personal memories would be considered to understand the dream more fully. To Jung, the function of dreams is compensatory, a way

Figure 11. Dreams Depict Emerging Compensatory Patterns.

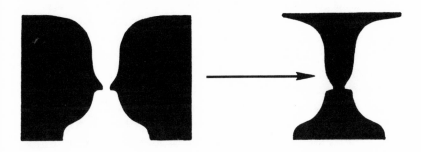

the unconscious expresses in symbolic form a homeostatic reaction to the one-sided position of the conscious mind. The dream is seen as a self-representation of the psyche, emerging as part of the continual regulation of one's psychological processes (Hall, 1982).

Despite their differing positions on many critical issues, Freud, Adler, and Jung all saw the dream's function as facilitating some type of resolution or equilibrium within the psyche. While Freud was more likely to emphasize conflict and Adler and Jung focused on balance, all three found dreams to be clinically useful. Later clinicians continued to acknowledge the unconscious determinants of the dream but generally emphasized ways the dream directly mirrored the dreamer's concerns and problems (Krippner, 1980a). More attention is now given to the *purpose* of the dream than to the dream's *cause.* Contemporary dream-workers acknowledge the ability of dreamers to avoid undue self-deception and defensiveness when attempting to understand their dreams. The conception of the dream as an authentic presentation of personality rather than a disguised product is common to most current dream interpretative schools (Fosshage & Loew, 1978, p. 293). This notion would have been ridiculed by early psychoanalysts, who took the position that only the therapist could tell a client what his or her dream signified.

Rapid Eye Movements

As early as 1892, G. T. Ladd suggested that there might be a relationship between night-time eye movements and dreams. In 1938, Edmund Jacobsen, a specialist in relaxation procedures, predicted that if a sleeper whose eyes were moving were to be awakened, he or she would report a dream. These suggestions were ignored for many years until Eugene Aserinsky and Nathaniel Kleitman (1953) initiated laboratory work on eye movements. Aserinsky, a medical student, had joined Kleitman, a renowned sleep researcher at the University of Chicago, to investigate the night-time activity patterns of infants. Observing that there were occasional periods of rapid conjugate (or yoked) movements from the infants' eyes at various intervals, the two partners speculated that this could be related to dreaming. They followed up their hunch by awakening adult subjects whenever they demonstrated rapid eye movement (REM) activity during sleep. Collecting data from ten subjects, Aserinsky and Kleitman reported that awakening them during REM sleep produced dream reports 74% of the time; awakening them during non-REM sleep produced dream reports 7% of the time.

A young physician, William Dement, joined Kleitman and began to investigate the type of dreams reported by schizophrenics. Dement made the interesting discovery that whenever Stage REM occurred, it was accompanied by a distinctive brain wave pattern marked by low amplitude and moderately rapid tracings on the electroencephalograph machine (EEG). Dement and Kleitman (1957) divided sleep into Stages 1, 2, 3, and 4, in addition to what was later called Stage REM (or REM sleep) on the basis of EEG tracings. REM sleep occurs about every 90 minutes; the initial Stage REM is quite brief but the final REM period may last from 25 to 40 minutes. Newborn infants spend about half their sleep time in Stage REM but the amount decreases to about 25% by the age of five (Fiss, 1979). Stage REM is also marked by arousal of the sexual organs, irregular respiration and heart rates, and muscular relaxation (sleepwalking does not typically occur in Stage REM because the muscles temporarily have lost their ability to coordinate movement).

Further investigation differentiated "tonic" from "phasic" events during sleep. Tonic events are continuously maintained neurophysiological components of sleep; they are the long-lasting characteristics of sleep. Most of the EEG patterns defining various sleep stages reflect tonic events; brain temperature changes and muscular activation and suppression are tonic events. Phasic events are discontinuous, episodic flurries of activity such as the REMs themselves, small muscle twitches, and irregularities of breathing and heart rate. Tonic events are stable background characteristics upon which momentary bursts of physiological activity (phasic events) are intermittently superimposed. Phasic events may be more closely related to the experience of dreaming than the REM periods themselves (Fiss, 1979, pp. 27-28).

Investigators of the psychophysiology of sleep were rarely psychotherapists. It is not surprising, therefore, that they developed their own theories of dream function, which they called "Stage REM function." Because prematurely born infants often spend most of their sleep time in Stage REM it was hypothesized that REM sleep serves to develop and maintain binocularity, the ability of both eyes to work together (Berger, 1969). There appears to be a biological need for REM sleep; when sleep subjects were deprived of Stage REM by awakening them as soon as the eyes began their yoked movements, a "rebound" effect occurred. REM time markedly increased during the first night their sleep was not interrupted; this did not occur with control subjects who were awakened an equal number of times during non-REM sleep (Dement, 1960). This effect has been repeated several times, yet any negative physical or psychological effects of REM deprivation appear to be minor. Psychologist Harry Fiss (1979) frankly states,

> It is very difficult . . . to draw any firm conclusions regarding the function of REM sleep on the basis of REM deprivation studies . . . All we can say with certainty at this point is that REM sleep must serve some vital function, since there is an obvious need for it. (p. 35)

Fiss points out that several studies appear to demonstrate a problem-solving function of dreams (p. 57). Indeed, a productive approach to dream study has been the investigation of Stage REM and its impact on learning. Aphasic patients learning to speak again have higher proportions of REM sleep than patients who are not recovering their speech (Greenberg & Dewan, 1969). A somewhat similar relationship between REM sleep and cognitive activity is suggested by the observation that severely retarded adults and children have lower than normal proportions of Stage REM, as well as delayed onset of REM sleep, and fewer REMs than normal. Those scoring lowest on IQ tests show the least amount of REM activity (e.g., Feinberg, 1968). College students given a visual memory test immediately before and after a brief sleep did better on a retest if REM sleep occurred (Barker, 1972). Some studies demonstrate an increased proportion of REM sleep following traumatic experiences, complex learning activities, or other forms of stress (Fiss, 1979, pp. 35-36).

These studies support the position that the function of REM sleep involves information processing and storage. A series of experiments by Rosalind Cartwright (e.g., 1974) demonstrate that this role is probably more significant when the material to be processed is emotionally or personally meaningful. Cartwright administered to a group of students three types of problems, ranging from neutral to emotional (crossword puzzles, word associations, and story completions). There were two experimental conditions. In one, there was a waking interval between the time the students began working on a problem and the time they finished it. For the other, there was a sleep interval, which included Stage REM, between trials. Since dreaming often allows for a synthesis of unconscious elements, Cartwright felt REM sleep might alter the results.

The findings were clear. There was no difference in crossword puzzles or word association test results whether the subjects had been awake or dreaming between trials. There was a decided difference in the story completions. In other words, the more emotional the material, the more impact REM sleep had upon the completions.

The way in which Cartwright's subjects changed their perception of the problem came as a surprise. After staying awake, most subjects gave stories a happy ending; the main character achieved gratification, sometimes at the expense of others. After a period of sleep, however, the story's main character was less successful. Sometimes the ending implied that matters did not work out very well. Cartwright suggested that her subjects were better able to recognize and speculate on negative possibilities following dreaming–possibilities they seemed to avoid while awake. Since dreamers need not take any direct action during sleep, they may be able to consider and prepare for unpleasant circumstances. Thus, REM sleep appeared to help subjects face reality, which they tried to avoid during wakefulness.

A different problem was approached by David Koulack, Francois Prevost, and Joseph de Koninck (1985), who studied how dreaming could help one adapt to a stressful intellectual activity. They reported that subjects who incorporated elements from a presleep stressful event into their remembered dreams showed less adaptation on awakening than subjects who did not. For stressful experience, uninterrupted sleep appeared to have more short term adaptive value than a procedure which enhanced dream recall through awakening the subject. It is likely, they suggested, that awakenings during dreams trigger an information processing system whereby dreams are not only better recalled but are also fitted into a framework of waking thoughts. But this process appears to be antithetical to mastery because it forces the material into a single track of conscious thought. On the other hand, when subjects remain asleep during their dreams, they may have at their disposal a number of different and integrative ways of dealing with the stressful event.

Several studies with animals demonstrate that REM time increases as a result of new learning, such as finding the way out of a maze. This relationship is evident in work conducted with cats, mice, rats, and newly hatched chicks (Fiss, 1979, pp. 36-37). Therefore, Stage REM appears to play an important role in the consolidation of such cognitive activities as learning, memory, and problem-solving for both humans and other organisms which engage in REM sleep. On the basis of these studies, sleep researcher Ernest Hartmann (1973) proposed that REM sleep's purpose is to restore one's mental operations after the trials and tribulations of wakefulness. Hartman claims REM sleep does this by providing recuperation to the neurochemical systems in the brain, which have become depleted while one is awake. Non-REM sleep plays its role by restoring the physical effects of waking and preparing for the action of REM sleep.

Ernest Rossi (1972) also emphasizes the role of learning in dream production, connecting it with an underlying biological process. For Rossi, new protein structures are being synthesized in the brain during dreaming. These organic structures are the forerunners of creative change in dreamers and how they view themselves and their world. This is the biological foundation for a naturally occurring process of constructive change in personality and behavior. To Rossi, the evidence is clear that the initiation of Stage REM comes from the brain stem; it then extends itself over the entire brain cortex (p. 142). Because animal experiments indicate that protein synthesis is present in new learning, Rossi hypothesizes that it also takes place during dreaming (pp. 143-144).

Some theorists have used computer analogies to describe dream functioning. For example, neuroscientist Jonathan Winson (1985) proposes that REM sleep is akin to "off-line processing" in computer science, the acquisition of input information and its temporary storage in computer memory until processing components are available. Information about the day's events is gathered and stored until the onset of Stage REM when it can be "processed," i.e., integrated with memories and formed into strategies for the future. According to Winson's theory, the theta brain rhythms produced by the hippocampus during Stage REM signal that information processing and future planning are taking place.

Winson notes that the spiny anteater (or echidna) was an early mammal whose sleep pattern shows no REM activity. The echidna's brain, however, had a huge prefrontal cortex, presumably used to integrate new experience with older experience. The mammals that evolved later were able to handle this task more efficiently during REM sleep; as a result, their brains were smaller—a more productive direction for evolution to follow. This problem did not exist in the earlier reptilian species; their behavior consisted largely of reflex activity, something that was adequately handled by a small brain with a neocortex (pp. 204-205).

Winson feels that dream recall is generally a matter of chance; however, he states that Freud perceived and pursued these chance occurrences, organizing them into a rather coherent working model. Dreams, then, can serve as a window on the neural processes whereby—from early childhood on—strategies for behavior are being set down, modified, or consulted. This process and the mechanisms involved were termed the "unconscious" by Freud and can be used advantageously in the clinical setting by Freudian and non-Freudian psychotherapists and other dreamworkers.

Adaptive Functions of Dreams

Montague Ullman's theory on dream function was the first to be derived from both clinical and experimental research, from his experiences as a psychiatrist and psychotherapist, and his experience as a sleep laboratory director and dream researcher (Jones, 1979, p. 291). In addition, Ullman stressed the importance of the dream's social roots, the way in which cultural forces and world events are reflected in dream content.

For Ullman (1958), the fact that REM periods are biologically controlled and humans share them with other animals has important implications. From an evolutionary point of view, a sleeping animal is more vulnerable to danger than when it is awake. Stage REM is a time of arousal; wakefulness can follow the REM period or the animal can enter another period of non-REM sleep. This is somewhat like having a built-in watchman check out the situation for possible dangers. Ullman (1961) referred to this explanation of dream function as the "vigilance hypothesis." For Freud, the dream was a "guardian of sleep," and kept a person from awakening to cope with troublesome impulses the dream was

Figure 12. Ullman's Model.

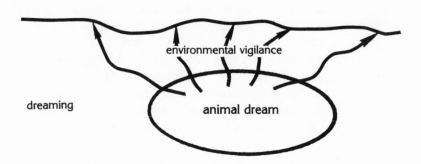

waking

environmental vigilance

dreaming

animal dream

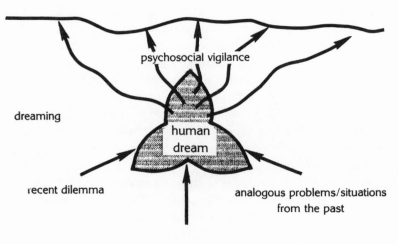

waking

psychosocial vigilance

dreaming

human
dream

recent dilemma

analogous problems/situations
from the past

cultural mores

able to discharge. For Ullman, dreams do not preserve sleep so much as they maintain an optimal state of vigilance; they may be oriented toward bringing about full arousal or playing a role in the return to non-REM sleep.

Humans focus on their social environment rather than on animal predators. The vigilance hypothesis suggests that people use the dreaming phases of the sleep cycle to explore the potential impact of dream content upon their lives. For Ullman, dreaming serves the purpose of seeking solutions to one's problems by embedding a recent dilemma in a network of analogous problems and solutions from the past, and related situations in the present. In addition, people are continuously trying to understand themselves, while at the same time trying to make sense of the world around them. As a result, cultural mores, social standards, and world events may find their way into the dream. Ullman (1973) is critical of therapists who take the personal truth out of the dream and discard the rest (p. 289).

Ullman (Ullman & Zimmerman, 1979/1985, pp. 87-89) uses as an example a soldier guarding an encampment at night, sitting before a radar screen ready to detect approaching enemy planes. When a blip appears on the screen, the soldier has to identify it for what it is and not for what he wishes or hopes it to be. He must keep it in focus until he has gathered enough information to assess the situation. Dreamers are in a somewhat analogous situation. Their attention is drawn to some residual feeling. They, too, are faced with a challenge too ambiguous to act on without further information. They also have a great deal at stake in assessing the issue for what it really is.

The soldier must decide whether or not to arouse the camp; dreamers must decide whether or not to arouse themselves and wake up. This is no small decision. It involves interfering with an important biological need and results in a radical transformation of consciousness. The decision must be based on facts. For dreamers, the facts are the truthful reflections of their feelings. Their dreams reflect how they relate to others, not the way they like to think they relate. After all, vigilance operations would be meaningless unless they were able to arrive at the truth.

Suppose a recent event results in tension which continues to trouble the dreamer. The feelings connected with it surface during REM sleep and are represented in the initial images of a dream. It is as if the dreamer is asking, "Now that I have the opportunity to be aware of my inner life, about *what* should I be aware? What is happening to me right now?" Faced with the decision of whether or not it is safe to remain asleep, the dreamer has to check out the intruding stimulus by exploring how the past can shed light on it. The dreamer pulls upon his or her memory bank, which is programmed with the initial images of the dream and the feelings associated with them. A flock of images from the past swiftly emerge. These images sometimes go all the way back to childhood, and are in some way related to the current issue.

Once the dreamer has expressed in imagery the information needed to assess the current predicament, he or she can turn to the last question: "What can I do about it?" At this point, the dreamer moves on to create relevant imagery to explore new solutions. If he or she fails, that is, if the feelings connected with the imagery are too intense to be compatible with the continuation of sleep, the dreamer awakens. So, in a sense, what the dreamer does during REM sleep is to form the basis for a yes or no decision about interrupting this state. Ullman (1961) sees dreaming as a complex and remarkable way for obtaining the data needed to arrive at this decision.

It is likely that dreams serve several purposes. Paramount among them seems to be a problem-solving function. By connecting information from clients who tell dreams to their therapists with data accumulated in laboratory settings, and by pointing out the need to understand this material within the cultural framework, Ullman provided a comprehensive dream theory. There is a consensus that dream content has three basic sources: biological, psychological, and social. Dreamwork must include all three if it is to provide a comprehensive approach to a better understanding of both the dreamer's psyche and the dreamer's world.

Figure 13.

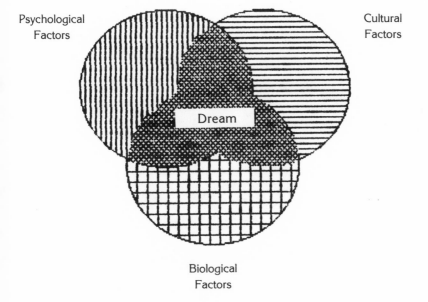

Psychological Factors

Cultural Factors

Dream

Biological Factors

In Summary

- From the middle ages to the beginning of the 20th century, many philosophers considered dreamwork to be a regression into superstition and the occult.
- Freud asserted that dreaming is relevant to mental health, claiming that dreams provide an outlet for disturbing thoughts and feelings.
- Adler considered dreaming to be a working through of unresolved problems from waking life.
- Jung thought dreams tried to correct unbalanced or inadequate daytime experience. For Jung, both emerging forces within the individual and future patterns of behavior are reflected in dreams.
- Most laboratory dream research dates from a 1953 publication

by Aserinsky and Kleitman showing an association between dream reports and rapid eye movements. Laboratory studies subsequently determined the stages of sleep and the biological bases of dreaming.

- One line of research has focused on the relationship of REM sleep and cognitive activity. Some studies indicate that dreams may help people resolve issues that they have avoided, ignored, or unsuccessfully pursued during wakefulness.

- Montague Ullman, integrating clinical practice and laboratory research, emphasized the adaptational role of dreaming as a means of maintaining vigilance during sleep. REM sleep can evaluate and provide a successful adaptation to waking conditions perceived as threatening.

- Dream content's three basic sources are biological, psychological, and social. Dreamwork should encompass all three.

Exercises

1. *Freud, Adler, and Jung.* Review your dream notebook. Did you find examples of wish fulfillment and/or apparently disguised material, the kind Freudians would expect? Were there examples to support Adler's view? These would be cases of continuity between dreams and wakefulness, of dream-style matching waking life-style. Or, as proposed by Jungians, did you find instances in which your dream-style appeared to compensate for some personal limitation? Did your dream behavior contradict your waking-style? Were any dreams primarily prospective, concerning emerging forces and solutions? These directions are all hypothesized by Jungians. Or perhaps your dreams were more Freudian in that they rehashed the past. Keep in mind that studies have demonstrated the flexibility of dreams; clients undergoing Freudian psychoanalysis actually begin to dream in Freudian symbols, while those seeing Jungian therapists began to dream in ways fitting Jung's model (Ehrenwald, 1966, p. 108).

2. *Your Own Theory.* This chapter has presented various theories about the functions of dreams. Why do *you* think people

dream? Which of these theories makes most sense to *you*? Perhaps you suspect they are all missing an important element. If so, what is it? Or, perhaps you believe there is not enough evidence to produce a believable theory now. If not, what additional evidence is needed?

3. *Understanding Negative Issues.* Rosalind Cartwright's study indicates that dreaming may help people understand negative issues they often avoid while awake. Review your dream notebook. Do any of your dreams help in identifying and comprehending unpleasant or difficult issues in your life?

4. *Solving Problems.* Despite differing opinions among dream theorists, the theme of problem-solving runs through most of their writings. Inspect your notebook to see if any of your dreams clearly focus on attemps to solve a problem, possible solutions to a problem, or solutions you had considered while awake that may not be as satisfactory as you had thought.

5. *Using Artwork in Dreamworking.* Even if you have no special talent for sketching, artwork can be a useful procedure in utilizing dream content to solve problems. A first step is to record the dream, write down any associations you might have, sketch the major scenes in the dream, and write down any associations you might have to your drawings. Secondly, ask yourself such questions as: "Who does what to whom? With what? Where? How do they feel about it?" Do your answers to these questions parallel anything going on in your life currently? Third, give each scene in the dream a title; ask yourself what *role* is being played in each scene and what *goal* is being sought. What *rules* or social constraints help or prevent the dream characters in their attempts to attain their goals? Fourth, identify the *problems* the dream appears to be portraying. How many of the dream characters (and their roles, goals, rules, and problems) represent a part of yourself? Finally, determine the effect of one character's actions on the other. Can competing dream characters get what they want or are they in conflict? Is there a way to create harmony

among competitors? Are there similar conflicts within yourself and are does the dream suggest ways balance can be attained? This exercise attempts to show how dreams express "the interaction between the cognitive and emotional systems" and how equilibrium can be established within the organism, or between the organism and the environment (Baylor & Deslauriers, 1986-1987, p. 115).

4

Dream-Style, Life-Style

You eat, in dreams, the custard of the day.

— Alexander Pope

You may be asking how your dreams could be so bizarre and yet so relevant to learning and problem-solving. Contrary to popular opinion, most dreams are not exceptionally unusual. One researcher asserted that the typical dream reported in his laboratory is "a clear coherent, and detailed account of a realistic situation involving the dreamer and other people caught up in very ordinary activities and preoccupations" (Snyder, 1970, p. 148).

We have found this to be true in our clinical and educational work with dreams. Here is a dream from Margo, one of our clients:

I need to take my car to the dealer to get it fixed. I drive to lots of different places which could not take care of it. I seem to have a time constraint because I must get to work by a certain time. I finally find a phone book, look up where I need to go, and take my car to an appropriate dealer who I know will do a complete and thorough job. I feel confident my car's needs will be addressed within the allowed time.

Margo needed to have her car repaired for several days before having this dream. During the night she was apparently engaging in problem-solving to determine how best to accomplish this task.

Not all dreams approach problems. There is good reason to assume that some dreams, like some waking thoughts, are trivial. In addition, dreams may fail to accomplish their work, as in the case of some nightmares or, perhaps, some recurrent dreams (Klein, Fiss, Scholar, Dalbeck, Warga, & Gwozdz, 1971).

Many nightmares successfully inform us of a stressful element in our lives we may be ignoring, just as some dreams repeat themselves until we have acted upon their message.

Some dreams may be incomplete and others may even be noxious. Just as not all sleep is physiologically restorative, not all dreams are psychologically restorative (Fiss, 1979, p. 64). A dreamer may awaken from a night of disturbing dreams wishing that he or she had never dreamed at all. In other words, dreams run the gamut from banal to sublime, from the important to the unimportant, from those which drain one's energy to those restoring it.

Dreaming can be defined as cognitive activity occurring in sleep, marked by imagery and narrative. Thus, one can make the case that dreams are part of an elaborate and intelligent feedback system. Dreams may contain some or all the hallmarks of intelligence, e.g., sequential thinking, metaphor making and symbolization, story telling, inductive and deductive reasoning, memory and recall, analysis and synthesis of information. In addition, dreams feature the innovative association of a wide variety of facts, experiences, and feelings. These are the reasons why dreams can provide insights in an ongoing way.

The Content Analysis of Dreams

If it is true that your dreams reflect your waking actions, emotions, and thoughts, then they automatically become relevant to you. They are capable of addressing those concerns to which you devote a considerable amount of your time. As you review your recent dreams, you will probably discover that most routinely deal with people you know, in places and activities that are not completely unknown or unfamiliar.

Studies of dream content among Americans have uncovered some fascinating material. For example, women are more likely than men to dream about being indoors in familiar settings with known people. The clothes, faces, and appearances of other people are clearer in the reported dreams of women than men. Female dream aggression is likely to be nonphysical and verbal while men are more likely to engage in physical violence, usually with men they do not know. Women have fewer sexual dreams than men; when they do, they usually dream about known men rather than strangers. Men have more sexual dreams and dream frequently about strangers. Women report more dreams containing emotion, colors, and values. Men's dreams are more likely to emphasize action, vocational activities, and themes of success and failure.

Women are more likely to dream about cats, and men about birds; both dream about dogs and horses, but children have more animal dreams than adults (Van de Castle, 1971, p. 37). Furthermore, the dream content of American men and women has become more alike in recent years, paralleling what has occurred in American society. Indeed, content analysis research indicates that dreams appear to mirror the same types of interests, activities, and personality attributes that differentiate between the sexes in waking life. This finding supports Alfred Adler's (1958) insistence that one's dream-style is congruent with one's life-style.

Young children report dreams that are not particularly frightening nor unpleasant. The most commonly occurring characters in children's dreams are family members and peers. When strangers appear, they have the same function as persons known to the dreamer. The most commonly observed settings in children's dreams are home and various outdoor recreational areas. The most common plot sequences involve everyday forms of social interaction, with a particularly strong emphasis on play (Foulkes, 1982; Witty & Kopel, 1938). David Foulkes (1982), as a result of his research, questions Freud's contention that children's dreams are unconsumated wishes. He contends that children's dreams more often reflect the exploration and manipulation of the environment. Nor did Foulkes find that children's dreams are populated by exotic creatures and monsters as some Jungians would contend. Animals are common in children's dreams, but they are usually the domesticated variety.

By the time they are six, girls populate their dreams with an equal number of men and women. Boys have fewer people in their dreams, with twice as many women than men. This pattern persists into and throughout adulthood. Girls report more social events and more happy emotions in dreams than do boys. Both girls and boys are more often victims in their dreams than adults are in theirs. Children's dreams are shorter, simpler, and less well organized than those of adolescents and adults (Garfield, 1984, chapter 2).

Dream content changes during menstruation and pregnancy. One of the leading experts in content analysis, Robert L. Van de Castle (1971, p. 40) once obtained dream reports from 50 nursing students, dated accordingly to their menstrual cycles. He found that menstrual dreams contained more references to rooms (perhaps symbolizing the uterus) and to anatomy, as well as more infants, children, and mothers. Several investigators have studied pregnancy dreams (e.g., Krippner, Posner, Pomerance, & Fischer, 1974), finding that pregnant women's dreams tend to contain more references to architecture, shopping centers, the human body, and babies of various shapes and sizes. There is evidence that dream content changes from the first to the third trimester of pregnancy; anxiety and fear may be present in the last trimester, especially for women expecting their first child (Stukane, 1985).

Cross-cultural studies have revealed important differences. The dreams of Cuna Indians in Panama demonstrate very little aggression against others, a trait also noticeable in their daily lives (Van de Castle, 1971, p. 41). People in developing countries who live in areas with high density populations where food is often scarce have an unusually low frequency of food consumption in their dreams (Monroe, Monroe, Nerlove, & Daniels, 1969). Both of these studies support Adler's position on dreams and refute Freud's notion that most or all dreams demonstrate "wish fulfillment." If dreams expressed unfulfilled wishes, why would there not be more food in dreams of chronically hungry people?

Adler's theory of dream/wakefulness continuity has also been supported by a project conducted by Robert LeVine (1966), an anthropologist. LeVine studied three different groups of male students in Nigeria, finding that dream content differed in relation to their educational and professional achievements. For example, the Ibo culture has a value system and social structure favoring upward mobility of its members. The Hausa culture does not support social mobility and individual achievement while the Yoruba culture takes an intermediate position. Dreams of Yoruba students contained more achievement themes than those of Hausa students, but less than those of the Ibo students, exactly what LeVine predicted.

There are many ways to identify content in dreams. The first was proposed in 1838 by a German investigator, G. Heermann, who studied the dream imagery of blind subjects (Van de Castle, 1971, p. 34). You might want to use a practical method that we adapted based on a system devised by Calvin Hall and Robert L. Van de Castle, who classified elements from 1,000 different dreams. Everything in your own dreams should fall into at least one of these eight categories:

1. *Characters* describe any human being, as well as any other living organism or mythical creature with a clearly discernible personality. Examples include Hercules and the satyr from Alexander the Great's dreams, Hilprecht's Babylonian priest, and Mohammed from Tariq Ibn-Ziyad's dream.

2. *Settings* refer to the time and place of a dream. Examples are Howe's presumed place of execution and Tubman's "Underground Railroad" passageways.

3. *Nature* refers to any vegetable, animal, or mineral. Examples are the snake, smoking clouds, and lightning in Hannibal's dream; Mendeleev's chemical elements, and Agassiz' fossil.

4. *Objects* would be anything made by humans. Examples are the spears in Elias Howe's dream, the wall in Alexander's dream about Hercules, and the airplanes in Parkinson's dream.

5. *Activities* refer to any behavior carried out in the dream. Examples are Genghis Khan and Tariq Ibn-Ziyad receiving instructions in their dreams; Julius Caesar sleeping with his mother; and Bismarck's ride on the narrow Alpine path.

6. *Modifiers* include any type of description, such as Hannibal's "huge" serpent, Bismarck's "endless" whip, Hilprecht's

"small" fragments of agate, and colors used as adjectives.

7. *Sensations* include such sense perceptions as tastes, smells, tactile impressions, and music. Examples are Hitler's choking sensation and the feeling of warm blood flowing down his chest (keeping in mind the dubious validity of this dream).

8. *Emotions* refer to any experienced mood or inner feeling. Examples are Howe's frustration at not being able to complete his invention and his fear as his execution drew near.

Content analysis has' served valuable purposes in dream research and it may be useful for you as well. Observing the content of your dreams in an entire collection may be useful. Jungians typically interpret a dream in the context of a series of dreams in which it is embedded. They note that misunderstandings and misinterpretations at an earlier stage can be corrected by later dreams (Hall, 1982, p. 132). Changes in content could be significant as well. If you notice a sudden absence of settings in your dreams, this may suggest a time when you are uprooted or uncertain. If you begin to record more emotional references, you may be in contact with strong inner feelings. Do not be upset if you experience a preponderance of unpleasant emotions as you engage in content analysis. Hall and Van de Castle observed that sadness is more common than happiness in most people's dreams and that sadness and anger are twice as frequent as joy and happiness. If dreams tend to focus on life's problems, we should expect this lopsided emphasis.

The Two Faces of Janus

Janus was a Roman god with two faces, one facing the past, the other the future. He was god of the gates, of departure and return, and the promoter of all initiative. Albert Rothenberg (1979), a psychiatrist specializing in studies of creativity, described *Janusian thinking* as the process which actively conceives two or more opposite or antithetical ideas, images, or concepts simultaneously. Rothenberg stated that Janusian thinking is essential to creativity; but unlike dreaming, one's rational and logical faculties are fully operative at the moment simultaneous oppositions and antitheses are formed. For Rothenberg, creativity is a mirror-image process; its contents resemble the reversals and multiple opposites found in dreams, but its psychological characteristics and functions are the obverse of the dream. The creator consciously uses the mechanisms and processes characteristic of dream thought but uses them to abstract, conceptualize, make ideas concrete, and to reverse the effects of unconscious censorship.

Rothenberg points out several ways dreaming and creativity form an obverse relationship. Dreaming occurred fairly early in human evolution while creativity appeared much later, beginning with the first cave drawings. Dreaming is an involuntary biological activity in which creativity must be invoked. Although creative thought sometimes appears to flow spontaneously and effortlessly, the reverse is usually the case. Extreme effort and conscious intention mark the creative process more than any other type of cognitive activity. However, Rothenberg sees creativity as functioning to arouse the creator, just as Ullman hypothesized that dreaming is a state of partial arousal. Rothenberg points out that those who appreciate a creative product are also aroused and speak of "having our eyes opened" or "being waked up" by a book, painting, or scientific breakthrough.

Whether or not one agrees completely with Rothenberg, one must admire his diligent attempt to compare the dreaming process with the creative process. When artists, entrepreneurs, inventors, scientists, and other innovators engage in Janusian thinking, they unearth unconscious material. Dreams can also tap some of this unconscious material, making dream content itself available for creative work. Mendeleev had set out to categorize the elements before having his dream; Howe had been working on a prototype for a sewing machine years before his dream. Both men had a high degree of technical knowledge that was evident in their dreams and the way their dream images developed into the final product.

Perhaps Rothenberg drew too rigid a line between the cognitive processes in dreams and waking creativity. Freud assigned dream thought to the category of "primary processing," which consisted of nonlogical thought, time and space distortions, the concretization of abstract problems (usually in visual symbols), and other ways instinctual drives manifest themselves psychologically. In "secondary processing," logic and reason are evident, distortions are minimized, and abstract linear thought prevails.

Most dream activity could be categorized as primary processing. However, there are many exceptions, especially in regard to highly creative people. Antonio Ludovico Muratori, an 18th century scholar, reported that he dreamed about composing a Latin verse, a pentameter which ordinarily would require complex use of metric technique (Arieti, 1976, p. 9). Although this feat resembles secondary rather than primary processing, Muratori's dream seems to have accomplished both.

Otto Loewi's demonstration of the chemical mediation of nerve impulses is usually attributed to a dream he had in 1920. However, if his report is read carefully, one can raise a legitimate question about whether the insight actually occurred in Stage REM. Loewi (1960) recalled:

> The night before Easter Sunday of that year I awoke, turned on the light, and jotted down a few notes on a tiny slip of thin paper. Then I fell asleep again. It occurred to me at six o'clock in the morning that during the night I had written down something important, but I was unable to decipher the scrawl. The next night, at three o'clock, the idea returned. It was the design of an experiment to determine whether or not the hypothesis of chemical transmission that I had uttered seventeen years ago was correct. I got up immediately, went to the laboratory, and performed a simple experiment on a frog's heart according to the nocturnal design . . . . Its results became the foundation of the theory of chemical transmission of the nervous impulse.

This account suggests that Loewi's waking mind was not aware of the contents of his night-time insight, for which he later received the Nobel Prize. But Loewi does not use the word *dream* to describe his insight, and gives no indication of visual imagery or dreamlike narrative. Nor does a secondhand account of Loewi's discovery indicate that it appeared in a dream:

> *Otto Loewi . . . once told me the story of his discovery. His experiments on the control of a beating frog heart were giving puzzling results. He worried over these, slept fitfully and, lying wakeful one night, saw a wild possibility and the experiment which would test it. He scribbled some notes and slept peacefully till morning. The next day was agony—he could not read the scrawl nor recall the solution, though remembering that he had had it. That night was even worse until at three in the morning lightning flashed again. He took no chances this time but went to the laboratory at once and started his experiment.* (Gerard, 1955, p. 227)

If the idea had occurred in full wakefulness, Loewi should have been able to recall it the next day. Though it is impossible to determine Loewi's exact state of consciousness at the time of his discovery, these accounts suggest it may have occurred during non-REM sleep.

Apparently, Immanuel Kant was able to differentiate between REM and non-REM mentation, the latter being of greater value to the philosopher:

> *Ideas in sleep may be clearer and broader than even the clearest in the waking state . . . . Dreams, however . . . , do not belong here. For . . . man . . . finds in them only wild and absurd chimeras, since ideas of* phantasy *and external sensation are intermingled in them.* (in Fromm, 1951, p. 139)

Kant believed that dreams were "simply caused by disordered stomach" and of little value (p. 138).

When sleep laboratory subjects are awakened from non-REM sleep, they report some type of mental experience about 15% or 20% of the time (Van de Castle, 1971, p. 29). The typical non-REM report is brief and nonemotional, contains a minimum

Figure 14.

of sensory imagery and very few characters, and is frequently described simply as "thinking about something." Yet the discovery of non-REM mentation indicates that sleeping individuals are almost constantly engaged in some form of cognitive activity, and that there is probably no period when the mind is a "blank." Except for coma or near-death states, it is likely that there is no time during a 24-hour cycle when people are completely "unconscious"; awareness continues throughout the cycle, albeit in changing forms. Furthermore, some individuals have emerged from coma or from near-death experiences with remarkable tales of mental activity and imagery, even though people around them considered their inner life to be temporarily or permanently at an end.

Some dream reports have been elicited in non-REM sleep and some reports resembling non-REM mentation have occurred in Stage REM, especially when there is a minimum of eye movement activity. Thus, the correspondence of dreams with Stage REM is not absolute. In the meantime, we need to entertain the possibility that the night-time creations of Loewi and Muratori were non-REM reports. If so, the head of Janus, used by Rothenberg as a metaphor for waking creative thought, might close its eyes from time to time, and engage in Janusian thinking while asleep.

Emotions in Dreams and Wakefulness

Ilene Wasserman and Bonnie Ballif (1984) conducted a study to determine what types of interactions took place between dreams and wakefulness. We will present this study in some detail to demonstrate that important work can be done in this field without expensive equipment and to encourage others to conduct similar investigations.

Wasserman and Ballif asked 20 male and female graduate students to complete a questionnaire and mood scale each morning for 28 consecutive days. The subjects selected the most influential cause of their moods from a list including dreams, environmental factors, events and activities, interpersonal relationships, personal concerns, physical factors, school, and work. The subjects indicated whether their selected cause was pleasant, neutral, or unpleasant, and whether they exerted control over it. They also indicated whether they recalled at least one dream from the previous night, even though the investigation was not presented to them as a dream study.

Of the 544 daily reports collected from the subjects, 190 were recorded on mornings of dream recall. Of the cited mood causes, 14 of the 190 attributions were to dreams. Three were labeled pleasant, three neutral, and eight unpleasant. One dream attribution was felt to have been controllable.

Wasserman and Ballif then initiated another study, with 30 male and female graduate students. The procedure was similar except that each attribution was rated on a seven-point scale. This time, there were 741 reports over a 28-day period; 296 were recorded on mornings of dream recall. Of these 296 reports, 42 listed dreams as the most influential cause of morning moods; 22 were pleasant, 6 were neutral, and 14 were unpleasant.

Eight dream attributions were labeled controllable, a surprising number since a shift of consciousness is supposed to be characterized by an interruption of volition. Because most of the controlled dreams were rated unpleasant, Wasserman and Ballif suggested that control may be a useful strategy to deal with stressful internal stimuli. People tend to perceive negative events as controllable to believe that they can be avoided in the future. Sometimes called "lucid dreaming," voluntary control of dream content has been reported throughout history.

The results of the seven-point scale indicated a wide variation in the degree to which subjects felt the dream had influenced their morning moods. Some subjects insisted dreams influenced their mood even when they could not recall any specific content. The combined data from both studies determined that dreams represented the fourth "most influential" cause of morning mood. Thus, there is not necessarily a clear-cut division of awareness between sleeping and waking.

These studies also emphasize the importance of emotion in dreams. Not only is emotion a content element in its own right, but one that may permeate waking awareness the next morning. If a dreamer awakens with only a feeling, then this aspect of the dream can be used advantageously to represent the tone of the night's final dream.

The results of Wasserman and Ballif's studies support one of Adler's key contentions about dreams. He believed that dreams produce emotions which can carry over into waking life. Adler also believed that the purpose of the dream is achieved by use of emotion and mood rather than reason and judgment. When one's life-style comes into conflict with reality, a dream often arouses feelings and emotions to bring that conflict to one's attention. Adler held that "people frequently get up in the morning argumentative and critical, as the result of an emotion created by the night's dream" (Ansbacher & Ansbacher, 1956, p. 361).

Samuel Lowy (1942) conceived of dreaming as an emotion-producing as well as an emotion-regulating process. Dreaming attempts to bring about homeostasis during sleep, thus regulating feelings but also producing images evoking feeling. This self-regulating procedure occurs largely outside waking awareness. According to Lowy, although "the dream is not primarily destined for conscious memory, it is clear . . . that it is definitely destined for being 'consciously' experienced during sleep" (p. 5). Since the primary function of dreaming pertains to the production and regulation of emotion, the interpretation of dreams must draw the dreamer's attention to the feeling associated with dream memories.

Julius Segal (1974) speculates that repeated dreams can be attempts to come to terms with particularly intense emotional material. Ernest Rossi (1972) calls the repetitive dream "an unsuccessful channeling of an emotional conflict; the imaginative drama of the dream cannot structure and transform the emotional process evoking it" (p. 147). Both perceive the role of emotion in repeated dreams and Rossi states that dream imagery can function as a representative or container of emotion.

Montague Ullman and Nan Zimmerman (1979/1985) assert that dream images evoke feeling during the night and dreamwork allows these feelings to be re-experienced during the day. As a result, dreamers can come upon less familiar and often disowned parts of themselves. An "emotional healing" can occur to repair the dreamers' relationships with others. Ullman and Zimmerman conclude, "Emotions register the state of our relations with others.

Figure 15.

It is this aspect of our lives that dreams monitor most sensitively"
(p. 98).

In Summary

- Contrary to popular opinion, most dreams deal with mundane
  life events.
- Dreams reflect intelligence. Indeed, dreaming can be defined
  as cognitive activity occurring in sleep, marked by imagery and
  narrative.
- Dream content varies according to age, sex, feelings, interests,
  culture, educational level, and socioeconomic status.
- Calvin Hall and Robert L. Van de Castle developed a useful
  method for categorizing dream content. Our adaptation of their
  system can help you identify trends in your dream life and
  allow you to compare your dream content with that of other
  dreamers.
- Jerome Rothenberg pointed out that people use creative
  thought to balance their ordinary waking approaches to problem-solving. Some aspects of this creative process are often
  observed in dreams.
- The discovery of non-REM mentation indicates that sleepers
  may be involved in some form of cognitive activity most of the
  night.
- Dreams are a sensitive monitor of emotions, and the feeling
  tone of a dream is a crucial content area to be considered for
  dream interpretation.

Exercises

1. *Content Analysis.* Apply the content analysis technique to several of your dreams. You might keep score on a simple chart to determine whether there are pattern changes from month to month. Which of the content categories seem to be most closely connected to those portions of your dreams you consider to be attempts at problem-solving?

2. *Dream Content and Computers.* Some dreamers have started to use their computers for content analysis. For example, Warren King (of Santa Cruz, California) wrote us: "I have recently undertaken the task of transcribing eight months of dream reports onto my Macintosh Apple computer with a program named 'Fact-Finder.' I am able to enter material that I can retrieve by date or key words. I also enter what time I recorded the dream, the process of remembering it, where I slept, and a tentative interpretation that expands in the following weeks. I then enter the key words that describe the major images, feelings, and other content material. I can ask the program to find one key word (e.g., 'horse') and all the dates of dreams with that content will be displayed. With the program 'Macpoint' I can also add material that I associate with each dream image. Each dream is named by its date and a short title that will elicit the dream most readily." Those of you who own a home computer might try to utilize it in this way to store your dreams and to study dream series.

3. *Janusian Thinking.* Have you ever engaged in Janusian thought? Try to recall your most recent creative project. Rothenberg believes Janusian formulations occur early in the creative process and serve to guide ensuing ideas and developments. Look for the simultaneous appearance of two or more opposite concepts, ideas, or images and their creative combination. Also remember that there are several *levels* of creativity and that Janusian thinking generally applies to the higher levels.

4. *Day Residue.* Select any one of your recent dreams. Ask

yourself, "What recent event or day residue could have produced a state of tension with which this dream might attempt to deal? How might dream images from my past help me understand this dream?" Consider all alternatives presented, even if they seem unproductive or even destructive.

5. *Awareness.* If it is true that you are aware—to some degree—almost all the time, perhaps you engage in creative problem-solving in your dreams (or during non-REM sleep). Has it ever happened that you did not recall a dream but awakened with the answer to a question? If so, dreamworking may have provided you with the solution.

5

Imagery In The Twilight Zone

We must at least agree that the things seen by us in sleep are . . . like painted images, and cannot have been formed save in the likeness of what is real and true.

— René Descartes

Carl Jung is well known for his description of introversion and extraversion, which he considered to be the two major personality orientations. The extraverted attitude supposedly orients a person toward the external, objective world, while the introverted attitude orients a person toward the inner, subjective world. Jung also described what he considered to be the four fundamental psychological functions: thinking, feeling, sensing, and intuiting. According to Jung, thinking is intellectual and deals with ideas; by thought, people attempt to comprehend the nature of the world and themselves. Feeling focuses on the value objects and activities have for people. Feelings provide people with subjective experiences of pleasure and pain, as well as such emotions as anger, fear, joy, and love. Sensing is the perceptual function which yields facts and representations of the world. Intuition is perception by way of unconscious processes and subliminal information. Usually, an individual has developed one of these four functions more highly than the other three. The intuitive person, for example, goes beyond facts, feelings, and ideas in his or her search for the essence of reality and the nature of existence.

Suppose a tourist is standing on the rim of the Grand Canyon. If the feeling function predominates, she will experience awe, grandeur, and breathtaking beauty. If she is controlled by the sensation function, she will see the Grand Canyon as a photograph might represent it, and marvel in the colors, shapes, and

Figure 16.

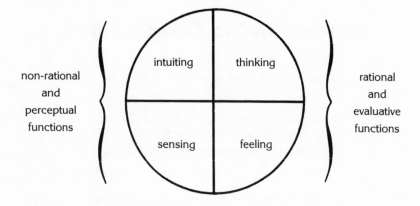

non-rational
and
perceptual
functions

intuiting   thinking

sensing   feeling

rational
and
evaluative
functions

details. If the thinking function is in control, she will be struck by the geological history of the canyon. If intuition prevails, she may see the Grand Canyon as a mystery of nature possessing deep significance. According to Jung, one or more of the other three functions would act in an auxiliary way, further enriching the tourist's experience.

Thinking and feeling are referred to as *rational evaluative* functions because they use judgment, abstraction, and generalization. Sensation and intuition are considered to be *nonrational* and *perceptual* because they are based on one's perceptions of the concrete, specific, and particular. Jung (1933) stated:

> *Sensation establishes what is actually given, thinking enables us to recognize its meaning, feeling tells us its value, and finally intuition points to the possibilities . . . that lie within the immediate facts.* (p. 107)

Donald MacKinnon (1978), a psychologist sympathetic to Jung's ideas, observes that everyone senses and intuits, thinks and feels. However, each person comes to prefer one function while growing up and uses it more often and in a more differentiated and modulated way than the others. The preferred function is called the *primary* function and the *secondary* one is the aux-iliary function. Extraverts use their primary function in dealing with the outer world of objects and persons; introverts use their primary function in dealing with their inner world of concepts and moods. But extraverts, too, have an inner life, and introverts have external situations with which they must cope (pp. 115-116).

The Importance of Intuition

Intuition is relevant to all fields of study and walks of life, but has barely begun to be investigated. In his landmark study of intuition, Tony Bastick (1982) claims:

> *Intuitions are responsible for every creation, device, and man-made system of civilization to date. Some might say that it is our reason that has brought civilization this far, but reason is only the servant of our intuition.* (p. 2)

Unlike purely logical thought processes, intuition does not sort through facts one at a time. Yet, one of the founders of quantum physics, Max Planck, wrote in his autobiography the creative scientist must have "a vivid imagination for ideas not generated by deduction but by artistically creative imagination" (in Koestler, 1967, p. 147).

Jung's description of intuition was one of several that have been put forth throughout the years. Behaviorists have attempted to explain intuition on the basis of learning principles, referring to it as "one-trial learning." For the Gestalt psychologists, intuition was a perception of the essential requirements of a problem so past experience could be brought to bear appropriately on the present (Anderson, 1959, p. 165). Starke Hathaway (1955), a research psychologist, defined intuitions as inferences in which the source of the inference could not be completely identified (p. 233).

To Jerome Bruner (1960), a leading researcher in cognitive psychology, intuitive thinking "characteristically does not advance in careful, well-planned steps" (p. 57). Instead, it tends to involve maneuvers based on an implicit perception of the total problem.

An answer may be right or wrong, but the thinker has little awareness of the process by which the answer was reached (p. 58).
M. L. Bigge and M. P. Hunt (1965) assert that intuitive judgments
usually are not based on publicly verifiable data. Supporting evidence for the intuition is hidden or vague, and the judgment,
often false or debatable, is typically based on personal conviction
(p. 105).

Digestion provides a humbling example of the limits of the
rational mind. Nutritionists and physiologists can explain some
of the processes which occur while a meal is being eaten. But
the phenomenon occurs without the hungry individual assigning
logic and reason to it. Indeed, if people had to rely on logic to
digest their food, they would starve to death in short order! Just
beneath the fragile surface of conscious control is a network of
instinctual behavior and habit on which individuals rely every day
of their lives.

When someone turns a corner while driving a car, he or she
is not using logic. Instantaneously, the driver takes into account
a multitude of such simultaneous variables as size, light, speed,
weight, obstacles, inertia, muscular coordination, gravity, and purpose. Because people use this ability routinely throughout the
day, they often consider it to be rational and logical. They can
provide plausible explanations for what they did to turn the corner
at the right time or why they responded as they did to a maverick
driver. But they ignore the remarkable fact that a barrage of data
is almost instantaneously processed that surpasses one's rational
capabilities. This ability probably reflects Jung's sensing function;
those for whom sensing is the predominant function sometimes
act so quickly that it seems like a force of habit. In fact, it probably
reflects the laws of learning at work in a manner outside one's
awareness.

Intuition often occurs in a similar fashion. Intuitive judgments
may seem to come in a flash, all at once. Intuition is experienced
as a single event as opposed to a series "a snapshot as opposed
to a motion picture" (Goldberg, 1983, p. 32). Typically, these
judgments represent the ability to consider a large amount of
data in a parallel manner. It is likely that each piece of information

is not individually considered in intuition. Instead, a "Gestalt," or collection, of stimuli is considered together. For example, a person may meet someone to whom he or she is immediately attracted. The newcomer's tone of voice, posture, and appearance are not individually evaluated. Yet this immediate attraction often is validated by future events and the person who trusts his or her intuitive judgment may not even realize what processes are at work.

Some writers (e.g., Goldberg, 1983, p. 39) insist that intuition depends on an accurate idea or concept. In her book, *Awakening Intuition,* Frances Vaughan (1979) states that when a hunch turns out to be incorrect, it should be labeled a "bad guess" rather than an intuition. There is no unanimity on this criterion, and most investigators are as interested in the process of intuition as they are in the results. Implied in the use of the word is something unexpected and out-of-the-ordinary. The amount of information a person has to make a decision based on intuition often appears to be scanty and less than what would be required to make a rational judgment on the same issue.

Sidney Parnes (1981) describes how creative problem-solving becomes the task of finding the greatest number of inter-relationships among internal and external resources, and connecting them in obvious and not-so-obvious ways (p. 59). The more remote the relationship, the more likely that originality plays a part in the idea, and the greater the opportunity for intuition to play a role in solving the problem.

Some creative persons never know when an intuitive leap will surface into awareness. Wolfgang Amadeus Mozart reportedly claimed that some of his musical inspirations occurred when he was taking walks. He observed:

When I feel well and in a good humor, or when I am taking a drive or walking after a good meal, or in the night when I can not sleep, thoughts crowd into my mind as easily as you could wish. Whence and how do they come? I do not know and I have nothing to do with it. Those which please me, I keep in my head and hum

> *them . . . . Once I have my theme, another melody comes, linking itself to the first one, in accordance with the needs of the composition as a whole: the counterpoint, the part of each instrument, and all these melodic fragments at last produce the entire work.* (Hadamard, 1945, p. 16)

Breakthroughs which rely on the inspiration phase of the creative process typically involve intuition. This is apparent in mathematics, dancing,[1] skiing, painting, investment, and many other fields. Though a person may not be able to explain how the idea was generated, it often proves to be useful or correct when the evaluation phase of creativity is applied. Then a person may claim the insight is finally "understood" by his or her rational and logical faculties. Before, however, one just *knew,* without being able to step back and explain the insight.

Of course, insights need not depend on intuitive processes. One can work with material in a rational, step-by-step manner to solve a problem. In these instances, the individual is usually able to explain quite eloquently how an idea was generated. This type of person represents Jung's "thinking" type. In addition, some people switch back and forth between both problem-solving styles, while others combine them. In his book, *The Intuitive Edge,* Philip Goldberg (1983), an industrial psychologist, emphasizes the symbiotic relationship between rationality and intuition (p. 33). Unfortunately, most educational systems assume that thinking, logic, and reason represent the *only* way in which problems can be solved (Rowan, 1979, 1986).

Law schools, for example, teach their students a base of knowledge. This educational system is rational, intellectual, and verbal; it assumes that students know how to gather, assess, and implement facts from which they can make appropriate decisions. But this system leaves little room for other problem-solving approaches.

In a study of engineering students at Yale University, grades from the last two years of school were correlated with employers' ratings of their originality. A perfect one-to-one correlation would

Figure 17.

EB

have been 1.00; instead, a correlation of .26 resulted. A similar study of 56 physicists produced a correlation of only .21 (Blakeshlee, 1980). It would appear that the original thinkers succeeded in spite of their education rather than as a result of it.

Intuition rarely can replace a solid base of knowledge. If a sizable data pool is available to a person, an appropriate insight will likely be offered by his or her intuitive processes. This ability to solve problems intuitively can make the difference between mediocrity and outstanding achievement. Some people have the reputation for being "lucky" in love and in work; it is more likely that they have learned how to use intuition properly, even if this learning has taken place outside their awareness.

Twilight States and Intuition

Bastick (1982) has detected an association between intuition and hypnagogic reverie, the thoughts and images occurring during the onset of sleep. There is a similar association between intuition and hypnopompic reverie, which occurs as one awakens (Paupst, 1975, p. 171). These "twilight" states, to use Thomas Budzynski's (1976) term, resemble dreams in that both are marked by primary process thinking and contain visual, auditory, and/or kinesthetic imagery. However, material from these twilight states is not typically characterized by narration, as are dreams.

Writer and artist Carolee Schneemann, who has used hypnopompic imagery in her work, states: "The source of all my work is poised between dreaming and waking" (in Coxhead & Hiller, 1976, p. 42). Schneemann describes how she once scrawled on the walls without opening her eyes to preserve dream imagery. This evolved into a more effective technique in which she would arrange pencils, pens, notebooks, and a tape recorder by her bedside. Sometimes Schneemann would not recall a dream, but while working on a project would remember it, once her concept began to take shape. Another artist, Jerry Schrier, claimed he virtually moved back into the dream state while making drawings (Evans, 1985, p. 224).

Hypnagogic imagery was a critical factor in one of the great discoveries of biochemistry. Without success, the 19th century chemist Friedrich August Kekule von Stradonitz had been attempting to conceptualize the structural formula of the benzene molecule. Two episodes of altered awareness led to a creative breakthrough, the first taking place when he was returning home by bus. Kekule recalled, "I fell into a reverie, and lo! the atoms were gamboling before my eyes . . . . I saw how, frequently, two smaller atoms united to form a pair; how a larger one embraced two smaller ones; how still larger ones kept hold of three or even four of the smaller; whilst the whole kept whirling in a giddy dance" (Harman & Rheingold, 1984, p. 41). Many years later, Kekule turned his chair to the fire and reported seeing structures "in long rows, sometimes more closely fitted together, all twining and turning in snake-like motion. But look! What was that? One of the snakes seized hold of its own tail and the whole form whirled mockingly before my eyes" (Rothenberg, 1979, p. 396). Kekule soon realized he had articulated what became known as the "benzene ring," a hexagonal structure with alternate single and double bonds between the carbon atoms. His discovery laid the foundation for biochemistry and molecular biology (Partington, 1972).

Another daytime experience resulted in an important development in mathematics. While a teenager, Karl Gauss had an insight on how to construct a 17-sided polygon. This experience reportedly occurred during an afternoon hypnagogic reverie while he was resting in bed (Cartwright, 1955). By the time Gauss reached 21, he had initiated his theory of complex numbers. During his career, he claimed to be subject to such a constant stream of imagery that he could barely pursue all the ideas generated. Gauss would often obtain proof for his theorems in a manner he compared to "a sudden flash of lightning" (Hadamard, 1945, p. 15). Gauss appears to have discovered the law of induction while in a hypnopompic reverie; he recorded in his notes that the law came to him "at 7 a.m., before rising" (Rothenberg, 1979, p. 106).

Twilight imagery may contribute to various forms of creativity (Rallo, 1974). William Blake claimed that images of spiritual beings started coming to him as a child and served as the basis for many of his later drawings. Blake also related that while searching for a less expensive means to engrave his illustrated songs, he dreamed that his dead brother appeared to him and described a process of copper engraving, which he immediately verified and put to use (Raine, 1971).

Henry Wadsworth Longfellow related how he began his poem, "Ballad of the Schooner Hesperus," about midnight. Upon retiring, he could not sleep because "new thoughts were running in my mind, and I got up to add them to the ballad" (Harman & Rheingold, 1984, p. 35). Harriet Beecher Stowe, the author of *Uncle Tom's Cabin,* was seated in her church pew during a communion service when the death of the venerable black slave seemed to pass before her. She was so affected she could hardly keep from weeping. That afternoon, she locked the door to her room and wrote the chapter, "The Death of Uncle Tom" (Prince, 1963, p. 174).

The British physicist Michael Faraday lacked a formal mathematical education but used "visual intuition" to develop the first dynamo and electric motor. These inventions apparently originated in Faraday's images of the universe as a composite of curved tubes through which energy radiated. Faraday also laid the foundations of modern field theory with ideas developed out of his images of "lines of force" surrounding magnets and electric currents (Goldberg, 1983, p. 76).

Elmer Green and his associates at the Menninger Foundation were intrigued by reports by Faraday, Kekule, and other creative people about twilight states and intuition. Noting that hypnagogic and hypnopompic images were accompanied by theta and low-frequency alpha brainwaves, they (Green, Green, & Walters, 1970) taught a group of 26 subjects how to enter these states through biofeedback. There was an expected increase in the subjects' awareness of internal imagery and dream recall. What was unexpected was that 20 subjects reported an increase in their "integrative experiences" and "feelings of well-being." Positive changes in subjects' personal lives were reported, changes Green and his associates noted were amenable to intuition, insight, and creativity. Green himself developed a personal hypnagogic imagery technique and used it successfully to solve a mathematical problem in psychophysics (Green & Green, 1977, pp. 296-297).

Thomas Budzynski (1976), after reviewing research literature suggesting that twilight states are conducive to assimilating newly learned material, proposed that these states could be produced at any time of the day through biofeedback. According to Budzynski, "Computer-assisted teaching programs augmented by a biofeedback produced twilight state might constitute an educational breakthrough" (p. 110).

Facilitating Intuition

The greatest opportunity for people's mental activity to escape rational control occurs during sleep. Bastick (1982) hypothesizes that the psyche's tendency to combine emotional sets during sleep is one of the reasons that dream sequences are frequently surrealistic. This type of imagery is necessary to match the contradictory feeling states of the dreamer. The combination of emotions also explains the intuitive solution of problems during sleep. Just as imagery can skillfully combine different experiences into a single symbol, so can the successful solution to a problem combine elements of the puzzle which were earlier perceived as contradictory. It is Koestler's (1967) position that "bisociation," a mental occurrence simultaneously associated with two habitually incompatible contexts, underlies creativity. Rossi (1972) suspects that intuition is based upon "synesthesia"—perceptions synthesized from two or more sensory avenues, such as "hearing flavors" or "smelling colors" (p. 175). And Arieti (1976) described "tertiary processing" as a creative combining of properties found in primary and secondary processing mechanisms (p. 12).

Bastick believes the day's emotional events need to be processed along with the dreamer's other experiences. It is not uncommon for differing, even contradictory, emotions to be processed and combined in a dream. This typically results in a reduction in the dreamer's anxiety, just as would the tying up of loose ends in a story, the resolution of a musical phrase by an appropriate chord, or the punch line of a joke (p. 380). However, this positive feeling would not have been evoked had there not been a series of emotional experiences to serve as its base. Nor would a night-time solution to a problem be possible unless the dreamer had become immersed in the factors needed to produce an eventual solution.

Goldberg (1983) finds that many people censure intuitive ideas which could yield outstanding results. Some people are afraid of censure, others yield blindly to authority, are too demanding or self-critical, or are simply afraid of novel concepts. However, he cites the case of James Couzens, a Detroit clerk who saw a noisy contraption rolling down the street in 1893. While his neighbors laughed, Couzens acted on intuition and put the thousand dollars he had saved into stock in the inventor's company. He also made a commitment to raise another $9,000 to bring his stock up to one hundred shares. In 1919, Couzens sold his stock in Henry Ford's company for 35 million dollars (p. 195).

In the original manuscript describing his sun-centered cosmos, Copernicus mentioned the possibility that planetary motion might be elliptical rather than circular. He crossed the idea out! Johannes Kepler is given credit for the discovery but even Kepler admitted he had turned his back on the concept for three years before accepting it. He wrote, "The truth of Nature, which I had rejected and chased away, returned by stealth through the back door, disguising itself to be accepted." Kepler finally opened the door to elliptical motion, but, in turn, closed it to universal gravitation, leaving that discovery for Isaac Newton (Goldberg, 1983, p. 196). These incidents are reminiscent of Brewster Ghiselin's (1952) comment, "Every creative act overpasses the established order in some way and in some degree" (p. 13).

Intuition rarely occurs unless the individual has become deeply immersed in the subject. Psychologist Rollo May (1959) observed that insights in reverie reflect "the encounter of the intensively conscious human being with his world" (p. 68). He sees creativity as the process of "bringing something new into birth" and as "the most basic manifestation of man's fulfilling his own being in his world" (p. 57). For May, creativity may occur in full awareness or in dreams and reverie:

> But let it be said immediately that . . . the answers to problems that come in reverie, do not come hit and miss. They come only in the areas to which the person is intensively committed in his conscious living . . . . We can not will to have insights, we cannot will creativity; but we can will to give ourselves to the encounter with intensity of dedication and commitment. The deeper aspects of awareness are activated to the extent that the person is committed to the encounter. (pp. 62-63)

In Summary

- Intuition is a possible route to creativity; it is probably latent in every individual.

- Dreams which exemplify problem-solving may represent intuition at work.
- Reason and logic complement intuition; intuition complements reason and logic. Together, they can bring a creative idea into useful expression.
- Creative insights sometimes occur in hypnagogic and in hypnopompic states.
- Immersion in the details of a problem before going to sleep probably enhances the relevance of dreams to that concern.

Exercises

1. *Pre-sleep Procedures.* It is quite likely that problem-solving occurs in your dreams whether or not you remember them. Before you go to sleep, review the elements of a personal dilemma, a task you have been unable to complete, or a project on which your progress has been blocked. Use as many sensory modalities as you can. *Read* any material pertinent to the task. *Speak* out loud as you consider alternative solutions to the problem. *Draw* diagrams which illustrate the problem. *Feel* any emotional concomitants of the dilemma you face. In the morning, review your dreams to determine whether any relate to your night's activity. If you do not recall a dream, approach the task again. You might be surprised to find that a solution is now available which was not apparent before your pre-sleep exercise.

2. *Twilight Imagery.* Pay special attention to your twilight imagery during the next few days. When does it occur? Does it contain useful or interesting material? You might want to attempt a content analysis of the imagery to determine how it resembles your dream content and how it differs.

3. *Synesthesia.* Try to determine whether synesthesia affects your dream recall. Think of a color. Visualize it as the sky above you, magnificently painted in that shade. Now imagine that the color has an odor. What is it? As you inhale, allow the smell to become stronger and stronger. Think of the last time you were

late for an appointment. If that feeling had a taste, what would it be? Let that taste fill your mouth now. When was the last time you had a creative insight? If the idea was a color, what would it be? If it were a taste, what taste would it be? What sound or smell would it be? Repeat this exercise, or a variation of it, while drifting into the twilight state tonight. In the morning ask yourself if your dreams were different, or if your waking mood was different. Repeat this procedure for a week to see if it has a discernible effect upon your level of creativity.

4. *Jungian Dream Interpretation.* James A. Hall (1982), a Jungian analyst and dreamworker, outlined the basic steps in Jungian dream interpretation. These may give you additional ideas for your dreamwork. The dream report should be as complete as possible. The dream should be placed in the appropriate context (e.g., the situation of the dreamer, the series of dreams in which it occurred). Motifs and themes in the dream should be amplified in terms of the dreamer's personal associations, associations related to the dreamer's culture, and the mythological associations which reflect the human condition in all cultures. The dream should be examined to see if it fits into a dramatic structure. Jung observed, "The dream is a theatre in which the dreamer is himself the scene, the player, the prompter, the producer, the author, the public, and the critic" (in Hall, 1982, pp. 151-152). The decisions and actions of the dreamer—in the dream—should be noted, as well as the responses other dream characters make to those actions. The dream can then be related to the overall life situation and development of the dreamer. Finally, Jung admitted that no dream is ever completely understood (p. 313).

5. *The Limits of Intuition.* No problem-solving strategy is perfect. Record your intuitions and hunches for about two weeks, whether you act on them or not. Upon reviewing the list, evaluate their accuracy. Were any of these sudden insights as appropriate as solutions occurring more slowly, in a step-by-step fashion, while you were fully aware of the problem-solving process? If so,

which ones? What did this exercise teach you about the value of your intuitive processes? According to Jung, even thinking, feeling, and sensing types can develop their intuition to some extent. One practical way to attempt this task is to engage in dreamwork.

6

The Night's Visitation

Dreams result from the penetration through the pores of the dreamer's body of the images that are continually emitted by objects of all sorts and especially by living persons . . . . By their impact they communicate and transmit to the recipients the opinions, thoughts, and impulses of their senders.

— Democritus

Alder's conception of a continuity between dream-style and waking life-style appears to be valid insofar as creativity is concerned. Joseph Adelson (1960), a psychotherapist, noted that his less creative clients generally described simple, conventional dreams while his more creative patients recalled highly imaginative dreams. One client, described by Adelson as insensitive to artistic work, was reported to be on guard against any mode of experience which was not logical, rational, and coherent. Another client, whom Adelson thought to be highly creative, related complex and fanciful dreams.

Stimulated by these examples, Adelson conducted a formal study of 15 college women who were taking a creative writing course. The eight who were rated by their instructor as "highly imaginative" had more exotic dreams than did the seven "uninventive" students. Some of the "highly imaginative" students' dreams took place in such settings as an African jungle, an Arabian mosque, and a Parisian bistro. The characters' identities were often transformed in dreams so the dreamer was portrayed in unusual roles. Humor, sexuality, and color were more prevalent in their dreams. By contrast, the "uninventive" students usually dreamed about their immediate environments and more conventional and stereotyped interests. When sexuality appeared, these dreamers expressed more apprehension in the dream about its possible discovery than members of the "highly imaginative" group.

Psychological Studies

Psychologist George Domino (1976) studied two groups of high school students. The groups resembled each other in age, sex, and educational background. However, one group had scored more highly on creativity tests and received higher creativity ratings from teachers. Both groups kept dream diaries for two weeks, which were then evaluated by five clinical psychologists for the presence of primary process thinking. Not only did the dream reports of the more creative group exhibit more primary process thought than the other group but they also showed greater symbolism and more unusual combinations of dream content elements. both groups showed a statistically significant relationship between primary process thinking and creativity test scores.

Domino (1982) later asked two other groups of high school students to complete a questionnaire about their attitudes toward dreams. More so than the less creative students, the highly creative students endorsed beliefs that dreams have hidden and symbolic meanings, can produce inventions and artistic creations, can sometimes predict the future, and can be programmed. Members of the creative group also claimed to make a greater effort to remember their dreams than the other group.

Domino (Sladeczek & Domino, 1985) next queried 200 college students and found that students who scored highly on creativity tests relaxed more easily and fell asleep more rapidly than those with lower scores. These results were explained on the basis that both creative behavior and falling asleep involve relinquishing control and letting go of everyday, rational awareness. Further, 93% of the more creative group claimed to have solved problems in their dreams compared with 63% of the less creative group.

Domino (Sladeczek & Domino, 1985) also studied 40 adults belonging to "creative" professions (e.g., architect, novelist, research scientist) and who had been rated "creative" by various judges. A similar group of "less creative" professionals was formed. Both groups kept dream diaries for a week. After analyzing the diaries, judges found that the "creative" group's dreams contained more regressive dream content, more dream distortion, and more visual imagery—all of which are examples of primary process thought.

In another study, a group of New York psychologists administered creativity tests to 105 college students who had been recording their dreams. It was reported that art students remembered their dreams more frequently than did science and engineering students. In addition, there was a statistically significant relationship between dream imaginativeness and scores on creativity tests (Schechter, Schmeidler, & Staal, 1965).

Ease of dream recall has been studied with the result that those who generally deny or ignore their inner world during wakefulness recall fewer dreams than those who accept and use this dimension of experience (Foulkes, 1966). However, these investigations have not been repeated often enough to be considered completely reliable. There are many reasons why people do not recall their dreams; chief among them is the fact that industrialized nations place no social reward on dream recall and this behavior is rarely reinforced.

The Adlerian notion of a basic similarity between waking and sleeping mentation is also confirmed when an experimenter awakens the sleeping subject before REM activity begins. Non-REM thoughts have been found to closely resemble mental activity during wakefulness (Rechtschaffen, Verdone, & Wheaton, 1963). However, Adler appears to have erred in agreeing with Freud that individuals dream in proportion to the intensity of their personal problems. The data indicate that REM sleep occurs in a highly predictable pattern with few variations for each individual studied (Foulkes, 1966).

In treating clients, a skilled psychotherapist can use dream content advantageously because emotional problems are often reflected in Stage REM mentation. However, most of the research data do not support the notion that one's psychodynamics precipitate REM periods or that disturbed individuals have more frequent and longer occurrences of REM. To the contrary, some researchers have reported that acute schizophrenic symptomatology is associated with decreased REM time, while remission of symptoms is related to an increase in REM time (e.g., Gulevitch, Dement, & Zarcone, 1967; Kupfer, Wyatt, Scott, & Snyder, 1970).

The normal sleep/dream cycle for adults reflects an alternation of non-REM and REM sleep on an approximately 90-minute rhythm, an increase in the length of REM periods throughout the night, and an increase in the density of eye movements with these REM periods. Rosalind Cartwright (1983; Cartwright, Lloyd, Knight, & Trenholme, 1984) investigated the sleep/dream cycles of 29 recently divorced women. She found that those who were the most depressed manifested greater variations from the normal cycle, entering their first REM period more rapidly and showing irregular phasic eye movement activity (REM density). Cartwright also investigated the sleep/dream cycles of nine women who claimed to be happily married. Their amount of REM sleep was within the expected limits. However, the depressed group gave more dream reports following the same amount of REM time than the married group or the divorcing group that was not depressed.

Cartwright suspected that the depressed women needed to undertake considerable "emotional reprogramming" and used their dreams for that purpose. Their dream content showed marked differences as well; the women who were divorcing had more negativity in their dreams than the married subjects. For Cartwright, Stage REM is a time for sifting through the fragments of feelings recorded in one's short-term memory but unexamined during the day; new information is reconciled with old memories in preparation for the coming day (Cartwright, Lloyd, Knight, & Trenholme, 1984, p. 259).

Some psychotherapists give severely depressed patients drugs to cut down on REM sleep. However, G. W. Vogel (1975, 1983) simply put his patients in a sleep laboratory and awakened them as they entered Stage REM; their state of mind improved considerably. In fact, REM reduction worked about as well as the most effective anti-depressant drugs and in roughly the same time (three weeks). Vogel reasoned that in depressed people, the brain mechanisms which mediate pleasure, appetite, and motor behavior might be active during dreaming and inactive during waking. Depressed people, if Vogel is right, are dreaming their waking lives away! By depriving them of considerable amounts of REM sleep, he has provided the night-time inhibition that they lack, thus improving their mental health during wakefulness.

Convergent and Divergent Production

J. P. Guilford (1977), one of the pioneer researchers on creative thinking, notes that the value of stored information depends on its future usefulness (p. 92). Many different abilities are involved in searching one's memory for necessary information. One set of these abilities, which Guilford termed "convergent production," is concerned with satisfying a restricted requirement in which there is only one right answer. Another set of abilities, "divergent production," applies to broad searches in which alternative ideas are required. Guilford uses the term "production" when discussing these cognitive processes because one is expected to "produce" an answer. In real-life situations, one is not given a series of answers and asked which is correct; the answer must be generated, i.e., produced.

Convergent production prevails when the input information is sufficient to determine a unique answer. Only *one* answer is considered correct in convergent thinking. But in divergent production, many alternative answers are desired. For example, if a person is asked, "What is the opposite of soft?" the answer "hard" would be a result of convergent production. If the question had been, "Name several objects that are soft," divergent production would have been required (Guilford, 1967, chapters 6, 7).

Both types of production are needed for problem-solving. However, Guilford believes that divergent production is especially important in creative thinking where many alternative ideas are necessary. Thomas Edison apparently had outstanding divergent production skills. When one of his experiments failed, he was able to suggest a number of ideas for new experiments. Winston Churchill is said to have been able to offer several alternatives instantly whenever a political problem was raised (Guilford, 1977, p. 94).

Convergent production tends to be literal, clear, exact, focused, specific, logical, precise, serious, and consistent. Divergent production tends to be metaphorical, ambiguous, approximate, diffuse, general, non-logical, fuzzy, humorous, and paradoxical. Students at the University of Edinburgh were classified according to their cognitive style and divided into two groups: highly logical, convergent thinkers and less logical, divergent thinkers. In a sleep laboratory, they were awakened when their eye movements indicated they had been dreaming and were asked to describe their dreams. The convergent group types recalled dreams 65% of the time, the divergent group 95% of the time (Austin, 1971). Although the reason for this difference is still unknown, the divergent group may have already been accustomed to drawing on their dreams to generate ideas.

Divergent production is especially important in the illumination phase of the creative process when one is generating ideas.

Figure 18.

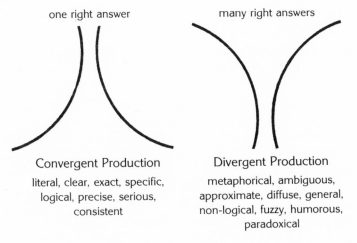

one right answer

many right answers

Convergent Production
literal, clear, exact, specific, logical, precise, serious, consistent

Divergent Production
metaphorical, ambiguous, approximate, diffuse, general, non-logical, fuzzy, humorous, paradoxical

Convergent production is best used in the evaluation phase when one is focusing on practical refinements, running risk analyses, and preparing to carry the idea into action. If convergent production is attempted earlier in the creative process, it tends to limit options, stifle spontaneity, and rule out any number of unorthodox but valuable, approaches.

On the other hand, divergent thinking in the evaluation phase can prevent the successful execution of an idea. In this stage, firmness and directness are preferable to ambiguity. One does not pass a mathematics examination by approximating answers. Sending an earth satellite into orbit cannot rely on intuition. Many creative breakthroughs appear logical and obvious only in retrospect. The light bulb, the automobile, the airplane, and the television were all denounced as impractical by many "authorities" before they won acceptance.

Creativity involves the proper use of both convergent and divergent production. Each by itself is an incomplete approach to the generation and implementation of new ideas. The dreams of Elias Howe and Dmitri Mendeleev produced original ideas, but practical evaluation was needed before the visions could be actualized.

Pattern Recognition

Convergent and divergent production are not the only cognitive skills needed for creative problem-solving. Donald MacKinnon (1978), a prominent researcher on the role of personality functioning in creativity, remarks that "creativity" is simply a convenient label for a complex set of cognitive, motivational, and emotional processes involved in bringing something new into existence (pp. 46-48). These processes include thinking, perceiving, remembering, imagining, appreciating, planning, and deciding. These are found in everyone, although qualitative and quantitative individual differences exist.

One important process in creative problem-solving is pattern recognition. If asked to describe the contents of your home, you would probably rely more on your visual than your verbal memory.

You would visualize patterns, go through your house in some type of sequential order, and convert your images into a stream of words to give your response. If you were shown photographs of several houses, you would have no trouble selecting your own. Instead of examining each detail of the photographs, you would probably compare Gestalts, or wholes. Pattern recognition would enable you to make this discrimination as well as others that are more challenging.

Psychologists who study pattern recognition examine how people compare input configurations with a variety of standards until they note a sufficiently close match (Green, 1963). In pattern recognition, a person has a set of hypotheses about the correct response, rejects possible responses which are inconsistent with the hypotheses, and makes a response once the hypotheses appear to be confirmed. This process may take place outside awareness. It can be illustrated in the way some physicians can identify illnesses very quickly by matching the patient's Gestalt against a number of possible diagnoses.

Albert Einstein seemed to have used a similar process. He once asked,

> *What, precisely, is thinking? When at the reception of sense impressions, memory pictures emerge, this is not yet "thinking." And when such pictures form series, each member of which calls forth another, this, too, is not yet "thinking." When, however, a certain picture turns up in many such series then precisely through such return it becomes an ordering element for such series, in that it connects series which in themselves are unconnected .*
> *. . . For me it is not dubious that our thinking goes on for the most part without the use of words.* (In Schlipp, 1949, p. 7)

Einstein apparently suggested that thoughts could be patterns of repeating images. This type of mental activity characterizes dreams as well, enabling those engaged in dreamwork to learn pattern recognition as a creative problem-solving skill.

Figure 19.

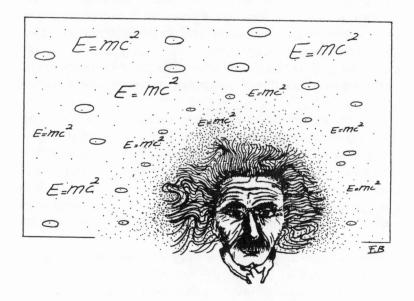

One way to use pattern recognition in dreamwork is to search for visually encoded patterns of emotions and activities. You can then match these with patterns occurring in your waking life. Jonathan had a dream in which he was running away from something; the harder he tried to run, the slower he ran. The pattern of this dream was one of increasing fear and accompanying loss of power. Jonathan recognized a similar pattern at his job. He was trying to win the approval of an unreasonable employer, but the harder he tried, the more he was criticized. Once he understood the meaning of the dream, he stopped running, confronted his employer directly, and was able to obtain an apology and a promotion. He knew he was taking a risk, but decided that losing his job would be better than coping with ever-increasing stress.

Another potential use of pattern recognition in dreams is the ability to foresee emerging trends. What business executive would not like to know what the stock quotes will be next week?

What government would not like to know the hidden purposes behind its adversary's actions? What lover would not like to know the genuine feelings of his or her beloved? Sometimes the answers are available but are not recognized by the rational mind. In dreams, however, the Gestalt often falls into place and the pattern is recognized.

Maria dreamed she visited her Aunt Hilda in a hospital, even though the aunt appeared to be in good health at the time. However, a few weeks later, Hilda was hospitalized for a stroke and Maria found herself acting out the behavior foreseen in the dream. Was the dream prophetic or coincidental? Most likely it was neither. Maria may have noticed her aunt's skin color undergo a change, her gait begin to slow, and her speech begin to slur. Pattern recognition enabled Maria to match this behavioral Gestalt with her knowledge of previous stroke victims, producing a dream which prepared her for the emergency. Dreams are capable of forecasting possible events, based on a multitude of perceptual data obtained both in and out of awareness.

Anomalies in Problem-Solving

Sometimes a dream will contain information about the future that is quite difficult to explain on the basis of the dreamer's past experience. On the morning of May 25, 1968, Alan Vaughan (1973), a so-called "psychic sensitive," recorded two dreams in his dream journal. In one of them, "an American Indian fired a rifle through a grating to murder a person." In the second, "Robert Kennedy became me, walking through a hallway; dirt fell from an overhead grating, which I associated with a kitchen hallway in my boyhood home." Vaughan wrote down his associations as well: "A single rifle shot from a grating might be connected with the dirt shifting down from the grating in the second dream. It may be precognitive, but in a very distorted form. The dirt coming down seems ominous . . . . The assailant will not be a member of a group commonly thought of as anti-Kennedy" (p. 46). On June 5, 1968, Kennedy was assassinated by a Jordanian immigrant.

Unlike Maria's dream of her Aunt Hilda, Vaughan's dream probably was not inferential. Either it was a bizarre coincidence, or it was "anomalous" in that it obtained information in a way not easily explainable in terms of contemporary science's concepts of time, space, and energy. A number of such dreams exist, among them a November 1937 dream by a Dutch "psychic sensitive" who reported, "Everything I saw was clear like crystal so that I cannot forget it . . . . A car comes along at a terrible speed . . . . A tire bursts and the car crashes at full speed against . . . the truck behind it. The driver of the car was killed immediately. I saw his face when he was lying there, it was Prince Bernhard" (Vaughan, 1973, p. 112). Two days later, Prince Bernhard of the Netherlands was severely injured when his speeding car hit a truck. He recovered, thus negating the most tragic detail of the dream.

Harriet Tubman was a historical figure who claimed to have had anomalous dreams. One of them was said to have predicted her escape from the pre-Civil War plantation where she had been held as a slave. Another concerned a three-headed serpent which attempted to speak to her. She recalled that one head resembled John Brown, the abolitionist leader, and the others looked like young men. A crowd rushed in and severed the serpent's heads. Shortly afterwards, John Brown and his two sons were killed at Harper's Ferry—a raid which Tubman had been invited to join, but had declined (Bradford, 1869/1981).

Not all anomalous dreams deal with death. A stockbroker dreamed, "A man was trying to sell me a radio. Someone put poison on the doorknob of my door and urged me to come and touch it. I was terribly frightened. He tried to force me to touch the poisoned knob. Struggling, I woke in a cold sweat." The American "psychic sensitive" Edgar Cayce interpreted the poison in this dream as a warning that the stockbroker should "refrain from investing in stocks, bonds, or anything pertaining to radio work for the next sixteen to twenty days" (Sechrist, 1968, p. 43). The 1929 Wall Street crash took place a few weeks later, but the stockbroker had failed to take Cayce's advice.

When Igor Sikorsky was ten years old, he dreamed of coursing the skies in the softly lit, walnut-paneled cabin of an enormous flying machine. Sikorsky later became an eminent aircraft designer and, three decades after the dream, went aboard one of his own four engine clippers to inspect a job of interior decorating done by Pan American Airways. With a start, he recognized the cabin as identical to the one in his boyhood dream (Krippner, Dreistadt, & Hubbard, 1979, p. 460).

These reports are provocative but must be viewed with skepticism. Not only might they be coincidental, but they may also reflect distortions of memory, confused time sequencing, unknown sensory cues, or even deliberate falsification. Dreams and other accurate premonitions about a future event may be divided into five general categories: 1. coincidental; 2. inferential, in which the dreamer intuitively puts together data—often perceived outside of waking awareness—that congeal into a correct assessment of a forthcoming event in a dream; 3. self-fulfilling prophecy, in which the dreamer unconsciously behaves in such a way that the dream comes true; 4. pseudo-anomalous, in which the dreamer deliberately lies or unconsciously fabricates or distorts the facts; and 5. anomalous, in which the information obtained appears to transcend what is scientifically known about space, time, or energy.

Montague Ullman developed a laboratory approach to the study of anomalous dreams. On eight nonconsecutive nights, the "psychic sensitive" Malcolm Bessent attempted to dream about an experience that was actually structured for him the following morning. A theme was randomly selected from a collection of several hundred possibilities; a multisensory experience constructed around this theme was then provided for Bessent. Outside judges were able to match descriptions of these post-sleep experiences with transcriptions of Bessent's dreams at statistically significant levels (Krippner, Ullman, & Honorton, 1971).

Ullman and his associates attempted a further experiment with Bessent, this time including eight nights on which he was given the multisensory experience *before* he went to sleep. Once again, the outside judges were able to match descriptions of the post-sleep experiences with Bessent's dreams at statistically significant levels. However, their matching of pre-sleep experiences with the ensuing dreams attained little better than chance results. In other words, Bessent's anomalous dreams contained more information about a future experience than comparison dreams contained about his activities just before he retired for the night (Krippner, Honorton, & Ullman, 1972).

One night, Bessent dreamed about "studies with birds . . . , ring-tailed doves, Canadian geese . . . , a few ducks." His concluding statement was: "I just have a feeling that the next target material will be about birds." Bessent's post-sleep experience consisted of tape-recorded aviary noises of bird calls accompanied by a slide presentation of various types of birds. The judges had no difficulty matching this experience with the correct collection of dream reports (Ullman, Krippner, & Vaughan, 1973, pp. 186-187).

Ullman and his associates also studied anomalous dreams in which attempts were made to obtain information at a distance. For example, a psychologist attempted to dream about a picture a laboratory staff member was concentrating on in a distant room. Over an eight-night period, her attempts were not statistically significant. However, a different psychologist obtained significant results in two separate eight-night studies. In one, a print of Marc Chagall's painting, *Paris from a Window,* was employed. In several separate dreams, the psychologist dreamed of "the French Quarter," "a French policeman's hat," "French attire," and "the French area" (Tolaas & Ullman, 1979, pp. 179-180). In this instance, the psychologist and the staff member were also separated and the target picture was randomly selected once the psychologist had gone to bed.

The Greek philosopher Democritus is credited with the first attempt to demystify anomalous dreams of this type. His view of distant information transfer is derived from the thesis that everything is made up of tiny particles he called *atoms.* These atoms constantly emit images of themselves which, in turn, are composed of still more atoms. According to Democritus, the images projected by living organisms, when emotionally charged, can be transmitted to a dreamer. When the images reached their destination, they were believed to enter the body through its pores. Images emitted by people in an excited state were especially vivid and likely to reach the dreamer intact and undistorted because of the frequency of emission and the speed of transmission (Dodds, 1971). The importance Democritus assigned to emotion is in keeping with present-day anecdotal and laboratory data.

Obviously, these studies need to be replicated by other investigators and extended to consider the many variables which might be operating. In the meantime, Ullman (1972) has observed that one of the characteristics of dreams is a backward scanning of remote memory stores that tries to link the impact of a present situation to past experience. The result of this information search is organized along lines of emotional contiguity rather than in temporal and spatial categories. The data on anomalous dreams suggest that this scanning process, on occasion, may conduct a forward or a distant scanning to provide the dreamer additional relevant information.

In Summary

- Highly imaginative people not only tend to remember more dreams but also report more creative dreams.
- Dreams generally address waking concerns.
- Bizarre dream content is not unusual and is more often associated with creativity than with personality fragmentation.
- Convergent production is a type of thinking which searches for one right answer. Divergent production searches for many alternative answers. While both types of cognitive activity are necessary for problem-solving, divergent production is especially suitable for idea generation.
- Dreamwork can teach pattern recognition, an important aspect of creative thinking.
- Some dreams so clearly identify future events that they are mistakenly thought to be prophetic. Actually, they consolidate

data that the dreamer has assimilated outside of his or her waking awareness.

- Anomalous dreams containing information not easily explainable by current scientific concepts may well occur but need to be approached with skepticism and be subjected to rigorous investigation.

Exercises

1. *Dialoging with Characters.* Your dreams routinely deal with past experiences, whether they involve the pizza you ate an hour before going to sleep or a game you played as a child. Any emotionally pertinent event may be used to produce a mood associated with a current, ongoing life issue. Even when dream activities took place a long time ago, the dream may be attempting to speak to your present actions, feelings, and thoughts. According to Carl Jung, dialoguing with characters in the dream is an effective way to clarify these connections. Arthur told his dream group that all he remembered of his dream was that he was staring at a box. By imagining that he was the box, Arthur was able to get in touch with the part of himself the box represented. The response surprised him as he stated: "I am a big, strong container. You are inside of me, fighting to get out. The more that you fight, the more tired and ineffective you are in your work. I am the budget expenditures that have boxed you in at work. You are fighting me and not getting anywhere. I suggest that you make the best of being inside me for the time being. If you do, you will find that you will quickly outgrow me without fighting." Examine your own dream notebook and use the same technique to understand a puzzling dream image.

2. *Divergent Thinking.* Consider one of your long-term goals. Does it express itself in one or more of your dreams? Examine the dream for divergent production to determine whether it suggests changes in your life that could facilitate attainment of the goal.

3. *Pattern Recognition.* From your notebook, select a dream

containing a past experience. How are the feelings and thoughts related to that event reflected in the dream? Use a pattern recognition approach rather than making an item-by-item analysis.

4. *Anomalous Dreams.* Have you ever had an anomalous dream that appeared to bridge time or space? Perhaps you dreamed about a future event or a situation a loved one was experiencing at the time of your dream. Consider what ordinary explanation could have accounted for the dream. If you decide that the dream was, indeed, anomalous, ask if it was characterized by any unusual content (e.g., strong feeling tone, vivid colors). Should you have additional anomalous dreams, determine whether they can be differentiated from your other dreams on the basis of their content.

7

Metaphors In Motion

Dreams and beasts are two keys by which we find out the secrets of our own nature.

— Ralph Waldo Emerson

Roger dreamed of an enormous black dog holding him by the neck in its jaws. Upon engaging in dreamwork, Roger realized that the beast reminded him of his supervisor at the office. The supervisor's rigid rules and demands seemed to be choking his creative processes. This metaphor led Roger to reevaluate the reasons for his career choice, resulting in a change in occupation, giving him greater opportunity to engage in creative thinking.

Metaphors are figures of speech in which one object is likened to another by speaking as if it actually were the other. Metaphors in dreams use images to draw comparisons emphasizing certain shared features. Usually these images are visual in nature, and represent a conceptualizing process using concrete imagery to arrive at the abstraction. For example, meditative practice can be depicted as a balloon ride, anger as a burning house, unfair criticism as a child being sent to bed without any dinner, procrastination as incarceration in prison, fear of failure as sitting for an examination but remembering nothing, engaging in dreamwork as exploring a cave. Perhaps the psychoanalytic notion of primary processing in dreams places too much emphasis on the primitive nature of dream imagery without giving it credit for the type of thought necessary for the production of metaphors.

The Impact of Metaphors

Jaime dreamed he was walking around in the abdomen of his

brother-in-law. He saw some pillars made of white ligaments. Several were broken in the middle. He thought to himself, "That doesn't look very good." Upon working with this dream, Jaime realized he admired his brother-in-law's weight-lifting ability. He recalled that he had experienced a strenuous workout at the local spa the previous day, and exercised his abdominal muscles for the first time. The dream seemed to be telling him he should not let his admiration for his brother-in-law cause him to overexert himself and expose his muscles to possible danger.

Charles Darwin (1871) was intrigued by dreams, suggesting that they were a "rest of the mind" (Gruber, 1974, p. 322). He recorded several of his own, including one on September 28, 1838. In this dream, someone had been executed first by hanging and then by decapitation. Somehow the character survived, "having faced death like a hero." This dream has been interpreted metaphorically to reflect Darwin's awareness that he was approaching a revolutionary idea that would initially subject him to harsh criticism but ultimately to praise and renown (p. 238). The double aspect of the execution also could have been a metaphor; the dream took place at the time of his impending marriage – a commitment he may have thought would supersede the time he could devote to science (Colp, 1986).

Being "like a hero" could represent Darwin's decision to continue his theorizing on evolution. Indeed, on September 28, he recorded his first insight on natural selection in his notebook, speculating that it could work in a positive direction. On November 11, he proposed marriage. In the decades that followed, Darwin was able to organize his daily schedule so that he could be an affectionate husband and father, and still engage in his scientific work. The lack of support for his theory about evolution was associated with psychosomatic illnesses, yet Darwin persisted, publishing the *Origin of Species* in 1859.

Montague Ullman (1969) described the essential characteristics of metaphor in dreams: Metaphors involve using images in improbable contexts; metaphors express meanings newly arrived at; metaphors provide a greater impact and more revealing presentations of life issues than literal statements. If a character in Jaime's dream had told him, "Take care so you do not damage your muscles," the dream might have been forgotten, and if recalled, might not have been taken seriously. If the dream had not been recalled, it is likely that the metaphorical presentation would have had a greater chance of unconsciously influencing Jaime's behavior than would a purely verbal admonition.

The appearance of images in incongruous situations is a major difference between most REM and non-REM mentation. Dreams also contain inappropriate relationships between objects. Ernestine was concerned about whether to take on a certain man as a business partner. There were many logical reasons why he would make a fine partner and Ernestine went to bed having tentatively decided to inform him of her decision the following day. However, she awoke the next morning remembering a strange dream. Ernestine recalled:

> I am standing on my back porch step talking to my neighbor. We are looking out at my garden. I notice that all of the lettuce is gone and ask her what happened to it. She said, "You know that man you hired as a partner? Well, he picked all the lettuce and left."

Ernestine felt that gardening was a metaphor for her business activities and that picking lettuce was a metaphor for handling money. She decided not to form a partnership with the man and, years later, discovered that he had become involved in one failed business enterprise after another.

Dreams characteristically express meaning newly arrived at through metaphors. Ullman observed that the model used by orthodox psychoanalysis is basically a closed system in which dreamers are limited in their expression of novelty to their own particular repertoire of artful camouflage. True novelty is not possible because psychoanalysis insists on linking unchanging instinctual energies to infantile wishes to account for dream content. Instead, according to Ullman, feelings are present which had not come clearly into focus while the dreamer was awake. In this sense they are new; they motivate the dreamer to express relations never before experienced. The dreamer is physiologically predisposed for this process, being in a state of arousal.

The dreamer's physiological state also forces the utilization of a sensory mode for constructing metaphors; one's biological system establishes the sensory vehicle for the metaphor while one's psychological system establishes the specific content. REM sleep also represents a period of vigilance, perhaps once needed for survival purposes. Vigilance demands correct information, not infantile wishes. Ullman (1969) feels this is why dreamers are so often concerned with fundamental questions, e.g., "Who am I?" "What is happening to me?" "What can I do about it?" Hence, dreams reflect dreamers' active efforts to reflect the immediate aspects of their own existence. "The dream is a metaphorical explication of a circumstance of living explored in its fullest implications for the current scene" (p. 700).

Day residue, reappearing in the dream, confronts the dreamer with either new and personally significant data or forces a confrontation with heretofore unrecognized, unintended consequences of one's behavior. What follows is an exploration, with the immediate issue polarizing relevant data from the past in an effort to explore the implications of the intrusive event and to arrive at a resolution. When unknown elements gain expression in a dream, they do so with the most appropriate metaphor the individual is capable of constructing to describe the feeling.

Ullman observes that hypnagogic images often are metaphorical in nature, yet are rarely as dynamic, complex, or evocative of the past. The hypnagogic image may be likened to a word which, no matter how unique or colorful, hardly compares in richness and expressive potential to the fully developed sentence (p. 701). Dreaming can be conceptualized as thinking in a sensory way, precisely because a sensory effect is needed.

An orthodox Freudian psychoanalyst interprets either hypnagogic or dream images to "stand for" something else by virtue of certain standard characteristics. Hence, projecting shapes are usually interpreted as male sex organs and receptive shapes as female sex organs. From this viewpoint, the psychoanalyst, not the dreamer, is held to possess the wisdom and objectivity to interpret dream images correctly. To Ullman, this type of interpretation is a misuse of the metaphor because it tends to obscure, hide, and conceal. Instead, the dream metaphor should be a potential instrument for self-learning and self-understanding. If properly appreciated, a dream may reveal metaphors within metaphors, forcing dreamers to take the risk of saying something new about themselves. If ignored or turned over to an outside "authority," the dream metaphor may die, and remain unread and unappreciated, its power to enhance self-awareness dissipated (p. 703).

The Shadow Knows

In 1909, Carl Jung (1961) had a dream about a house that contained a salon decorated in rococo style. The lower floors seemed older, dating from the 15th or 16th century. Descending into the cellar, Jung found walls dating from Roman times. Noticing a stone slab, he lifted it and saw a narrow stairway. Descending into a cave, he discovered two human skulls, "obviously very old and half disintegrated" (pp. 158-159). He later interpreted this dream as a metaphor of his own psyche. His conscious awareness was represented by the salon, and the various levels of his unconscious by the lower floors, cellar, and cave. These deeper levels of the psyche, according to Jung, contain "archetypal" or universal mythic symbols, such as the skulls with their representation of the primitive roots of human behavior.

Other archetypal symbols Jung observed over the years were wise old men and women, healers, and the "divine child," whose creative energies could transform the individual or the world. Each archetype is said to have negative as well as positive aspects; the reverse of the benevolent deity is the wrathful god or the avenging goddess, the opposite of the healer is the charlatan, and the flip side of the divine child's creative force is the apocalypse. The dual nature of archetypes is well illustrated by the "trickster," an archetype that supposedly represents human consciousness itself, simultaneously wise and foolish, imbued with self-deception yet with the capacity and knowledge by which human creativity manifests itself (Taylor, 1983, p. 165).

Whether or not one agrees with Jung that there are universal symbols in cultural myths and in night-time dreams, one can appreciate many of his concepts. He used the term "shadow" to refer to an archetype that represents the disowned aspects of an individual. All too often, however, these rejected aspects of the psyche contain important creative potentials. Teresa was tormented by dreams about wanton women and prostitutes; their behavior in her dreams contrasted sharply with her professed sexual conservatism. Teresa and her husband were seeing a marriage counselor, and the dreams took place as the discussions began to focus on the couple's unsatisfactory sex life. As their sexual behavior altered, Teresa's shadow elements made fewer appearances. In retrospect, Teresa felt that the "scarlet ladies" in her dreams represented an important part of her that was finally finding expression and becoming integrated with her total psyche.

Giuseppe Tartini, the Italian composer who invented the modern violin bow, dreamed that the devil had become his associate. Upon requesting assistance with an incomplete sonata, Tartini recalled, "How great was my astonishment when I heard him play with consummate skill a sonata of such exquisite beauty as surpassed the boldest flights of my imagination." Upon awakening, Tartini recalled the music as best as he could. The result, often called "The Devil's Sonata," is his most often performed composition but Tartini lamented, "The piece . . . was the best I ever wrote but how far below the one I had heard in my dream" (Ellis, 1911, p. 276).

As a child, Robert Louis Stevenson (1925) had vivid dreams and was terrified by them. Ultimately, he gained some control over his dreams, especially through the "little people" or "Brownies" who told stories and frequently assisted his creative processes. About his celebrated short story, "The Strange Case of Dr. Jekyll and Mr. Hyde," Stevenson recalled:

I had long been trying to write a story on . . . man's double being, which must at times come in upon and overwhelm the mind of every thinking creature . . . . For two days I went about racking my brains for a plot of

*any sort; and on the second night I dreamed the scene
at the window, and a scene afterwards split in two, in
which Hyde, pursued for some crime, took the powder
and underwent the change in the presence of his pur-
suers. All the rest was made awake, and consciously,
although I think I can trace in much of it the manner of
my Brownies.* (p. 172)

Not enough information is available to claim with certainty
that Tartini's devil represented the shadow archetype and that
Stevenson's Brownies were archetypal tricksters. However, both
Tartini and Stevenson exhibited some control over these dream
characters, who may have originally represented unwelcome elements, and harnessed them for creative purposes. To facilitate
contact with the shadow, tricksters, and other archetypes, Jung
would ask the dreamer to "be" the various figures and objects
in his or her dream. In this way, the dreamer could make contact
with potentially worthwhile aspects of the psyche that would otherwise be neglected or rejected (Greene, 1978).

The Gestalt psychologists later utilized the same technique,
often combining it with psychodrama. Ann Faraday (1972)
pointed out other similarities between Gestaltists and Jungians.
Both insist that any particular dream has reference to the
dreamer's particular life situation, as well as to his or her basic
character structure formed by early childhood experiences. Both
look for the dream's existential message in the "here and the
now," bringing in the past only when necessary (p. 155). However,
Gestaltists prefer such colloquial terms as "topdog" and "underdog" to Jung's archetypal designations which are considered
excessively esoteric (Fantz, 1978).

One might be tempted to categorize Howe's ferocious king
as a shadow archetype and his savages as tricksters who ultimately led him to his great discovery. Like other representations
of the shadow, Howe's fierce ruler initially appeared as evil and
frightening. Closer examination, however, revealed that in the
middle of the shadow's darkness was the very element which
had been lacking for Howe's further creative development. The

shadow knows what the dreamer needs, but to receive its gift, the dreamer must overcome whatever fear and repugnance is experienced with this repelling part of oneself (Taylor, 1983, p. 160).

From a Jungian point of view, one might speculate about whether Hilprecht's Babylonian priest may have represented the archetype of a wise old man. A similar case would be that of Sriniwasa Ramanujan, a mathematician. From time to time, the image of Namakkal, a Hindu goddess, would appear to Ramanujan in his dreams. Upon awakening, he would record the mathematical formulae provided by Namakkal and would verify them (Newman, 1948). Perhaps the Hindu goddess represented the archetypal wise old woman. Though, like the Gestaltists, one may prefer to use other terms to describe Jungian archetypes, the fact remains that they can serve as important teaching functions in using dreams for creative problem-solving.

New Ways of Being

Nanhoi had been very successful in business, but did not consider himself a happy individual. One night he had an exceptionally vivid dream that he later related to one of us:

> It is medieval times. A king is giving an audience on an island in the middle of his kingdom. It is evening and his subjects surround him as he sits on his throne. The glow of torches lights the scene. The monarch's left leg is broken and in a plaster cast, resting on top of a stool. Suddenly, archers appear, seize the king, and take him hostage, demanding either his treasury or his kingdom for ransom. The king does not know what to do because there is no gold in the treasury. The fact that it is empty has been a well-kept secret for generations. It appears that the king will have to surrender his throne.
>
> At this suspenseful moment, one of the subjects shouts, "The king's leg! Look at the king's leg!" In the torchlight, the glint of gold is shining through a part of

the cast where the plaster had been rubbed off when the archers seized the king. Slowly, the king realizes what had occurred. Many generations earlier, the kingdom had been in danger of invasion. The monarch of that era developed an extraordinary plan to save the wealth of the kingdom. He had all the gold in the treasury taken to the royal foundry where it was melted and beaten into the shape of common objects—stools, hinges, doorknobs, bowls—then covered with natural materials to hide their worth. He had these objects distributed throughout all the houses of the kingdom. The gold had remained safely hidden under the noses of the kingdom's citizens all these years.

The king explained the story to his captors. He said that he did not have the wealth that gave authority to his right to rule, but that all the treasure anyone could possibly need was available and at hand within most of the houses in the realm. The archers sensed that this account was true. Should the king be deposed because he had no gold? Or should he be restored since holding him at ransom would accomplish nothing? With greed no longer an issue, the archers were able to judge the king on his merit. Had he been a wise ruler? Did he represent their interests fairly? The archers decided that he did, and the king was allowed to continue his reign.

Nanhoi recognized what Ullman termed "the metaphors within the metaphor." All his life he had sought status and wealth for legitimacy and power. Deep down, he realized that these possessions would not bring happiness. In retrospect, he realized he was most joyous when sharing what he owned and knew. He needed only to scratch through the mundane nature of his world to discover an unlimited source of richness and worth. Even so, this treasure was not all in one place but in everything around him, if he could only take the time to appreciate it. He had always looked upon this aspect of himself as a weakness; but just as the cast covering the king's broken leg turned out to be made of gold, so Nanhoi's "weakness" was revealed to be of great value. The archers represented a part of himself that was even more aggressive, a part which lost its greed once new priorities were established.

It is not unusual for a dream metaphor to call into question the rules the dreamers follow in making life decisions. Yet new ways of being are often needed to surmount creative blocks, and dream metaphors can often suggest them. These dreams are sometimes called "breakthrough dreams" because of the power of their metaphors (Hart, Corriere, Karle, & Woldenberg, 1980). Their transformative power differentiates them from other dreams and is contained in the shifts in emotion experienced while dreaming. The metaphors in breakthrough dreams are powerful, and often require a minimum of interpretation.

Hannah dreamed she was driving up a hill in a police car. There was a ceiling at the top of the hill and she felt it marked the limits to how far she could go. Suddenly, her car turned into a rocket ship and blasted through the ceiling into space. After working on the dream, Hannah concluded that the police car represented her carefully regimented life in which she obeyed all the traditional "rules." The ceiling was a self-imposed limit, but one she could break through if she altered her vehicle, that is, if she broke some of the rules which may no longer have applied to her.

It is likely that the source of dream images is the neurological firing mechanism described by Hobson and McCarley. This explains why dream images are primarily visual and why there is a rapid juxtaposition of the images taking place primarily during REM sleep. But this neurological process provides the dreamer with images blended to produce a metaphorical effect, facilitating the individual's constant process of self-confrontation. It produces what Ullman (1969) refers to as metaphors in motion, a series of changing images which express and evaluate the vigilance needs of the sleeping human organism. As a result, dreams can highlight the creative interplay of old patterns and newly evoked responses, an interplay which can become "a widely developed and broadly applied medium for self-understanding" (p. 702).

Shamanic Dreams

The first dreamworkers were the shamans of the prehistoric and ancient hunting and gathering societies. These individuals were men and women who believed they could voluntarily regulate their attention to communicate with the "spirit world." From this world they would bring back power and knowledge they used in attempts to help and heal tribal members. Jung pointed out that dreams became less important as a resource for social guidance when political control was taken away from the tribal chiefs and shamans by Western invaders (Hall, 1982, p. 130). However, some shamans still exist in native cultures and continue to work with dream metaphors.

For example, a friend of ours visited Rolling Thunder, an intertribal medicine man living in Nevada. He presented the shaman a recurring dream about a battle between a white buffalo and a black buffalo. He was surprised when Rolling Thunder asked him, "What part of yourself do you think the white buffalo stands for and what part does the black buffalo represent?" By paying attention to the metaphor in the dream, our friend was able to identify an ongoing internal conflict of which he had been only dimly aware. Rolling Thunder's experiences with dream metaphors, however, permitted him to focus on the dream's meaning and ask questions to guide the dreamer to a helpful interpretation.

The Wintu and Shasta tribes of California hold the dreams of dead relatives to mark one's call to shamanism. Among two other California tribes, the Diegunos and Luisanos, future shamans supposedly are identified as early as age nine on the basis of their dreams. Among several other Native American tribes, initiatory dreams contain such creatures as bears, deer, eagles, and owls which instruct the dreamer to draw upon their power and begin shamanic training.

In the case of the Washo initiate, power comes through a dream in which the dreamer is awakened by a whistle. The initiate follows the whistle, which gradually changes to a whisper and issues a command. For example, the initiate might be told to bathe each morning and treat a sick person on four successive nights. If the ill person recovers, the initiate's status as a shaman will be confirmed (Rogers, 1982).

Among the Northern Algonquian Indians, mothers may ask their children if they dreamed that night. This practice encourages children to pay more attention to their dreams. In return, future dreams supposedly will favor the dreamer with more accurate information and on more frequent occasions, just as a friend would supply more and better guidance if listened to and respected. However, not all dreams are regarded as equally important; only those having special qualities of vividness are taken seriously (Tooker, 1979, pp. 89-90). Many Native American tribes believe in entities resembling the Jungian trickster archetype; tricksters often attempt to fool dreamers by giving them incorrect information.

Among Peru's Cashinatua Indians, tribal hunters request herbalists to give them medicines to keep them from dreaming because they believe the process interferes with their skill in hunting. Cashinatua shamans, however, believe that the more dreams they have, the greater their power will become. Thus, they develop methods to "pursue dreams." Unpleasant dreams are held to cause disease among the Maricopa Indians, bringing on colds, diarrhea, and aches. Paviotso Indian children can fall ill if their parents' dreams are unfavorable or if unpleasant dreams occur to visitors in the house. In either event, shamanic intervention is required to halt the effect.

In the Caribbean, members of the Taulipang tribe call upon the shaman to interpret their dreams. When the Cuna Indians of Panama dream about impending illness or disaster, the shaman administers a variety of cures to prevent the incident from occurring. Shamans of various tribes have used their own dreams, as well as those of tribal members, to diagnose and treat illness, create songs and dances, discover new charms and cures, locate lost objects and solve crimes, and name newly-born children (Krippner & Hooper, 1984).

The Senoi shamans in Malaysia were said to have assisted tribal members in working with dreams on a daily basis. However, recent evidence indicates that the earlier reports were exaggerations (Domhoff, 1985; Faraday & Wren-Lewis, 1984). Nevertheless, dreamwork based on the purported Senoi techniques does seem to be helpful for many people (Williams, 1980).

However, there is little doubt about another shamanic tradition. The Iroquois of North America had a sophisticated theory that dreams represented one's hidden desires. Therefore, dreams could provide clues to the shaman about what could be done to restore a person's health by fulfilling these desires in a manner consistent with the tribal social structure. There even were cases in which sexual dreams were acted out, under certain circumstances. A yearly Festival of Dreams was held in which everyone was given the opportunity to relate important dreams. Sometimes, a dream involved a gift, and the dreamer—by tradition—could not identify the gift. Instead, the dreamer needed to use gestures or give hints until the donor understood what was to be done. This festival often lasted for three days and was socially approved for the release of one's inner wishes (Roheim, 1952, pp. 192-193).

Like Freud, who distinguished between the "manifest dream" (the dream story recalled by the dreamer) and the "latent dream" (the dream's real message, presented metaphorically), the Iroquois believed the dream's meaning was hidden in its images. And like Freud, the Iroquois used free association techniques to decode the dream's intention. Unlike Freudians, however, the Iroquois attempted to understand their own dreams and would only call upon the shaman if the metaphor was too puzzling.

Psychoanalyst Erich Fromm (1951) pointed out that native people often view the dream not as a psychological phenomenon but as the voice of spirits or ghosts (pp. 109-110). The Iroquois believed dreams could be divine messages as well as the dreamer's wishes. In either event, they paid attention to their dreams and their legacy represents a sophisticated approach to dreamwork.

Figure 20.

In Summary

- Dreams routinely use highly personalized metaphors to draw analogies to waking life.
- By expressing life issues metaphorically, dreams may affect waking life even if a dream is not remembered.
- While REM mentation is filled with images which can yield metaphors, non-REM mentation has fewer images.
- There are physiological and emotional reasons why dreams address issues relevant to waking life which may have been related to survival in the early days of humankind.
- Jung used the shadow concept to convey the idea that dreams sometimes contain characters to depict both fears and possibilities of which the dreamer is unaware. Understanding these elements can defuse stress-related concerns as well as help dreamers capitalize on previously unsuspected abilities.
- Shamans were a society's first dream specialists; many of their procedures were highly creative as well as useful.

Exercises

1. *Metaphors.* Construct a metaphor to represent the history of your country. What form does the metaphor take when you try to summarize historical development into a sentence or phrase? What are the messages of that metaphor for you? Now construct a metaphor around your life history. What messages are revealed? Would it have been easier to create a visual symbol representing your country's history or your life history? Attempt both and think over the differences.

2. *Forms.* With a pencil and paper before you, focus on a personal or professional problem. Allow your hand to move the pencil and see what form emerges. Work with this form, allowing it to take its own shape. When you are finished, compare the form to your problem to see if it captured certain elements of the dilemma. Imagine that this form has appeared in a dream.

Could it be perceived as a symbol of a possible solution to the problem?

3. *Feelings.* What emotional feelings characterize your episodes of greatest creativity? Are you more or less creative when angry, confident, confused, relaxed, having fun? What prevents you from engaging in these creative feeling states more often? Which dreams have reflected those emotions and what can be learned from them to enhance your creativity?

4. *Archetypes.* Examine your dreams from a Jungian perspective. Do any contain what Jungians might consider archetypes? Be especially aware of those archetypes which are supposedly associated with creative insights, e.g., shadows, tricksters, wise old people. Keep in mind that Jungian approaches are complex and should not be treated superficially. For example, shadow archetypes are held to be the same sex as the dreamer. Wise old people may resemble, but are not identical to, such other archetypes as "great fathers" and "earth mothers." Activities such as journeys, initiations, and transformations can be archetypes as well as dream characters, so can deeply emotional states such as awe-inspiring or dangerous experiences. For additional information, you may want to read some excellent books containing discussions of this material, e.g., Fordham (1953), Hall and Nordby (1973), Jung (1974), Mahoney (1966), Singer (1973), Stevens (1982), Taylor (1983), von Franz (1964), Watkins (1976), Whitmont (1978).

8

Blocks To Creativity

It was night, and I made a careless movement inside the dream; I turned too brusquely the corner and bruised myself against my madness.

— Anais Nin

Biases and distortions of reality can block creativity. Attaining personal and professional goals can elude one's grasp if a strong belief system fosters failure instead of success. One can hardly expect solutions to problems to spring full blown from one's dreams like children from the head of Zeus. Preparation and incubation are necessary if illumination and inspiration are to occur in dreams. However, dreams have been known to respond to a request for help by delineating fears and doubts blocking a resolution. This can be done by identifying "personal myths" which may be helping or hindering a creative insight.

Self-Deceptive Strategies

Psychoanalyst Ernst Kris (1956) was the first to introduce the term "personal myth" into psychotherapeutic literature. He did so to describe certain elusive dimensions of the human personality for which psychoanalysis needed to account if it was to make lasting behavioral changes. Carl Jung (1961) discussed his personal myth in the autobiographical work, *Memories, Dreams, Reflections* (p. 17). David Feinstein (1979) developed the concept of personal mythology as a central dimension of personality which is related to both the pervasive myths of the culture and the inner psychodynamics of the individual.

Dick McLeester (1976) advocated using dreams to discover one's personal myth, defined as "the story we tell by living, the threads of meaning and continuity underlying our daily lives" (p. 8). Montague Ullman and Nan Zimmerman (1979/1985) were the first to make extensive applications of the personal myth concept to group dreamwork. They pointed out that it is the nature of the dream to expose and puncture dysfunctional personal myths, illuminating self-deceptive strategies one uses to avoid initiating a more functional behavior pattern. Common dysfunctional myths are those of personal invulnerability (e.g., "I can take anything the world throws my way"), over-protection (e.g., "Curiosity is dangerous; obedience is safe"), and fear of failure (e.g., "I can't possibly succeed, so I won't even try"). Ullman and Zimmerman point out:

> The gap between the true and the false, the known and the unknown, forms the subject matter of our dreams. An aspect of ourselves that we have taken for granted is up for critical scrutiny. A part of our personality that ... we consider invulnerable and inviolate is now revealed as flawed. A personal myth has been punctured. (p. 156)

Personal mythologies consist of people's ever-changing systems of complementary and conflicting personal myths—those cognitive-affective structures (patterns of thinking and feeling) giving meaning to the past, definition to the present, and direction for the future. A personal myth serves the functions of explaining, guiding, and sacralizing experience for the individual in a manner analogous to the way culture myths once served those functions for society (Feinstein & Krippner, 1981). Defining myths as cognitive-affective structures allows using principles established by cognitive psychologists to better understand how personal myths operate. For instance, psychologists have found that cognitive-affective structures may be coded verbally or pictorially; may or may not be within an individual's waking awareness; can be influenced by heredity and/or experience; may operate at various levels of human life (the trivial as well as the important); and may change as a result of new experiences during one's life.

Dreams appear to synthesize one's mythic structure with the data of one's life experiences. Frequently, when one's underlying mythic structure is incongruous with a personal experience, the dream's task is to resolve the difference. A dream can emphasize weaknesses in one's mythic structure, giving that structure an opportunity to adjust to the new experience. A dream can point out that a dysfunctional personal myth is not adequately accounting for the dreamer's experiences by revealing an emotional blind spot.

Personal myths serve the individual in the same way cultural myths used to function in primitive and ancient societies. One's personal mythology includes all interacting and sometimes conflicting thoughts and feelings a person harbors about the world, both in and out of awareness. These myths shape the actions people take and the interpretations they give to their experiences. A myth functions well if it provides an emotionally satisfying reflection of reality. It does the individual (and the society) a disservice if it obscures gaps between one's feelings and reality (Krippner, 1986).

An individual is most likely to become aware of a myth when a change is occurring in it. Maggie was a commercial artist who had terrifying dreams that she was fleeing from a huge, ugly monster. She was so troubled by these dreams that she tried to draw pictures of the monster but couldn't quite capture the image. The next time she had the dream, Maggie was so determined to remember what the creature looked like that she actually turned to face it, but the monster disappeared. The dream occurred again, but this time when the monster faded into the distance, Maggie ran after it, finally catching up and touching it. As she touched the monster, she screamed in terror and at that moment it turned into a beautiful horse-like creature. Maggie rode it, whirling in a sky of clouds, until she found herself in the embrace of a man.

Maggie awoke, realizing that she had once had the same feeling of terror in an early experience with dating. As a result, she had held herself distant and aloof from men, acknowledging that the sexual response was difficult for her. Taking clues from

the dream, Maggie allowed more sexual fantasy into her awareness and into her life. She finally was able to draw the sequence
of events in her dreams. Maggie began to open up to intimate
contact on both the emotional and sexual levels. Her old personal
myth's insistence that intimate contact was monstrous gave way
to a new myth stating that interpersonal closeness could transport
her to new realms of understanding, just as the flying horse did
in her dream.

Figure 21.

Personal Myths and Dreamwork

The mass media continually remind people that they are sur-
rounded by extremely talented individuals with skills in areas
about which most others know very little. Upon comparing oneself
with these celebrities, one finds it too easy to ignore or minimize
one's creative potentials. A person may know an area of expertise
thoroughly but it may have ceased to be new, unusual, or inspirational. Abilities are taken for granted, and unique capabilities
are ignored. Personal myths become constricted, limited, and
mundane. The hero's or heroine's journey, a common theme of
cultural mythology, is bypassed in favor of myths emphasizing
a habitual, passive existence. Yet, effective dreamwork is based
on the reality that creative potential is a nearly universal human
trait.

Dreams can be a constant inspiration to free expression,
outrageous exaggeration, and tolerance of ambiguity. Dreams
often give the dreamer permission to make mistakes, discard
old habits, and indulge in what is apparently spontaneous, impractical, irresponsible, fallible, and non-rational. Dreams can
point out the absurdity of the status quo limiting creative expression. The dreamer can become less concerned about other
people's opinions and about traditional ways of understanding
projects. If a business deal is successfully consummated in a
dream, the dreamer may become more confident in waking life.
The approach used in the dream may even reveal some hitherto
overlooked strategy which could yield success.

Henry James, in *The Turn of the Screw,* lived out a unique
personal myth which influenced this novel as well as his other
writings. When he was still in his cradle, James' father experienced
an anxiety attack so severe that it took him two years to even
begin recovery. During this episode, the elder James was convinced that he sensed a demon in the room. This notion that
people could be haunted by daytime ghosts remained a profound
family memory, and it was a frequent topic of conversation. It
affected Henry and his older brother William, who was later to
become the first American psychologist of eminence and a foun-

der of the American Society for Psychical Research. Indeed, William James as a young man had an experience reminiscent of his father's. While stepping into his dressing room, he was overcome with a profound sense of fear that transformed itself into the image of an epileptic patient had seen during his medical studies. This experience was added to the family legacy, joining that of the father.

Henry James had no waking experiences like those of his father and brother. However, he wrote in his autobiographies about a dream he experienced late in life in which he defended himself against an invader. Suddenly, amid thunder and lightning, the monster was racing away down a corridor filled with works of art. Apparently, James had told friends about similar dreams; in one of them, James found himself in a beautiful house. He wandered through the rooms, feeling a mysterious presence, until he arrived upstairs. Finding himself in a room in which an old man was sitting in a chair, James called out, "You're afraid of me, you coward." In both dreams, James began with a strong sense of fear or anxiety, then proceeded to defeat the entity that had evoked this feeling. Apparently, James drew upon this firsthand knowledge of fear in *The Turn of the Screw,* an unfinished ghost novel, *The Sense of the Past,* and his brilliant short story about preternatural forces, "The Jolly Corner."

Literary biographer Leon Edel (1982) observed that Henry James' ghost stories came from James' family experiences and his dreams. James' personal myth appeared to hold that humans are in an ongoing relationship with impenetrable and mysterious forces which are outside themselves and their control. His first group of stories are fairly conventional, but the second group, including *The Turn of the Screw,* represent James' years of anxiety and depression. In these tales, there are many "daylight ghosts," such as those reported by his father and brother. *The Turn of the Screw* concerns a young governess convinced that she sees daytime ghosts, and her efforts to protect the children she cares for from these ghosts actually allow greater forces of evil to enter their lives.

The last group of James' stories contain phantoms, both demonic and comical, and literary creations with no preternatural element, merely what Edel calls "the terror of the usual" (p. 304). An example would be James' last novel, *The Golden Bowl,* in which the heroine thinks of "the horror of finding evil" seated during a game of bridge where her husband and his secret mistress end up as partners. This is the woman's first experience with falsity, and "the most horrible kind of fright" occurs, paradoxically, in a quiet house on a Sunday afternoon (p. 307).

James' mythic conviction was that as long as one conceals the occult, "the imagination will run riot and depict all sorts of horrors, but as soon as the veil is lifted, all mystery disappears" (p. 304). This theme runs through James' ghost stories; the ghostly creatures are vaguely described, allowing readers to let their imagination supply the particulars. Taking the worn ghost story, James enriched it, showing how the phantasmagoric can be attached to one's daily existence. James did not rationalize the ghosts or the horror, just as he did not explain away his family's terrifying episodes or his own dreams. James believed that too much explanation would demystify wondrous events.

The interrelated themes of the James family's experiences exemplifies what E. B. Taub-Bynum (1984) referred to as "the family unconscious." Similar dreams, fantasies, and beliefs can produce a family myth which could run through several generations. Taub-Bynum recommends that family therapists should pay more attention to their clients' dreams, not only to open deeper levels of communication among family members, but also to help them better understand such common themes as autonomy, control, dependence, and separation among members of troubled families.

Old Myths and Counter-Myths

Personal myths appear to form in a manner which parallels how dreams develop (Feinstein, 1987). Hobson and McCarley hypothesized that dreams are related to the brain's propensity for language, imagery, and story-telling. As such, dreams play an active role in the ongoing revision of an individual's personal mythology. Though dreams probably serve many physiological and psychological functions, the one receiving the greatest attention in working with personal myths is the dream's role in synthesizing the dreamer's existing mythic structure with the data of personal life experiences. As Ullman (1979) notes, "Our dreams serve as corrective lenses that, if we learn to use them properly, enable us to see ourselves and the world about us with less distortion and with greater accuracy" (p. 410).

Frequently, a conflict in one's personal mythology affects his or her behavior, feelings, or thoughts, and a mythic crisis becomes apparent in that person's development. This crisis typically occurs when a prevailing myth becomes so outdated or otherwise dysfunctional that the psyche generates a counter-myth to organize perceptions and responses along different lines. When this occurs, the psyche is in conflict; each myth becomes a psychological entity which starts to dominate the same situation with its mode of perceiving and responding. Typically, the conflict between the old myth and the counter-myth proceeds outside of awareness. The counter-myth may become crystallized, developing within one's cognitive system and emerging in response to the old myth's limitations. It challenges the old myth and the two engage in a dialectical process. The old myth becomes the *thesis* and the counter-myth becomes the *antithesis.* The way that internal conflict develops is similar to the way that the Aztec religion (old myth or thesis) was opposed by the newly-arrived Catholic religion (counter-myth or antithesis); or the way Eastern thought (thesis) was confronted with Western thought (antithesis) when Alexander the Great invaded India; or the way Japan (thesis) was opened up by Commodore Matthew Perry (antithesis).

There are nine ways dreams seem to handle old myths and counter-myths (Feinstein & Krippner, in press). Three of these are attempts by a dream to strengthen an old, self-limiting myth, particularly when it is challenged. For example, this type of dream could emphasize past experiences validating the old myth. One man we know was told in a dream that, "You really are a failure and always have been, your promotion at work notwithstanding."

Second, a dream could force a fit between the old myth and daily experience: A woman who stays out later than she planned dreams about being berated by her husband, a punishment her old myth felt she deserved, even though her spouse never would have taken such an action. Third, a dream could preview the future according to the script of the old myth, often with a sense of irreversible fate: A young woman on the verge of moving away from her dominating parents dreams about herself ten years in the future, still living at home. Some people misinterpret these dreams as confirming the validity of the old myth rather than as reflecting and often caricaturing it.

On the other hand, there are three ways a dream may strengthen a counter-myth which has grown out of the old myth's deficiencies. First, the dream may rework old experiences and interpret them in a less self-limiting, more affirming manner providing an alternative to the old myth's template of reality. For example, a young man who had worked many years for an unstable, vindictive employer dreams about making the best of the situation, learning all he can before moving to another job. Second, the dream may accommodate the old myth to fit new experiences so the old corresponds more closely to the counter-myth: An aspiring vocalist, somewhat disappointed that her first engagement turns out to be a small night club, dreams about how much she can learn by trying out new material with her audience. Third, the dream may organize possibilities into a future with wish-fulfillment qualities: A newly arrived immigrant dreams about the possibilities she envisions for her life in the new country.

Finally, there are three ways the dream may facilitate an integration between the two myths. As ongoing experiences bring the two together, making them more compatible, the essential elements of each become integrated. The forces working against dissonance begin to unite the two. This is evident in dreams highlighting past experiences, in which the mythic conflict was evident, showing how it could have been integrated at the time. For example, a man works on resolving a new conflict by dreaming of a past psychotherapy session in which he resolved a related problem. Second, a dream may highlight the conflict as it has emerged in current experiences and show ways of resolving it: A woman dreams about a conflict with a neighbor, considers ways of resolving the problem in the dream, and is instructed to attempt one of these by an inner voice. Third, a dream may portend that the conflict is resolved: A woman, anxious because her children are about to leave home, dreams about how she will enjoy her free time once they go to college.

This integration of the thesis and antithesis is called *synthesis.* Although the Roman Catholic Church became the official religion of Mexico, syncretic underground rites developed in some parts of the country, combining Aztec deities with Catholic saints. After Alexander the Great left India, Greek themes continued to influence Indian sculpture. Western ideas had a major impact on Japan after the historic "opening" of Commodore Perry; the success of Japanese technology and industry is a more recent example of synthesis. Sometimes the counter-myth predominates, as in Mexico; sometimes the old myth retains most of its power, as in India; and sometimes a true synthesis is accomplished, as in Japan.

Once one learns how to interpret dreams on this basis, one can quickly identify which of these nine possibilities is present. Sometimes none of them will appear, while occasionally more than one will be present in a dream. This system also demonstrates the value of working with a *series* of dreams because the struggle between the old myth and the counter-myth is often played out in one's dreams over time.

This system interfaces with portions of several other dream theories. The counter-myth would be seen by Adlerians as the psyche's attempt to solve problems around dilemmas caused by the prevailing myth. Freud's wish-fulfillment notion involves the counter-myth as do Jung's compensatory dreams, which allegedly express an underdeveloped part of the psyche. Gestalt psychologists' view of dream elements as conflicting parts of the psyche focuses on the conflictual aspect of this system. The information theory approach to dreams is congruent with the adaptive function this system perceives dreams as serving.

Emotional tone and bodily feelings often give the dreamer

clues about the dream's function. Old myth dreams typically feel pessimistic, hopeless, and seem to drain the dreamer of energy and vitality. Counter-myth dreams usually feel hopeful, optimistic, and exhilarating. Integration or synthesis dreams tend to produce a calm, positive, assured feeling. Of course, emotion and mood in a dream are dependent on the dreamer's thinking and feeling style.

However, one cannot claim that all dreams revolve around personal myths any more than one can claim that a Freudian client's sexual dreams prove Freudian theory, or that a Jungian client's compensatory dreams prove Jungian theory. Ullman (1978) suggests that dream theories are basically waking metaphors for expressing, in highly condensed language, the therapist's preferred way of perceiving and understanding the client's predicament. When the therapist's metaphorical construct fits well with the metaphors of the client's dream imagery, a sense of contact between the dreamer and the therapist develops.

Indeed, Ullman (1978) suggests that professional help is needed when the dreamer's self-deceptive myths are so intrusive that he or she is not open to what is coming through in the dream. But for the dreamer who is in touch with internal processes, personal myths can be seen in dreams as accommodating developmental needs and unknown parts of the psyche. Personal myths capitalize on opportunities and strengths, and deal with a person's deficiencies. Personal myths can resolve polarities and enable a healthy dialectic to occur, leading the dreamer to higher levels of synthesis.

Creative behavior can reflect one's ongoing struggle or the mythic synthesis which marks the temporary end of the conflict. Maslow (1976) pointed out that a hallmark of creative people he studied was their ability to resolve dichotomies.

The great artist is able to bring together clashing colors, forms that fight with each other, dissonances of all kinds, into a unity. And this is also what the great theorist does when he puts puzzling and inconsistent facts together

*so that we can see that they really belong together. And
so also for the great statesman, the great therapist, the
great philosopher, the great parent, the great inventor.
They are all integrators, able to bring separates and even
opposites together into unity.* (pp. 89-90)

This same process marks the creative synthesis of two opposing personal myths.

Yet today's synthesis often becomes tomorrow's old myth,
a cognitive-affective structure which may outgrow its usefulness
as an individual continues to develop his or her latent capacities.
Dreams can provide continual access to one's ongoing development, allowing a creative use of each step in self-discovery.

In Summary

- Personal myths can block one's creativity if they are not understood and taken into account.
- Some dreams attempt to eliminate discrepancies between personal myths and daily life events. Other dreams point out these
  discrepancies.
- Whether a person is aware of them or not, personal myths
  structure one's actions as well as explanations for what occurs.
- The old myth states the accepted worldview of the dreamer
  while the counter-myth provides alternatives.
- Integrative dreams may state the procedure for synthesizing
  the old myth and the counter-myth.

Exercises

1. *Emerging Myths.* Emerging myths often require people
to take risks to test their potential value. These may be previewed
in dreams, as they give dreamers an opportunity to behave and
experience in new and unusual ways. Review your dream
notebook. Have you engaged in unusual activities in your dreams,
suggesting a novel opportunity for developing your personal or
professional life? Dreams typically reflect one's daily concerns
and customary life-style. A departure from conventional behavior

in your dreams may anticipate the possibility of a new direction in your life.

2. *Alternative Answers.* Dreams can present not one but several "right answers" by expressing a number of different points of departure in a single dream or series of dreams. Tonight you may be presented with alternative answers to a life dilemma. Examine which is the most feasible, and try to determine the basic personal myth each "right answer" reflects.

3. *Alternative Values.* Unquestioned attitudes and assumptions often reflect prevailing myths which have a paralyzing effect on your creativity. But waking ethical and moral standards can be violated with impunity in dreams. Priests may find themselves sleeping with nuns; judges may find themselves committing perjury; business executives may find themselves squandering the company's profits. The dreamer may feel futility and be horrified by such behavior, but these alternative value standards may reflect emerging myths attempting to gain the dreamer's attention. Examine your dreams; identify an instance in which your dream behavior was immoral by your waking standards. What was your dream attempting to tell you? Consider the possibility that what Jungians call your shadow might reflect an emerging myth.

4. *Alternative Role Models.* Carl Rogers (1970) stated that people's desire to actualize themselves is the mainspring in both creativity and psychotherapy (p. 152). This tendency can also be found in many dreams. However, one personal myth blocking self-actualization is the presence of inappropriate role models. Realizing that this is often a problem for contemporary women, Koch-Sheras, Hollier, and Jones (1983) wrote a book, *Dream On,* specifically for women. The authors say that to win psychological independence, women often must separate themselves from their family of origin and from the messages given by their parents and siblings. "For women, the negative messages often assume the form of disapproval and discouragement of developing such

traditionally masculine traits as independence, assertiveness, and risk-taking. Furthermore, we are often given mixed messages about the valuable characteristics we *are* allowed to develop, such as emotional expressiveness, nurturance, intuition, and sensitivity to others. The message we often get is that such qualities are really weaknesses making us unfit for taking care of and standing up for ourselves, or for doing anything but serving others" (p. 191). They recommend recording dreams, working with dreams, and sharing dreams, urging their readers to "learn the private language of your dreams and apply it to the specific needs and situations that arise in your life as a woman today" (p. 230). Have you identified with role models which are inhibiting your development? Do these represent old myths in your dreams? Do your dreams contain images of emerging myths challenging these role models? Do your dreams challenge messages provided in the past by people or institutions who supported your adherence to these role models?

5. *Alternative Myths.* The hero's quest is only one myth appearing in dreams, legends, and works of art. Some alternatives are myths of creation, destruction, nurturance, finding a community, overcoming obstacles, completing a task, attaining wisdom, reconciling opposites, and empowerment, initiation, and/or transformation. Find one or more in your dreams and construct a fairy tale reflecting your life situation. If you are interested in expanding your knowledge of personal myths, the appendix contains several additional exercises and examples which may be of interest.

9

Terror In The Night

*The first night I was in bed here . . . , I went to sleep,
and suddenly I felt my whole body* breaking up. *It broke
up with a violent shock—an earthquake—and it broke like
glass.*

— Katherine Mansfield

While in the French military, René Descartes had a nightmare
accompanied by acute physical distress and terror. His images
involved darkness and a tempestuous wind, haunted by strange
and spectral beings. Descartes awakened in pain, horrified that
an evil spirit had aspired to seduce him. After praying for forgive-
ness and protection, he fell asleep but was awakened by a loud
sound. He thought he saw a multitude of fiery sparks scattering
about the room. He fell asleep again, dreaming of a dictionary,
an anthology of poems, and a stranger who gave him a poem
and engaged him in a literary discussion. In his dream, Descartes
concluded that the dictionary represented the sciences, and the
anthology the union of philosophy and wisdom. To Descartes,
the sparks were the seeds of wisdom to be found in all human
beings. Upon awakening, he continued his interpretation, con-
vincing himself that the stranger—the Spirit of Truth—had intended
to open all the sciences to him (Brook, 1983, pp. 133-134).
Descartes eventually presented a unification of philosophy and
mathematics which was to change the intellectual history of the
Western world.

Nightmares which did not stimulate any apparent creative
work have been reported by such writers as W. H. Auden, Emily
Bronte, Rudyard Kipling, Doris Lessing, Katherine Mansfield,
John Ruskin, August Strindberg, and Virginia Woolf. Nightmares

do not have to be terrifying to upset the dreamer. Evelyn Waugh wrote:

> *A night disturbed by a sort of nightmare . . . is becoming more frequent with me . . . . Dreams of unendurable boredom—of reading page after page of dullness, of being told endless, pointless jokes, of sitting through cinema films devoid of interest.* (Brook, 1983, p. 194)

For a highly creative writer such as Waugh, terror would probably be preferable to boredom, especially in a dream.

Nightmares and Night Terrors

The association between nightmares and creativity has long been a matter of conjecture. In a questionnaire survey of 314 college students, art majors reported the most nightmares while physical education majors reported the fewest. Mathematics and science students were in between (Belicky & Belicky, 1982). Furthermore, students with frequent nightmares tended to report more visual imagery during awakening, became easily absorbed in aesthetic stimuli, and scored higher scores on a hypnotizability scale than did other students.

However, Rothenberg (1971) reported few recalled nightmares in his study of 20 established artists, either in their childhood or when they were interviewed. Rothenberg hypothesized that nightmares may be frequent among artists who have talent but are limited by psychological problems. For him, nightmares would not be expected among successful artists not constrained by inner turmoil. Rothenberg's results are inconclusive because only a few subjects remembered their dreams.

Different results were reported by Hartmann (1984), who studied the nightmares of 35 artists and authors who replied to a newspaper advertisement. Admittedly, the method of selection biased the results but Hartmann was left with the impression that "a sizable subgroup of creative artists frequently experience nightmares and that there is some relationship between nightmares and creativity" (p. 127).

Figure 22.

Nevertheless, highly creative people, like Descartes, have transformed potentially terrifying dreams into creative products. Mary Shelley based her best-known work, *Frankenstein,* on horrifying hypnagogic imagery. Bram Stoker, who wrote *Dracula,* is said to have had frequent nightmares and used them in his work. Both Dracula and Dr. Frankenstein's monster place the reader, or viewer, in the position of the helpless victim—the dreamer's position in the nightmare. The terrifying monsters of both novels are only half-human, and are reminiscent of characters from many people's nightmares (Hartmann, 1984, p. 122).

Andre Gide recalled having had horrible nightmares, especially as a child. Two other authors, Theodore Dreiser and Edgar Lucas White, wrote about their nightmares in some detail

(Hartmann, 1984, pp. 122-123). The 18th century philosopher Emanuel Swedenborg reported a nightmare: "I saw a man with a long sword coming toward me. I thought I also had a sword, one with a silver handle, but as the man came closer, I had no sword left, only a broken stick. The man jumped on my back and bit me. I kept calling for help, but no help came" (p. 124). This nightmare portrays the helplessness of the dreamer, a common characteristic of dreams that frighten the dreamer.

Nightmares can be defined as terrifying dreams. Typically, the dreamer awakens with a feeling variously reported as anxious, scary, or frightening, and overwhelmed with fear, dread, or horror. Nightmares are not to be confused with "night terrors" which are sudden arousals from non-REM sleep. In night terrors, the sleeper may have similar reactions as the dreamer awakening from a nightmare, but there is little or no dream recall (Fisher, Kahn, Edwards, & Davis, 1973). Sometimes a vague image is recalled (e.g., "something is sitting on me," "something is closing in on me," "I am choking"), but this may represent the accompanying bodily feeling rather than any dream content. It is likely that a night terror is not a long, ongoing process from which the sleeper awakens, but rather a phenomenon associated with awakening itself. One study demonstrated that a night terror could be induced in a child prone to night terrors by pulling him upright as he slept (Hartmann, 1984, p. 20).

Night terrors can be considered a minor dysfunction in the brain's sleep-wakefulness mechanisms that produce unusual arousals. In susceptible children, environmental and emotional factors may also play a part. Hartmann (1984) states, "Most often, no specific treatment is required. In cases beginning at the typical age in childhood, the condition is usually benign and the night terrors disappear spontaneously. Thus, reassurance to the parents is often the most important step" (p. 232). However, many well-meaning parents have taken their children, usually between the ages of three and eight, to psychotherapists at the onset of night terrors. When the child cannot remember the dream accompanying the scary awakening, the therapist often regards it as a sign of repression. When the child outgrows the night terrors, the therapist often claims credit and the parents are relieved.

Night terrors in combination with sleepwalking can be dangerous for the sleeper. The treatment should include making the surroundings safe for the sleeper and others. Glass windows, mirrors, and sharp objects should be removed from the vicinity of the sleeper. The sleeper should not sleep on a balcony or near the open window of an upper floor. Medication sometimes eliminates the incidence of night terrors but should be taken as a last resort because the condition can recur when the medication is withdrawn (Hartmann, 1984, p. 234).

Phenomena resembling nightmares have also been reported during twilight states, sometimes accompanied by a "hypnagogic jerk," in which a person is suddenly "jerked back" awake while falling asleep. "Sleep paralysis" can also occur as one is falling asleep; in sleep paralysis one becomes unable to move. In medieval times, tales were commonly told of the "incubus," a frightening creature who sat on the sleeper, preventing movement. It is likely that the victims of incubi suffered from sleep paralysis, conceptualizing the condition in terms appropriate to their era. Some hysterical women claimed that incubi had molested them sexually, and hysterical men said the same about "succubi," female cousins of the incubi. Indeed, the "mare" in "nightmare" is derived from an old German word for a monster who oppressed people while they were asleep.

Topdogs and Underdogs

Ann Faraday (1974) has found many instances in which nightmares were a form of self-punishment for some offense committed against an external authority or an inner ideal during the day. The nightmares usually took the form of imprisonment, execution, or being menaced by a wild animal or other dangerous creature. These animals, she concluded, could be interpreted by Gestalt psychologists as "topdogs" who are hounding the "underdogs" that have offended them during the day. On the other hand, the topdog might deny the underdog a basic need during waking hours, producing a night-time conflict (pp. 234-235).

F. C. Perls (1969) and other Gestalt psychologists claimed that all dream content represents various parts of the dreamer's psyche; by pretending to become each element in a nightmare, the dreamer could "re-own the energy" previously invested in demons, ogres, and other frightening characters.

Topdogs and underdogs might also be conceptualized as two conflicting personal myths, or as a shadow in conflict with one's "persona"—the image of oneself worn to impress or accommodate others. In *The Marriage of Heaven and Hell,* William Blake wrote, "The man who never alters his opinion is like standing water, and breeds reptiles of the mind." Blake could well be referring to a rigid, outworn myth that is no longer appropriate. The "reptiles of the mind" could be the resulting nightmares that attempt, perhaps in vain, to introduce a new mythic structure that would be more functional.

Because dreams typically use images to describe the emotional reality of one's life situation, there may be considerable exaggeration. Rae was afraid of gaining weight and dreamed she was riding a hippopotamus. Todd, a worker resenting management intervention in his job, dreamed of his parents breaking up a party and sending everybody home. Wambli was having difficulty expressing love to his mate; he dreamed of nearly dying during heart surgery. Teresa was excessively self-critical and dreamed of carrying around the frozen corpse of her aunt, who had excessively criticized her as a child, as she searched for some way to dispose of the body. All these dreams were considered to be nightmares by the dreamers who awoke in a terrified state.

But exaggerating a problem is sometimes necessary to confront a difficult situation. Such exaggeration is an example of using "artistic license" to make a point. Comics do this all the time. Playwrights will use artistic license in their plays; writers often will use it in their stories and books—even those based on fact. Therapists often have their clients exaggerate anger, sadness, and other emotions to get them to release and understand these powerful feelings. Children routinely exaggerate facts when they role play or relate an experience, but this trait is lost as they grow older. Exaggeration becomes taboo; it is labeled dishonest and all but disappears except from humor, drama, and dreams.

Freedom of expression is essential to the creative process. Dreams provide a conceptual alternative to linguistic descriptions of objects and events. A verbal description of internal topdogs and underdogs would not be as memorable as a dream scenario in which two different parts of the psyche are fighting to the death. Nor would a verbal description of one's feelings of being pursued by creditors have as much of an impact as a dream in which a steel robot is relentlessly chasing the dreamer. Because of the dream's visual emphasis, images make an impact not unlike the barrage of sensory input an infant constantly encounters.

Every so often this nocturnal barrage breaks through, often waking the dreamer. When it does, the experience can be transformative. Paulo reported a dream in which he saw a vibrant mass of color and form dancing before him. He sensed it was alive, and did not know if it would fly into the air, expand, shrink, change form, or attack him. The shape was awe-inspiring, incomprehensible, and—in a sense—sacred. Frightened, Paulo became aware of himself. Once again immersed in his mundane perceptions, Paulo realized he was looking at an ordinary oak tree, one of many at the edge of a forest. What had happened to Paulo? Did he have a regressive experience in a nightmare? Or did he have an expansion of consciousness, realizing that all forms somehow contain the powerful freedom symbolized in the whirling mass? From that day on, Paulo became convinced his waking perception was blinding him to the spontaneity and freedom that were potentially his. He determined that he would take steps to transcend his societal upbringing and make his life more meaningful.

Some would have been terrified by this dream, would have dismissed it as a nightmare, and would have forgotten it as quickly as possible. But for Paulo, it carried an important message; he began to view life as precious, and was able to prioritize his activities. Gradually, Paulo found himself engaging in both work and play he considered important, satisfying, and even holy.

Karen Horney, a psychoanalyst, stated that one of the most crucial questions therapists must ask themselves is "What is the disquieting factor from which this dream arises?" To answer the question, she felt therapists need to take into account the client's character structure, the factors evoking the dream, and how the dream's content deals with the evoking factors (Knapp, 1979, p. 347). This type of comprehensive approach is needed to deal with frightening elements in dreams.

Ambiguity versus Clarity

Clarity is highly revered in Western traditions. Science, education, and technology wage an eternal war against ambiguity in all forms. Research proposals should be clear and concise, experimental designs rigorous, and outcomes measurable. Although such traits are noble and highly advantageous in many situations, it is easy to forget that extremes tend to produce their polar opposites. The dialectic engages each extreme, attempting to find a useful synthesis. Is it surprising that in Western achievement-oriented societies, purposelessness is endemic? That people determined to be happy often suffer from bouts of depression and anomie? That individuals given a multitude of choices often choose not to make any?

The emphasis on clarity has ignored the equally valid condition of ambiguity. Creative people, according to Rothenberg (1971), can tolerate ambiguity, possessing an ability to conceive and use two or more opposite or contradictory ideas, concepts, or images at the same time. As a consequence, creative people are able to explore relationships and associations never entertained by those who worship clarity.

One learns to tolerate and use ambiguity when dreams are studied because the essence of metaphor is ambiguity. In Swedenborg's nightmare, the attacker's sword could have represented the insights of a critic, the sexual prowess of a rival, the wrath of a deity, self-punishment for failing to meet a publication deadline, or a combination of forces. The fact that the attacker used his teeth to injure Swedenborg rather than his sword could have meant that "his bark was worse than his bite," that a body part was a more intimate weapon than a sword, or that in close quarters the feared figure took on the image of a vampire, slowly draining the philosopher of his time, energy, money, and/or life. Swedenborg's broken stick and the stranger's leap onto the dreamer's back are also ambiguous at first glance. Yet this is the nature of dreams, and their secrets are worth the time spent unraveling the ambiguity.

Sexual imagery in dreams can be extremely ambiguous. Freud was probably correct in describing the symbolic forms sexual organs and functions sometimes can take in dreams. But sexual intercourse can also symbolize other activities, such as the reconciliation of one's own male and female parts. Jung referred to the feminine archetype in males as the *anima*, and the masculine archetype in females as the *animus*. The most "masculine" of men will often show surprising gentleness with children; "strong" men may be both sentimental and tender (Fordham, 1953, pp. 52-59). The most "feminine" of women may demonstrate strength and resourcefulness in the time of a crisis. Of course, gentleness, tenderness, and resourcefulness are basically *human* traits rather than male or female characteristics. But cultures typically harbor sexual stereotypes. One practical way of approaching the anima and animus is to consider them as aspects of one's psyche that the culture has not reinforced because of its prevailing sex roles.

Cynthia's parents told her that to fulfill her role in life she needed to serve her husband and children. Cynthia entered into marriage imbued with this personal myth, but it did not serve her well. Her husband abused her, mistreated her, left her for another woman, and then disappeared. Cynthia was considered a failure by her parents and had to take a job to support herself—a task for which her personal myth had never prepared her. She began to have nightmares in which a masked stranger would break through her window and rape her. Her response was to put extra locks on the doors and windows, and to install an alarm system in her apartment. But the dreams continued to terrify her.

After several months, Cynthia began doing well in her office, and her dreams began to change. No longer did the stranger break in through the window, but came to the door bringing her gifts and flowers. Their lovemaking became tender rather than forced. One day, Cynthia received a promotion in her office. That night the masked stranger again appeared in her dream; Cynthia removed the mask and discovered her own face. The stranger had been Cynthia's animus, her disowned capabilities of doing well professionally, living independently, and caring for herself. The animus had to force itself into her attention, by breaking into her apartment and making itself a part of her experience as symbolized by the rape.

Many Jungians would consider the "creative muse" spoken of by some creative males as their anima. They would consider both the anima and animus to reflect deeper levels of the psyche than the shadow. Maria Mahoney (1970) observes that some writers literally draw portraits by pen of the animus or the anima. Some have provided such excellent descriptions that Freud "wrote about his vexation with the creative writer's ability to look into the motivations of his characters with ease" (p. 130). In T. S. Eliot's play, *The Cocktail Party,* a character speaks to her lover, realizing that until that moment she had projected her animus upon him, which prevented her from seeing him as he really was: "I see you as a person whom I never saw before. The man I saw before, he was only a projection . . . something that I desperately wanted to exist." One does not have to use Jung's terms to recognize this common occurrence; people will project their images of an "ideal man" or "ideal woman" upon a loved one, often to their eventual disappointment.

Spontaneity versus Practicality

Some dreams are frightening because of their spontaneous nature. Dream imagery can be so alarming to some people that they awaken with a disturbed feeling. The crisis, or sudden turn of events in a frightening dream, can represent a choice available to the dreamer. The catastrophe in many nightmares may represent how the dreamer reacted (or would react) to an important insight or decision (Greene, 1979, p. 309).

For example, Chuck dreamed:

I am at a urinal, urinating. I look down and realize that I am a woman.

Other members of his dream group reported dreams which disturbed them as well:

I am at a party, eating appetizers. Suddenly I realize that they are grasshoppers.

I am walking near my home. I begin to float and rise high above the ground.

I am at a board of director's meeting. The president of the company gets up and starts dancing on the table. One by one, the rest of us join him, dancing in sheer abandon.

Fear of such spontaneous images causes many people to block their creativity as well as to remain apprehensive about their dreams. Free, unbridled expression can violate social and personal values and norms. Many claim they want to be creative (or that they want their children to be creative), but not in ways which seem to threaten their personality or their social relationships. The fear of losing control is often apparent in nightmares; it can also block spontaneity and, consequently, problem-solving ability.

Chuck was disturbed about his urination dream until he realized he had been denying a sensitive part of himself, what Jungians would call his anima. Other members of his dream group gained similar insights from their upsetting dreams. When Barbara had her grasshopper dream, she began to question the value of the constant round of cocktail parties she had been attending. Norman, who began to float as he approached his home in a dream, realized he had been trying to "rise above" some serious family problems rather than face them. Zelda felt constrained in board meetings and thought the company could do better if her fellow executives "danced in sheer abandon," took more risks, and showed more imagination.

Letitia awakened from the following nightmare: "I am walking around, trying to take care of business. I notice I am being followed by a slimy-looking salamander. I'm scared." When invited to role-play the salamander, Letitia incredulously discovered that it was not poisonous or threatening, but was merely there to help her "stay in control." Could fear be an asset, helping her maintain her stability? Letitia reflected upon some aspects of her life that were not "in control." By her sexual promiscuity, she risked acquiring sexually transmitted diseases. Letitia's spending habits were making it difficult for her to pay her bills. Her neglect of her health was contributing to feelings of exhaustion and burnout. Because she disliked and even feared "slimy" creatures such as lizards and salamanders, they were precisely the symbol needed to shock her into a recognition of her self-destructive behavior. Taking Jung's advice, she did some research on the mythological meaning of salamanders, discovering that they reputedly were able to survive flames. She also found out that the alchemist Paracelsus used the word to describe a spirit able to live in fire. Letitia adopted this meaning, seeing the salamander as her own route to purification by transmuting anger and frustration into beneficial rather than harmful behavior. Eventually, the notion that she had a "guardian salamander" was comforting and encouraging.

Elias Howe's nightmare contained the seemingly impractical image of holes near the tip of spears. Yet this creative insight later proved to be extremely useful. Miguel used an "impractical" image of a flying building to help his firm prevent an unwise investment. In Miguel's dream, his office flew through the air and crashed into the local courthouse. When Miguel checked further into the property in question, he discovered it had liens against it. Had he and his business associates attempted to acquire it, they would have crashed financially and ended up in the courthouse.

Figure 23.

Sometimes the presence of a child in a dream indicates the type of spontaneity and "impracticality" which might be needed for a creative breakthrough. For example, Robert Sun had been a devoted player of the parlor game Mah Jongg since he discovered the pastime at the age of four in his native country, China. Half a century later, he had almost given up trying to update the 3,000-year-old game when the solution came in a dream. Sun recalled, "A little kid came into my room and said, 'Why don't you make it simple and turn it into a deck of cards'?" Sun took the child's advice; *Games* magazine later awarded him the prize for "Best Game of the Year" (Dlaboha, 1985).

One person's nightmare can be another's creative breakthrough. The qualities of exaggeration, ambiguity, spontaneity, and freedom of expression are threatening and disturbing to some dreamers. To others, they might provide useful information that can be used in solving problems, composing music, or inventing games.

In Summary

- Nightmares often depict important truths or contain useful information to enrich our lives once we overcome our initial fear of dealing with them.
- Night terrors have little or no content, are less frequent than nightmares, and may reflect a neurological imbalance that is usually outgrown.
- Some nightmares may be conceptualized as self-punishment for disobeying a rigid personal myth during wakefulness.
- Dreams often use exaggeration as a type of "artistic license" to make a point.
- Creativity requires the ability to tolerate and use ambiguity. By working with one's dreams, the dreamer often can learn to make creative use of the ambiguity in his or her life.
- Dreamwork can teach dreamers to use spontaneity as a counterbalance to practicality. Spontaneity is often associated with creativity as well.

Exercises

1. *Evaluating Nightmares.* Harry Fiss (1979) suggests that nightmares often represent a failure of the dream to accomplish a piece of work. Recall your most recent nightmare. What could have been the issue in your waking life the nightmare failed to address or resolve? Give the same type of attention to a repetitive dream which Fiss believes may serve the same function. His view is important because it demonstrates that not all dreams successfully solve a problem. The unresolved elements in these dreams may have a nightmarish quality, or the dream may repeat itself, making a further attempt to attain closure.

2. *Nightmare Imagery.* Try to recall the most frightening nightmare you ever had. Reflect upon the imagery to determine

what you can learn from it. Dialogue the dream. Role-play the salamander, monster, or other scary character in the nightmare.

3. *Ambiguity and Spontaneity.* Find an instance of ambiguity in your dreams. Notice how it frustrates reason and avoids giving you a final answer. What creative aspects does it contain? Now find an instance of spontaneity in your dreams. Recall the feeling accompanying it. Think of a waking situation when you were spontaneous. Were the dream and waking feelings similar? What would your life be like if you had those feelings more often? Would your creativity suffer or be enhanced?

4. *Projecting Archetypes.* Think of someone you love. If it is a member of opposite sex, do you find yourself projecting your anima or animus, or your image of an "ideal woman" or "ideal man" on that person? If it is a member of the same sex, do you find yourself projecting your persona (the image you want others to have of you) or some archetypal figure on that person? Can you see how such projections prevent you from appreciating that person for herself or himself? Try the same exercise with someone you dislike. Could you be projecting your shadow (what you dislike about yourself) on that person? You may prefer to use terms other than those coined by Jungians, but remember, projections can keep you from dealing with people as they really are.

Dreams Of The Spirit

It is beyond dispute that I can fly in dreams. You too. I add "in dreams" because my efforts, like yours, have not succeeded . . . in crossing the frontier that separates the two worlds, only one of which we designate, arbitrarily, as 'real.'

— Colette

From time to time, people have dreams which they believe transport them into sacred experience, those aspects of one's existence considered to be most hallowed, holy, and inviolate. These dreams have been described in different ways—numinous (filled with "numen," or divine power), transpersonal (extending beyond personal concerns into those of all humanity), transcendent (establishing contact with higher, or "divine," knowledge), spiritual (pertaining to the "spirit" or the ultimate values of the human being). Jung spoke of the Self archetype as the center of the psyche. The Self attempts to integrate all opposing elements (conscious/unconscious, male/female, expressed/repressed) and transmute them into a unique entity representing all that a person is able to become.

In dreams, this process of integration (or "individuation") can appear as a flower (the Golden Flower of Taoism and the rose window of medieval Christian cathedrals); a geometric form (the circular mandala of such philosophies as Tibetan Buddhism and the Native American medicine circle); a jewel (the Blessed Pearl of Islam and the Jeweled Net of Indra in Buddhism); a person (Buddha, Jesus, Mohammed, Lord Krishna, a hero or heroine); or a common object which takes on new meaning (the wheel of Hinduism, and the drum of the Lakota Sioux). For

Jungians, the "ego" is the center of waking awareness, and appears in dreams as the evaluative, judgmental, decision-making part of the psyche. But the Self is the most direct route to the world of spirit, and Self archetypes in dreams typically indicate a striving for integration, synthesis, and transformation (Fordham, 1953, pp. 62-68).

Religion and Dreams

Dreams have played a major role in religious traditions throughout the world. The Carthaginian philosopher Tertullian wrote, "Nearly everyone knows that God reveals himself to people most often in dreams" (Savary, Berne, & Williams, 1984, p. 28). Christians are familiar with the biblical account of St. Joseph's dream in which the agency of Mary's pregnancy was revealed to him. Another biblical dream warned the Eastern Magi to return home without revealing the whereabouts of Jesus to King Herod. Joseph was warned in a dream to take Mary and Jesus to safety because Herod was seeking to destroy the child. In addition, the time when it was safe for Joseph to return to Israel was announced in a dream (Savary, Berne, & Williams, 1984).

Queen Maya, mother of the Buddha, is supposed to have had a dream in which a white elephant with six tusks entered her womb, indicating that she would give birth to an infant who would become a universal monarch. King Cudhodana, father of the Buddha, also dreamed about his son's path and was saddened by the separation it foresaw. Gopa, Buddha's wife, dreamed of catastrophic events and shared them with her husband who explained that world turmoil heralds the inner liberation that is possible (de Becker, 1968, pp. 31-32). Much later, in the 6th century, the mother of Prince Shotokutaishi dreamed that a Boddhisattva asked to take shelter in her womb. She soon became pregnant and gave birth to the man who was to establish Buddhism in Japan (p. 56).

The *Talmud* makes 217 references to dreams and the *Bible*'s Old Testament contains about 15 dreams, most of which herald the beginning of vital stages in Judaism's history (de Becker,

1968, p. 20). For example, Joseph attained eminence by interpreting the Egyptian Pharaoh's dreams. Earlier, his father, Jacob,
is said to have undergone a transformative experience as the
result of a dream. According to the Scriptures, Jacob was hardly
an appropriate figure to be the patriarch of Israel. At one point,
he refused to feed his hungry brother Esau until the latter surren-
dered to him the rights of the firstborn. In conspiracy with his
mother, Jacob undertook an elaborate deception to take advantage of his father's blindness and to cheat Esau out of a paternal
blessing.

Later, when Jacob made a journey, he had a powerful dream
in which he saw a ladder stretching from earth to heaven, with
angels ascending and descending the steps. At the top of the
ladder, God stood and proclaimed that He would give all the
surrounding land to Jacob and his descendents. Thus was the
apparently unrighteous brother chosen over the pious one. But
Jacob, shaken by the dream, slowly mended his ways and, years
later, offered Esau his wives, sons, servants, and animals. Esau
refused the gifts out of love, and the two brothers were reconciled.
Jacob's dream is an example of "theophany," a person's direct
apprehension of one's God, whether in a dream, vision, or other
circumstance; such experiences are often transformative in nature, altering a person's life.

Creative problem-solving in dreams is well illustrated in the
history of Islam. Mohammed claimed to have received his mission
in a dream, his famous "Night Journey" to heaven. Later, during
a six-month period, he was said to have received dream messages
about the format of his new religion, the *Koran* being revealed
in a series of dreams. This pattern was repeated by one of his
followers, Abdullah ben Zayd. Mohammed was eager to introduce
a recognizable call to prayer for the faithful, just as the Jews were
called to the synagogue with a trumpet and the early Christians
to church by the sound of a rattle. During prayers, ben Zayd fell
asleep and dreamed of a man dressed in green who was carrying
a rattle. Ben Zayd asked if he could buy the rattle to use as a call
to prayer. The man in green replied, "Call out, There is no god
but God and Mohammed is his Prophet." Upon awakening, ben

Zayd told Mohammed of his dream and the Prophet instructed him to teach the exact phrase he had heard to another follower, who became the first muezzin (Coxhead & Hiller, 1981, p. 17).

Dreams and Religious Conflicts

Francis of Assisi, the 13th century monk who founded the Franciscan order, was about to have an interview with the terrifying Pope Innocent III. It is reported that he dreamed he had grown as tall as a great tree and, as Innocent looked on in dismay, restored the balance of a Vatican basilica which was on the point of collapsing. This dream gave St. Francis the courage to tell the pope that his order was badly needed to restore vigor to the Roman Catholic Church. St. Dominic, who founded a rival religious order, reported a dream of being presented to Jesus and the Virgin Mary in the company of St. Francis. The two of them were jointly entrusted with conversion of the world (de Becker, 1968, p. 26).

Dreams can also illuminate intrapersonal religious conflicts; St. Francis had a dream series in which his fiancee, present in the first dream, was replaced by the Virgin Mary, signifying his rejection of secular life (de Becker, 1968, p. 29). Sometimes, dreams serve the purpose of pointing out a schism which has emerged between the religion in which the dreamer was raised and the spiritual values he or she has since adopted. From the standpoint of personal myths, the traditional religion represents the old myth while the new set of values (a different religion, or an abandonment of institutionalized religion) represents the emerging myth. The dream may suggest ways in which the dreamer's new experiences can be worked into a modification of the old framework. Or, the dream may point out the inability of the long-standing myth to account for new experience. In that case, there is a conflict and if it is to be resolved, the old myth must be either abandoned or synthesized in some way with the emerging myth.

Heidi faithfully attended the church in the small town where she was born and raised. She had always been interested in art and, at college, took considerable delight in painting, drawing, filmmaking, and art history classes. She became close friends with Vivian, an older student with similar interests, and they entered into a sexual relationship. Heidi kept this liaison a secret from her parents and hometown friends, knowing that they would never approve. In the meantime, she and Vivian attended plays together, went to museums, and saw films. Vivian taught Heidi a great deal about makeup, fashion, and even rearranged her dormitory room. One night Heidi had a dream in which her parents arrived at the university and began to rearrange the furniture in her room. They insisted it be put back in its original order, and even threatened to take Heidi back home with them if she did not comply. This dream forced Heidi to confront the shift in values that had taken place, and her need to clarify her beliefs and life-style.

There are cultural myths which demonstrate how dreams can illustrate conflicts with a society's values. A 12th century Jain text tells the story of Kesara and Vasanta. One night, Kesara dreamed that she married Vasanta, and that same night he dreamed that he married her. Both were delighted with the dream message and declared their mutual love. But Kesara's parents, as was the custom, had arranged her marriage to someone else, based on such traditional practices as favorable astrological signs. They considered their daughter's dream love an illusion and disregarded their daughter's pleas. Saddened, Kesara and Vasanta tried to commit suicide. Fortunately, they were rescued, escaped their parents, and lived together happily (O'Flaherty, 1982, p. 58).

In some eras, religious institutions have taken a hostile attitude toward dreamworkers and dreamworking. In some meditative disciplines, it is maintained that spiritually developed adepts do not need to dream. In the 5th century, St. Jerome's translation of the Bible from Greek and Hebrew manuscripts was marred by his substitution of "observing dreams" for "witchcraft" in several parts. Therefore, the new translation dogmatically stated, "You will not practice soothsaying or observe dreams." As a result, dreamwork was held in disfavor by the Roman Catholic

Church for the next 15 centuries; people were discouraged from turning to their dreams for insight, consolation, or hope. It is not known whether St. Jerome or church authorities were responsible for the error in translation; it appears to have been deliberate because the word "witchcraft" is correctly used in other portions of the translation (Savary, Berne, & Williams, 1984, p. 51).

Projection, Negative and Positive

Many individuals routinely project onto other people qualities of concern to them that the other persons may not actually possess. Projection is easily accomplished; it occurs every night in dreams and in the waking roles personified by one's dream characters, activities, articles, and objects from nature. However, projections are difficult to integrate because they are often tied up with the dreamer's body. Dreams frequently reflect what is happening in the body and dreams may project those feelings on to someone or something else (Mindell, 1985, p. 29).

Dreamworking can teach dreamers that much of what they dream represents aspects of themselves. Once they understand this, they can begin to withdraw their projections, stop blaming others for their problems, stop looking to others for their happiness, and start accepting responsibility for their well-being. They can then use their latent creative problem-solving abilities. Facing the world realistically, they may realize their behavior created many of their problems, and that other problems were due to external circumstances. In both instances, one's inner resources as revealed by dreams can enable the dreamer, as St. Francis of Assisi once counseled, to change what can be changed, to accept what cannot be changed, and to acquire the wisdom to know the difference.

It is not uncommon for individuals to project their shadow, animus, anima, or some other archetype upon other people. Sometimes a person will intensely dislike an acquaintance, attributing various vices and depravities to that person. Hortense had a dream about Suzanne, a woman she disliked because of her barbed tongue. Hortense described how, in the dream,

Suzanne was shooting darts from her mouth, an appropriate metaphor for her antagonist's indulgence in gossip. Suddenly, Hortense found herself playing a dart game with Suzanne, and doing just about as well as her rival. Upon awakening, Suzanne realized that she tended to cast aspersions on other people herself, but in a more subtle way than Hortense. She realized her behavior was even more insidious because it was carefully controlled and hidden. Realizing that Hortense, in the dream, represented her own shadow, Suzanne became less critical of the other woman and focused her attention on correcting her own behavior.

Ullman (1979, 1984) developed a way of using projections beneficially in experiential dream groups. Two principles governed the dreamwork conducted by these groups: The dreamer must remain in control of the process while his or her dream is being discussed. The group serves as a catalyst, helping and supporting the dreamer's efforts to understand the dream. Theoretical material is minimized, except for a few basic concepts, such as day residue, linkage of dream images to recent and remote past, the dream's use of a visual method to engage in metaphorical expression, and the tripartite structure of the dream: setting, development, and resolution.

Certain assumptions underlie the experiential dream group: A remembered dream has a useful application to waking life. The dream's imagery is generated as part of an intrinsic self-healing process. When a dream is recalled, the dreamer is ready to be confronted with the information it contains. Dreams do not invariably require the aid of a trained analyst for their appreciation (Ullman, 1979, p. 409). Ullman sees dreams as a normal dimension of human experience. The dream group is one way of helping dreamers realize, in a way which puts them in touch with their feelings, the relevance of the night-time images to the issues they face during the day. A social process is implemented to help put dreamers in touch with these images while respecting their privacy and authority over the dream (p. 42).

Ullman's system begins with a dreamer presenting the manifest content of his or her dream. Realizing that they will project their feelings and experiences into the dream, group members reflect back any feelings experienced both while listening to the dream and imagining they had just had it. Then the group turns its attention to each dream image, responding to it in a metaphorical way. The dreamer responds to the group's projections, some of which may have been helpful in increasing his or her appreciation of the dream. The dreamer recalls the events of the day before the dream to define the context which helped shape the dream. The dreamer and the group try to make connections between the dream images, the dreamer's life situation, and the contact between the dream and the dreamer's past experiences. The dreamer responds to the group's questions with as much self-disclosure as he or she feels comfortable, and the process continues until the dreamer feels a sense of closure.

Ming told her group about a dream in which she survived an atomic explosion and began seeking refuge. She headed toward a church but, when nearing it, heard a variety of evil voices coming from within. She bypassed the church and continued on her lonely way. Glen commented, "If this were my dream, I would relate it to the way that I survived the explosions in my family. The traditional institutions of my childhood stood for values I considered destructive, and so I set out to find my own way in life." Johanna said, "When I had this dream, I felt it related to my seemingly solitary concern about the fate of the planet and how most 'good' people, by ignoring the threat, are making the problem worse." After each group member treated the dream as his or her own, they discussed each image separately, e.g., the explosion, the church, the evil voices. At the end of the process, Ming thanked the group and was satisfied that she had grasped the basic meaning the dream had for her.

Ullman (1980) stated that his work with experiential dream groups made him aware of the "transpersonal dimensions" of dreamwork, of the great need people have to communicate with others at the level of intimacy and honesty which characterizes dreamwork. Individual psychotherapy, he notes, typically touches only briefly on the transpersonal qualities of the dream, neglecting a powerful source of healing. For Ullman, the human's main focus while awake is separateness and individuality. While asleep, there can be a shift to the more basic state of relatedness and connectedness to others. If individuality is considered analogous to waves in the sea, the waking state limits one's view to the crests of these waves. The view from the dreaming state, however, focuses on the troughs–the connecting medium between the crests. This is the transpersonal realm, and the degree of turbulence here is what most concerns the dreamer. Individuals need support in what is basically a self-healing process; the experiential dream group is one of the few social agencies available for this purpose.

An Ethic for Creativity

A person's morals and ethics (the application of one's values to real-life situations) are guided by one's spiritual framework and interface with creativity in several ways. Maslow (1976) found that the qualities of creative people typically include boldness, courage, freedom, integration, spontaneity, perspicuity, and self-acceptance. According to Maslow, creative individuals "emit" creativity "just like sunshine" (p. 91). Other researchers have observed additional traits, noting that creative people are motivated by a need for achievement, autonomy, curiosity, and order. They tend to be aesthetic, aggressive, critical, dominant, enthusiastic, independent, intuitive, and self-sufficient; they tend not to be conventional, inhibited, or repressed (Stein, 1974, pp. 58-60). One can think of these traits as providing the foundation of a possible "ethic" for creativity, recognizing the fact that individual differences exist and that a highly creative person *can* be neurotically timid, overly controlled, or even self-rejecting. For example, Louis Pasteur was dogmatic and conceited; Ignaz Semmelweis was irascible and tactless; Charlie Chaplin could be autocratic and cruel (Goertzel, Goertzel, & Goertzel, 1978; Stein, 1974).

Morris Stein (1974) once prepared a list of "commandments" for industrial researchers seeking the opportunity to pursue their creative interests in a work setting:

1. Be assertive without being hostile.

2. Take account of your superiors, colleagues, and subordinates as people without becoming too personally involved with them.

3. Keep your own counsel, but do not be isolated, withdrawn, or uncommunicative.

4. On the job, be congenial but not sociable.

5. Off the job, be sociable but not intimate.

6. "Know your place" with superiors without being overly acquiescent, timid, or submissive.

7. Speak your mind without being domineering.

8. Be subtle in achieving your ends but not cunning.

9. In your relationships at work, be diplomatic, honest, and sincere; but don't be unwilling to accept "shortcuts" if they come your way.

10. Intellectually, be "broad" without "spreading yourself too thin," be "deep" without being pedantic, be "sharp" without being over-critical (pp. 261-262).

Although Stein assembled this list for industrial researchers, he implies that it may be of value for all creative people who work within an institutional setting. Because creative people tend to be unconventional and uninhibited, working for a business firm, an educational institution, or a research company can force a type of discipline on them. Again, there are ethical questions: At what point must the creative person be true to one's principles rather than display behaviors necessary for job security? Perhaps paradoxical issues are involved in the creative person's behavior as well as his or her creative product.

Patrick, an engineer whose avocation was the invention of electrical gadgets, had frequent dreams about buffets, cafeterias, and smorgasbords, identifying the wide choice of foods as sources of possible nurturance for his creative life. One night, he dreamed he was at a meeting of inventors sponsored by the government. At first glance, the cafeteria had several appetizing dishes, but at second glance, they were varieties of pasta entrees and gelatin desserts. Patrick was dismayed and asked a fellow inventor why there were so few choices. The reply was, "All this food is government surplus; our work is not exactly high priority and so we must be grateful for what we can get." Upon engaging in dreamwork, Patrick concluded that his own internal "government" had placed his avocation very low in its priorities; he was not aware of this in his waking life as he was thankful for every spare hour he could spend tinkering in his laboratory. Indeed, the mass of wires resembled spaghetti and his ever-changing blueprints were about as stable as gelatin.

Patrick resolved to spend more time puttering around with his electronic circuitry. However, his work at the office began to suffer and his superiors began to complain. Patrick dreamed about another cafeteria in which a variety of foods were available. However, there was a discount on meat and potatoes. Patrick interpreted this "sale price" as a suggestion to pay closer attention to his professional duties. He was struck by the way the two dreams prepared him to find a balance between his daily work and his hobbies as both were important sources of nurturance for him. Patrick lost no time in revising his priorities and values to honor the guidelines provided by his dreams.

Many creative people who do not identify with organized religion have developed a set of ethical principles by which they live. They often claim this moral code is spiritual, as it emanates from the deepest part of their being and reflects values they hold most sacred. They also claim these ethical principles provide a framework within which their creativity operates, one which typically focuses around the injunction to respect the rights of others while their needs are fulfilled and their goals are pursued. In many cases, there is also a concern for the wider community and a commitment to contribute to the culture-at-large. This concern for the social fabric is the distinguishing mark of transpersonal experience for Ullman (1980). The ongoing dialectic between individual needs and group requirements is a perennial concern for creative individuals. Like so many other aspects of their experience, one's creativity is at risk if it veers too wildly in one extreme or another. Each major creative contribution overpasses the established order in some way. But if the creator is too blunt and audacious, the work may be ignored. If he or she is too reticent, it may remain unappreciated for different reasons. Those who have reached Selfhood, as Jung termed it, have found a way to deal with these paradoxes. Others can do no worse than search their dreams for advice about how to attain the delicate balances needed to foster and protect their creativity.

The Script and the Stage

Some writers conceptualize the world of spirit as mediating between the worlds of ideas and action. The world of ideas provides the script for creative behavior while the world of action serves as its stage. The world of spirit provides the inspiration and motivation to energize the actors who perform their script upon the stage. In much the same way, the philosopher Ken Wilber (1983) speaks of the "eye of flesh" (knowledge from the senses), the "eye of reason" (knowledge from one's mental processes), and the "eye of contemplation" (transcendent knowledge). Dreamwork can illustrate many ways in which these three worlds can be related.

Sometimes the world of spirit appears in anomalous dreams, seeming to contact some sort of higher intelligence obtaining information not ordinarily available to the dreamed. Naomi, a member of one of our workshops, reported this story:

> When I was 19, I became quite ill. I went to a physician and he told me that I was pre-diabetic. There was nothing that could be done at that time. Basically, he told me that I would have to live with the condition and eventually become dependent on insulin. That night I went to sleep while thinking about this problem and awakened following a remarkable dream.
>
> My mother's uncle—whom I had only met once before he died—was talking to me. He said that if I would eat heart of palm daily for a month, I would outgrow my pre-diabetic condition. He noticed my surprise and

*added that heart of palm could be found in the gourmet
section of most supermarkets.*

*I mentioned this dream to a friend who commented
that heart of palm was available at many grocery stores
as well as health food stores. My tendency was to dismiss
this experience as "only a dream," but I eventually decided that I had nothing to lose by trying some of the
remedy. I concluded that if it were easily available in the
market that it probably wouldn't hurt me.*

*So I went to a store and bought a month's supply
of the stuff. Before two weeks had gone by, I felt a lot
better. By the end of a month, my symptoms were completely gone. Now, some 25 years later, I still have no
signs of diabetes. I can eat anything I want without having
negative reactions. And I still occasionally eat heart of
palm!*

Anecdotal instances of this nature are familiar to many
dreamworkers. Naomi's return to health is remarkable, whether
explained as coincidence, misdiagnosis, the placebo effect, the
intervention of her dead uncle, or self-healing based on contact
with the "higher" intelligence in the "deepest" part of herself.
Vasily Kasatkin (1984), a Soviet physician, studied 8,000 of his
clients' dreams to determine ways dreams could warn of an
impending illness. Kasatkin took the position that signals of an
incipient disease sometimes are too weak to excite pain receptors
but strong enough to innervate the brain's sensitive optic area
which produces imagery showing up in dreams. Although this
proposed mechanism is a matter of dispute, Kasatkin's case
histories are impressive.

According to Kasatkin, dreams focusing on hypertension
begin to appear two or three months before the problem is
apparent. In the case of tuberculosis, the time averages two
months, and with some conditions a year or more. One of his
patients dreamed of fires and blood, and would awaken feeling
cold and anxious. A medical examination confirmed Kasatkin's
diagnosis of a rheumatic heart condition. One man who dreamed
of being buried under a collapsing building was later hospitalized

for hypertension; a woman who dreamed she was crawling through a narrow passage was diagnosed as tubercular (Krippner, 1980, p. 283).

Kasatkin's dream-based diagnosis has been used to determine whether alcoholics have fully recovered; if they continue to imbibe in their dreams, the prognosis for abstention is poor. Some disturbances rarely work their way into dreams; the atrophy of limbs is difficult to predict because dreamers can be quite active physically regardless of their oncoming disease. Kasatkin advises against self-diagnosis but believes that if a dreamer works with a knowledgeable physician, many ailments can be prevented or be treated in their early stages.

Kasatkin's work is reminiscent of that carried on by Arnold Mindell (1985), a Jungian psychotherapist who specialized in discovering how dreams mirror bodily concerns. One's gestures, tone of voice, speaking tempo, and facial expressions are reflected in dreams as well as the symptoms of physical health and illness (p. 3). Mindell works with a Jungian process called "amplification" in which both personal and cultural associations are made to dream images, followed by possible archetypal associations. This process differs from Freud's use of "free association" because it returns to the dream image time and time again rather than moving from the original image to a chain of associations (Hall, 1982, pp. 139-142). Mindell relates the case of a young girl, dying from a cancerous tumor on her back:

> The little girl came in and told me that she had dreamt that she let go of the safety fences around a very dangerous lake. Then she lay down on the floor and told me that she wanted to fly. She had a corset on her back because the tumor had weakened her spine and she said she couldn't fly with it on . . . . I phoned her doctor and . . . he told me . . . that she was such an unhappy child and as nothing worse could happen to her any more, I could go ahead and remove the corset. (p. 12)

After several sessions in which the therapist and the client engaged in "flying," the girl improved. Soon she could do without her corset and eventually the tumor disappeared. The use of amplification had touched the client at a profound level of her psyche, allowing self-healing to occur. This procedure could not be condoned if it had been attempted in place of proper medical treatment. But as an adjunct to medical treatment, these procedures sometimes are beneficial if carried out by competent practitioners.

Mindell refers to his process as "working with the dream body"; disease symptoms are frequently "dreams trying to come true" (p. 27) and through dreamwork one can discover this connection, amplify its channel, and turn the "symptom" into a "medicine." In a sense, Mindell's point of view receives support from Hobson and McCarley (1979), even though they ignore both anomalous and spiritual dreams. These researchers have presented evidence that neural generation can affect motor systems during the dream. The dream events of stepping, walking, and running may be linked to the brain stem pattern generator for locomotor movement. Vestibular stimulation may be associated with floating, flying, or spinning in dreams. Activation of high brain regions concerned with such emotions as anger and defensive behavior may provide important content material as well (p. 124). They refer to their point of view as the activation-synthesis hypothesis because it predicts a correspondence between the frequency and intensity of subjective sensations in dreams and the extent and intensity of physiological activation of brain nuclei related to these sensations.

The spiritual aspects of dreams were also undervalued by Freud, who was hostile to organized religion, and by Adler, who was hostile to anything smacking of the occult. Jung, on the other hand, spoke of "curing souls" and leading clients toward "experiencing the Self." Individuation, or attaining an integration of the Self, was seen by Jung as a lifetime goal. Jung believed that spontaneous religious experiences help to attain Selfhood, as do ritualistic practices (meditation, prayer, yoga), and dreamwork (active imagination, amplification, working with the dreaming body). Jung believed the dream can be thought of as being

Figure 24.

produced by the Self as part of the psyche's attempts at self-regulation and self-healing.

The self-regulating and self-healing aspects of dreams have
induced Ullman (1983) to refer to them as "an unappreciated
natural resource." Dreams are readily available but are rarely
used in a person's search for healing and growth. Ullman observed that the pragmatic social matrix found in industrialized
countries rates dreams rather low in its scale of priorities. Yet,
dreams continue to depict in metaphorical images both the existing emotional condition of the dreamer and clues of what con-

flicting emotional issue might be disturbing this condition. Dreams can also explore the impact of the impinging stimulus on a dreamer's life and the range of both healthy and neurotic defenses which can be mobilized to cope with the stimulus. The denouement is an effort to face the tensions and remove the disequilibrium evoked by the emotional material triggering the dream. The dreamer's spiritual resources can assist in resolving the issues posed by dream content, and in enhancing the dreamer's personal and social growth and development.

In Summary

- Some dreams contain spiritual elements directing dreamers toward personal integration.
- Key people in the founding of some world religions felt their dreams gave them spiritual insights.
- Some dreams attempt to reconcile the dreamer's waking assumptions with unfolding spiritual concepts.
- When dreamers recognize that dream content often expresses aspects of themselves, they may take greater responsibility for how they bring both happiness and sadness into their lives.
- Dreamwork can teach people how to recognize their projections and perceive events and people more realistically.
- Through dreamwork, one can develop an ethic for creativity to guide one's work relationships.
- Some dreams contain aspects that enhance self-regulation and self-healing.

Exercises

1. *Reaching the Spirit.* Have you ever had an experience you would describe as sacred? What feeling accompanied the experience? Did it provide information? If so, do you feel the information was valid and helpful? Have any similar feelings or pieces of information come to you in dreams? If so, how do they compare with your waking experiences?

2. *Examining Your Ethical Code.* What is one specific ethical

principle you attempt to follow? What is the source of this principle (e.g., your church, family, intuition, or life experiences)? Look over your dream notebook. Are there instances when this principle appears? If so, was it followed or flouted? If the rule was broken, what meaning does this have for you (e.g., the principle may need revision, the principle is still valid but you are beginning to disregard it or are associating with someone who does not share the same values)?

3. *Sexual Expectations.* According to Jungians, the bringing to consciousness one's opposite-sex (or "contrasexual") components is important in one's approach to totality and wholeness. Androgyny is seen by Singer (1976) as an archetype representing the principle of wholeness in human form. Falling in love often involves projection of the animus or anima on to the loved one. In the case of falling in love with someone of the same sex, the animus or anima is projected onto the "contrasexual" side of the loved one. (Of course, one does not have to have lovers of both sexes to be whole or androgynous; sexual behavior is only one area where rigid sex roles can be modified.) If the person doing the projecting is not aware of this dynamic, the romance might go sour as the loved one fails to meet the expectations of the projected animus or anima. Examine your dreams closely. Are there any examples of the androgyny archetype? Are there activities you refrain from because you associate them with the opposite sex? Are you unfairly projecting your image of an "ideal mate" onto people you love? Examine your dreams about your loved ones to determine whether this may be the case.

4. *The Dream Body.* Examine your dreams from the perspective of your body. Remember that emotions are closely associated with the body, and that these factors often can be observed together in dreams. Use amplification to understand those dreams at a more profound level. Act out any bodily movements occurring in the dream; exaggerate them and observe your feelings about them.

11

Problem-Solving, Incubation, And Lucidity

All that we see or seem is but a dream within a dream.

— Edgar Allan Poe

Alfred Maury, it is said, dreamed that a French military tribunal had sentenced him to death. As the blade of the guillotine dropped, Maury awoke to find that a headboard had fallen on his neck. He decided that the loose headboard was the single stimulus producing his dream. Maury later became one of those responsible for the widespread (and generally discredited) belief that dreams occur within a split second (Evans, 1985, p. 37).

In any event, the dreamer's ability to incorporate external stimuli was recognized by Freud, and has been demonstrated by experiments in which various auditory, tactile, thermal, and verbal stimuli were presented to subjects during Stage REM. In general, about one out of four stimuli presented is mentioned in a subsequent dream report (McCarley & Hobson, 1979, p. 109). These results could be interpreted to support the view that there is a psychological need to complete dreams; incorporating an external stimulus will prevent the dreamer from awakening prematurely.

In a different type of experiment, subjects felt more disturbed when awakened in the middle of a REM period than when awakened at the beginning or the end (Fiss, 1979, p. 55). However, dream reports after interrupted REM periods were usually equal in length to reports following completed REM periods. Fiss (1979) conjectured that the subjects must have compensated for the interruptions by cramming more dream activity into the shortened REM periods (pp. 56-57). He also conducted an experiment in which his subjects read a nautical story before going to sleep, and were tested on it the following morning. If the story influenced their dreams, or even if their dreams were unusually vivid (emotionally, with color, etc.), the subjects recalled more details about the story. This study demonstrates the impact of pre-sleep experience on dreams as well as illustrating some mechanisms behind the memory-serving function of dreams (pp. 60-61).

The influence of pre-sleep stimuli in dream content has been successfully attempted in experiments using hypnosis, subliminal stimulation, emotionally arousing films, and real-life stress situations (Fiss, 1979, p. 47; Moss, 1967). The results indicate that it is relatively easy to influence dream content in predictable ways. Cartwright and her associates (Cartwright, Bernick, Borowitz, & Kling, 1969) found that reaction to pre-sleep stimulation (e.g., erotic films) elicited dreams which provided emotional support for the dreamer's self-identity—a finding congruent with the thesis that one's personal mythology plays an important role in determining dream content. Another team of investigators (Breger, Hunter, & Lane, 1971) induced pre-sleep stress and observed that the resulting dreams contained feelings and moods of personal relevance. They concluded that dreams serve to assimilate emotionally arousing information into problem solutions embodied in existing memory systems.

Preparing for Breakthroughs

If it is possible for the experimenter to influence the course of a dream, then it should also be possible for the dreamer to influence the dream content. Recalling the dream incubation practices of ancient Egypt and Greece, psychologist Henry Reed (1976; 1985), developed an approach by which dreamers could attempt to incubate dreams which would respond to specific problems posed by the dreamers.

Gayle Delaney (1979), another psychologist, followed up on this by training a small group of people to select a night free from distractions and pressures, to incubate problem-solving dreams. Before going to sleep, Delaney's subjects wrote a few lines in their dream notebooks stating what they had done during the day and how they had felt. The subjects also wrote tentative answers to various questions about their problems: "What do you see as the causes of your problem?" "What are the alternative solutions you now recognize?" "What benefits might you be receiving by perpetuating this problem?" "How would your life be different if this problem were resolved?" The subjects then composed a one-line problem, question, or request (e.g., "Give me an idea for my next painting." "What are the dynamics of my current relationship?"). After the subjects went to bed, they lay quietly, repeating the question over and over to themselves before falling asleep. Upon awakening, they recorded any dreams they recalled as quickly as possible, and later engaged in dreamwork to determine whether the question had been answered.

Delaney's subjects reported a high degree of success and were satisfied with the incubation process. However, some critics of dream incubation claim that dreamers are unwise to tamper with their natural dream-making processes. After all, they point out, many creative people have attained remarkable results taking a passive rather than an active approach to their dreams. For example, writer Enid Blyton described how she allowed her characters to take her over while she worked on a book:

> I shut my eyes for a few minutes, with my portable type-writer on my knee—I make my mind blank and wait—and then, as clearly as I would see real children, my characters stand before me in my mind's eye. I see them in detail—hair, eyes, feet, clothes, expression—and I always know their Christian names but never their surnames . . . . I don't know what anyone is going to say or do. I don't know what is going to happen. I am in the happy position of being able to write a story and read it for the first time, at one and the same moment. . . . Sometimes a character makes a joke, a really funny one, that makes me laugh as I type it on my paper—and I think, "Well, I couldn't have thought of that myself in a hundred years!" And

then I think, "Well, who did think of it then?" (Evans,
1985, pp. 163-164; Stoney, 1974)

Although Delaney acknowledges this criticism, she says the
psyche has sufficient defenses to protect its integrity if incubation
becomes too controlled and restrictive. It can do this by giving
dreamers messages to modify or stop the incubation process,
or by refusing to cooperate with attempts at incubation. Further,
some highly creative individuals have obtained useful results from
pre-sleep preparation. Nobel Prize-winning biochemist Albert
Szent-Gyorgyi stated, "My work is not finished when I leave my
work bench in the afternoon. I go on thinking about my problems
all the time, and my brain must continue to think about them
when I sleep, because I wake up sometimes in the middle of the
night with answers to questions that have been puzzling me" (in
Dement, 1974, p. 98).

Composers Richard Wagner and Ludwig von Beethoven
and mathematician Henri Poincaré were three highly creative
people who inadvertently prepared themselves for creative breakthroughs in a way similar to that advocated by Reed and Delaney.
At age 40, Wagner was suffering a midlife crisis; his artistic career
was unsatisfactory, his marriage was dull, and his finances were
disastrous. Searching for new musical themes, he began to travel,
but only became exhausted. In September 1853, when all his
efforts seemed in vain, he had a creative breakthrough. Wagner
wrote to a friend:

*After a night spent in fever and sleeplessness I forced
myself to take a long walk through the country. It looked
dreary and desolate. Upon my return I lay down on a
hard couch. Sleep would not come, but I sank into a
kind of somnolence, in which I suddenly felt as though
I were sinking in swiftly flowing water. The rushing noise
formed itself into a musical sound, the chord of E flat
major, whence developed melodic passages of increasing motion. I awoke in sudden terror, recognizing that
the orchestral prelude to* Das Rheingold *which must*

Figure 25.

have been long lain latent within me, had at last been revealed to me. (Hock, 1960)

Inspired by this hypnagogic episode, Wagner was able to complete an entire opera, the first of his celebrated "Ring Cycle," by the following May.

This was not the first time Wagner had been so inspired. In describing his opera *Tristan and Isolde* to his friend Mathilde Wesendonck, Wagner wrote, "For once you are going to hear a dream, a dream that I have made sound . . . . I dreamed all this; never could my poor head have invented such a thing purposively" (Hock, 1960).

Beethoven reported obtaining inspiration for a composition in 1821. He recalled falling asleep in his carriage en route to Vienna; a "canon came into my head . . . but scarcely did I awake when away flew the canon, and I could not recall any part of it. On returning home, however, the next day, in the same carriage . . . , I resumed my dream journey, being on this occasion wide awake, when lo and behold! in accordance with the laws of association of ideas, the same canon flashed before me; so being now awake I held it fast . . . , only permitting it to be changed into three parts" (Shapero, 1955, p. 51).

Poincaré's (1913/1955) account demonstrates how intensive preparation can produce sudden results.

For fifteen days I strove to prove that there could not be any functions like those I have since called Fuchsian functions. I was then very ignorant; every day I seated myself at my work table, stayed on an hour or two, tried a great number of combinations and reached no results. One evening, contrary to my custom, I drank black coffee and could not sleep. Ideas rose in crowds; I felt them collide until pairs interlocked, so to speak, making a stable combination. By the next morning I had established the existence of a class of Fuchsian functions . . . . I had only to write out the results, which took but a few hours. Just at this time I left Caen, where I was then living, to go on a geologic excursion . . . . The changes of travel made me forget my mathematical work. Having reached Coutances, we entered an omnibus to go some place or other. At the moment when I put my foot on the step the idea came to me, without anything in my former thoughts seeming to have paved the way for it, that the transformations I had used to define the Fuchsian functions were identical with those of non-Euclidian geometry. I did not verify the idea; I should not have had the time, as, upon taking my seat in the omnibus, I went on with a conversation already commenced, but I felt a perfect certainty. On my return to Caen, for conscience' sake I verified the result at my leisure. (p. 37)

This process continued, and Poincaré experienced further break-throughs at the seaside, while strolling on a bluff, and walking down a street in a French town. Poincaré concluded, "The role of this unconscious work in mathematical invention appears to me incontestable . . . . The subliminal self is in no way inferior to the conscious self" (pp. 38-39).

Poincaré's use of black coffee is reminiscent of several ac-counts in which mind-altering drugs may have evoked creative insights (e.g., Krippner, 1985). Perhaps the most celebrated ac-count is that of Samuel Taylor Coleridge (1955), who had taken an opium preparation to check an oncoming bout of dysentery just before reading about the construction of Kubla Khan's palace in China. The drug induced a reverie in which "all the images rose up . . . as things." Coleridge estimated that he "could not have composed less than two to three hundred lines" of what was to become his poem, "Kubla Khan." However, he was roused prematurely from this reverie by "a person on business from Porlock," who detained the poet for over an hour. When the visitor left, Coleridge found he could recall only eight to ten scattered lines (Abrams, 1970). Yet "Kubla Khan," which contains the well-known lines, "For he on honey-dew was fed,/And drunk the milk of Paradise," is considered one of his most lyrical. Col-eridge's account of his reverie has never won universal accep-tance. Some skeptics (e.g., Schneider, 1953), unfamiliar with the effect of dreams of literature, regard dream and reverie poetry as impossible.

Inspired by these accounts of creative people and their suc-cesses in making breakthroughs in their dreams, Maxine, a de-signer, asked for a dream showing a toy she could sell commer-cially. She recalled no dreams for two nights and began to feel discouraged. But on the third night, she dreamed she was show-ing an official of a major toy company the prototype of a space-age doll, promising him it would be in great demand by children who had watched real or fictional space voyages on television and in films. Upon awakening, she drew the doll and later pro-duced a model similar to the one in her dream. Maxine was successful in selling her idea, and sales of the toy during the holiday season fulfilled the promise made in her dream.

When research in dream control moves from the anecdotal level to more rigorous types of inquiry, the results are not as encouraging. David Foulkes and M. L. Griffin (1977) taught 23 subjects "dream control" methods and asked them to dream about randomly selected topics. The subjects kept daily records of their dreams for 10 nights. Judges attempted to match dreams with the suggested targets; the matchings did not exceed what would have been expected by chance.

The same investigators designed a second study using 29 highly-motivated subjects who claimed some previous success in dream control or an interest in the topic. They spent 10 nights attempting to dream about assigned topics, but in this case they were allowed to select the nights on which they felt they could successfully control their dreams. Again, judges were unable to match the dreams with the topics. Griffin and Foulkes (1977) concluded that the results did not "disprove" pre-sleep dream control but did indicate that "if such control is possible, it must be much more difficult to achieve than enthusiasts . . . generally intimate" (p. 662).

Pre-sleep Suggestions and Image Control

In ancient Greece, over 400 temples were dedicated to Aesculapius, the god of healing and intermediary of dream incubation. A citizen was not allowed to drink alcoholic beverages for three days before entering a dream temple (Quinn, 1981, pp. 62-63). It was believed that useful dreams were unlikely to occur while the dreamer was under the influence of alcohol, a sentiment supported by recent research demonstrating that alcohol drastically reduces REM sleep (Luce & Segal, 1966, p. 154).

Some of the most interesting cases from the Aesculapian temples were recorded on votive tablets: "Alecetes of Alicos, blind, dreamed Aesculapius opened his eyes with his fingers. The next day he could see." "A man named Julian hemorrhaged from the lungs. In a dream he was told to go to the altar, mix pine nuts with honey, and eat them for three days. He was cured."

"Lucius' son was dying of pleurisy. The god appeared to him in a dream and told him to make a poultice of altar ashes mixed with wine, and apply it to his side" (Sechrist, 1968, pp. 73-74).

It is unlikely that pre-sleep suggestions could produce such dramatic effects today. Nevertheless, anyone who has had troubled sleep or nightmares after seeing a horror movie knows that pre-sleep experiences can have an impact on one's dreams. Family arguments, problems at work, and fears about the future may have an even greater influence.

Dream incubation was common among the American Plains Indians. Upon entering adolescence, an Indian boy would retire to a solitary location, expecting a dream about his guardian spirit or totem animal. An eagle or bear was often interpreted as the sign of becoming a future warrior, a wolf of becoming a successful hunter, a serpent of becoming a future medicine man (Coxhead & Hiller, 1976, p. 78).

In ancient China there was a tradition of dream incubation among artists. For example, in the 9th century, Kwan Hiu regularly engaged in a ritual of prayer to a particular holy person before falling asleep. He was rewarded by a dream of the saint, awakened with the dream image in mind, and proceeded to paint it (Garfield, 1974, p. 250). The most often played bamboo flute music, "Bell Ringing in an Empty Sky," was written by a Japanese Zen priest after attaining enlightenment in a dream (Delaney, 1987).

Neurologist W. B. Cannon said he rarely went to bed preoccupied by a problem without the solution being in his grasp when he awakened the next morning (de Becker, 1968, p. 84). Mathematician and philosopher Bertrand Russell would often work hard on an abstract mathematical problem to the point of exhaustion, and then go to sleep. He claimed the answer to his problem would frequently occur in a dream (Morris, 1985, p. 126).

Belgian artist René Magritte claimed his "self-willed" dreams, apparently experienced during wakefulness, were sources for many of the paradoxical images in his paintings. Italian artist Giorgio de Chirico referred to the dream as a "source of inspiration" and advised "constant control of . . . all the images that present themselves to our minds." Spanish surrealist Salvador

Dali also claimed to have a remarkable ability to induce and utilize his dreams (Coxhead & Hiller, 1976, pp. 88-89).

Not everyone can use dreams as springboards to vision quests or feats of artistic creation, but dreams can still help many people to live more fully integrated lives. In this way, dreams and psychotherapy have the same objective, that of augmenting the individual's capacity for adaptation and personal growth (Fiss, 1979, p. 58). One team of investigators (Greenberg & Pearlman, 1975) made a point of focusing on dream content during psychotherapeutic sessions held just before their clients entered a sleep laboratory where their dreams were collected. The following morning, another psychotherapeutic session was held. The data suggested that dreaming about a problem raised during the pre-sleep session positively influenced the way in which the clients dealt with that problem during their morning sessions.

The process by which pre-sleep suggestions operate can be constructive or destructive. If dreamers immerse themselves in positive, inspirational experiences before going to sleep, they are more likely to engage in creative problem-solving in their dreams. If they focus on negative thoughts and feelings, they may awaken drained and depleted. Adler maintained that dreams deal with ongoing and continuous problems of one sort or another. The individual creates a set of hypotheses about what his or her future may be like, and the kind of results expected. While dreaming, the individual plays with these hypotheses and tries to test them (Gold, 1979). If the pre-sleep experiences have been negative, the dreams will very likely attempt to work through this negativity, often at some psychological cost to the dreamer.

At its best, dream incubation can facilitate dreamwork, enhance waking intuitions, and even serve as a foundation for successful functioning the next day. There is a possibility that while people sleep, their dreams "rehearse" activities they have in mind for the upcoming day. Perhaps some cases of "déjà vu," when a person senses "I have done this before," can be explained as forgotten dreams anticipating the event. In formulating pre-sleep suggestions, one might remember the basic assumptions behind dream incubation:

1. Any action, feeling, or thought you experience during the day may affect your dreams that night.

2. Constructive actions, feelings, and thoughts encourage constructive problem-solving in dreams.

3. Destructive actions, feelings, and thoughts (e.g., chronic anger, dishonesty, fear, guilt, worry) tend to encourage dreams which disturb your sleep and interfere with most types of problem-solving. Sometimes dreams are produced which can assist the dreamer in identifying the sources and solutions to this negativity, but even these dreams would be clearer if the dreamer had followed Delaney's procedure and formulated a question about the destructive behavior.

Kevin's pre-sleep question was fundamental: "What do I need to do in order to facilitate creative problem-solving in my dreams?" He followed Delaney's procedure for a week before recalling the following dream:

I was walking along a beautiful sandy shore, beachcombing. I collected a variety of interesting objects—rocks, seaweed, shells, flotsam, and jetsam. I put each item into my bag and moved on. I became tired from the weight and took the bag back to my shack. I noticed that my shack was filled with bags of objects from previous days on the beach. I felt overloaded, but lacked the energy and motivation to sort and categorize what I had collected.

Kevin realized that although he faithfully recorded his dreams whenever he remembered them, he had not allowed enough time to engage in dreamwork. Therefore, he had dozens of dreams in his notebook which needed to be categorized and worked through, just like the bags of interesting objects in his beachcomber dream.

Sometimes dreamers will obtain stimulating ideas during their dreams, and record them in great detail, but will not put the new ideas into practice or even try them out. Sometimes it is necessary for the dreamer to return to dream incubation to ask why he or she is procrastinating on a plan that makes sense. Inconsistent thoughts, feelings, and actions reflect inner confusion and conflicts in one's personal mythology.

Mario went to bed early one night because he had an important presentation to give at a sales meeting the next morning, and wanted to be refreshed and alert. However, he had a troubling dream in which he forgot his presentation, his charts fell to the floor, and the staff walked out laughing. The next morning, Mario engaged in dreamwork to determine why such a dream should occur just before his big opportunity to present the sales campaign he had been planning for several weeks. Mario used a technique often found to be successful in cases of this nature. He reviewed his dream to the point where it stopped—when his superior expressed disappointment in Mario and said the promotion for which Mario was being considered was now out of the question.

Opening his eyes, Mario understood that his dream was trying to tell him that he could possibly undermine himself. Mario was afraid of success; he feared a promotion would give him responsibilities he simply could not handle. Once Mario was aware of this conflict, he confronted his anxiety, his negative self-image, and his reluctance to take on a more important job. He knew that though he could not work these through completely before his presentation, he could keep them from sabotaging what turned out to be an impressive and successful display of his sales ideas.

Dreaming Lucidly

Born in 1877, Edgar Cayce was a pioneer in the practice of teaching people how to request help from their dreams. Cayce's theory was remarkably comprehensive for its time, holding that dreams reflect physical conditions, past experiences, and/or spiritual forces. Cayce advised dreamers to make a firm decision about the topic on which they needed guidance before going to sleep. This decision, Cayce felt, directs awareness during sleep and helps to focus the dreamer's response (Bro, 1976; Thurston, 1978, 1986).

William Sechrist had studied with Cayce and admitted he needed guidance about where he should start a car rental venture. When Houston was recommended in his dream, he asked for what reason and was given three images: a star, a gushing water faucet, and a family on a houseboat. In dreamwork, Sechrist interpreted these images to mean that Houston would become the "star" of the South with ample water and increasing importance as a vacation center. Sechrist moved to Houston where he established a successful business (Sechrist, 1968, p. 47).

Sechrist's ability to ask a question in his dream is typical of those dreams in which dreamers appear to take an active role in the dream process. Some dreamers go a step further, realizing that they are dreaming and often manipulating the dream while still asleep. When a dreamer realizes he or she is dreaming, the dream is considered to be "lucid." The Tibetan Buddhist practice of "dream yoga" focused on the ability to remain aware and lucid while dreaming. However, the Hindu yogic dream tradition eschewed such dream manipulation in favor of a waking meditation practice described as "merging with the light" (Taylor, 1983, pp. 198-199). Aristotle (1952) knew about lucid dreams, noting that often when one is asleep, there is something in one's awareness that declares what is presented is a dream: "the sleeper perceives that he is asleep, and is conscious of the sleeping state during which the perception comes before his mind" (p. 706).

In the second edition to *The Interpretation of Dreams,* published in 1909, Freud noted that some people are clearly aware when they are asleep and dreaming, and are able to direct their dreams. While discussing what was apparently one of his own dreams, Freud (1909/1965) described himself in a sexually exciting situation. Attaining dream lucidity, he decided, "I won't go on with this dream any further and exhaust myself with an emission" (p. 611). Patricia Garfield (1979) took a different approach to her lucid dreams, two thirds of which were associated with "the flow of sexual energy." In nearly one half of these dreams,

Garfield experienced "an orgasmic burst." Her husband was usually her lover, but there were dreams in which images of other men appeared, as well as "a male angelic creature, a rare woman, or half man-half woman, and myself" (pp. 134-135).

Firsthand reports from lucid dreamers have produced a list of methods thought to be useful in facilitating the experience. Pre-sleep reflection was frequently mentioned; in other words, one can often incubate a lucid dream. Asking such critical questions as "Is this a dream?" and "Am I dreaming?" during a dream will often produce lucidity. Some dreamworkers encourage people to ask these questions at regular intervals during the day with the expectation that these questions will arise during the night. External stimulation is sometimes incorporated into a dream and triggers lucidity; again, this can be deliberately programmed (Gackenbach, 1985-1986, p. 41).

Psychophysiologist Stephen LaBerge (1985) studied this phenomenon in the laboratory, knowing that bodily musculature is virtually nonfunctional during REM sleep. LaBerge capitalized on the one major exception—the eye movements that are active during most night-time dreams. He recalled:

> I knew that lucid dreamers could freely look in any direction they wished while in a lucid dream, because I had done this myself. It occurred to me that by moving my (dream) eyes in a recognizable pattern, I might be able to send a signal to the outside world when I was having a lucid dream. I tried this out . . . . I moved my dream gaze up, down, up, down, up, to the count of five. As far as I knew at the time, this was the first signal deliberately transmitted from the dream world. (pp. 62-63)

LaBerge repeated this feat in a sleep laboratory and extended his work to include other subjects. Eventually, he trained individuals to dream lucidly and to demonstrate their success by moving their eyes in a manner determined before they went to sleep.

Keith Hearne had been conducting similar work in England, and soon other researchers replicated LaBerge's study. Emerging data revealed new information about the dreaming process:

1. Dreams do not occur in a few seconds, as once was thought. Although there are exceptions, dream time is similar to waking time, at least for lucid dreams.

2. Control of one's breathing is possible in lucid dreams, suggesting that variations in respiration during Stage REM might be related to changes in dream content.

3. Lucid dreamers who sang while dreaming demonstrated an activation of the cerebral cortex's right hemisphere similar to that of waking subjects. When lucid dreamers counted, the left hemisphere showed a greater activation which is typical with right-handed subjects (left-handed subjects usually demonstrate the reverse). Although the topic of hemispheric specialization is complex and often exaggerated by the popular press, there are some reliable differences. LaBerge demonstrated that these differences may also be found in lucid dreaming.

4. The use of vaginal probes and penile strain gauges (to measure blood flow into the sexual organs) has demonstrated a link between sexual activity in lucid dreams and activation of the sexual organs during the same period (LaBerge, 1985, pp. 72-90).

LaBerge and others have demonstrated that what happens in the inner world of dreams—and lucid dreams especially—can produce physical effects on the dreamer's brain and body that are no less real than those produced by similar events in the external world. This information is important for both theoretical and practical reasons. On the theoretical side, these data can demonstrate that subjective, mental events can closely parallel objective, physical events. On the practical side, these data support the use of mental imagery as an adjunct to psychotherapy and, perhaps, even in the treatment of such diseases as cancer.

Can lucid dreaming be learned by people who want to use it for creative problem-solving? Charles Tart (1979) presented some preliminary evidence that hypnosis and suggestion might help people dream lucidly. LaBerge (1985) cites motivation and satisfactory dream recall as the two essential requirements for lucid dreaming. His subjects have learned to engage in lucid dreaming by concentrating on it during the day. They think of waking experiences as dreams; they tell themselves "all things are of the substance of dreams"; they remain aware of the effect their daytime experiences may have on their night-time dreams. Before going to sleep, the subjects resolve to realize that they are dreaming during the dream itself. If subjects awaken from a dream in the middle of the night or in the morning, they go over the dream several times and tell themselves, "The next time I'm dreaming, I want to remember to recognize I'm dreaming." They visualize themselves returning to the dream, then repeat these last two steps, and attempt to fall asleep again. A majority of the subjects trained by LaBerge and his associates to use this technique eventually report lucid dreams (pp. 125-150).

Specific skills are sometimes learned in dreams. Jack Nicklaus, after winning a number of golf championships, found himself in a slump. He regained his form quickly, reporting:

> I've been trying everything to find out what had been wrong . . . . But last Wednesday night I had a dream and it was about my golf swing. I was hitting them pretty good in the dream and all at once I realized I wasn't holding the club the way I've actually been holding it lately. I've been having trouble collapsing my right arm taking the club head away from the ball, but I was doing it perfectly in my sleep. So when I came to the course yesterday morning, I tried it the way I did in my dream and it worked. (LaBerge, 1985, p. 171)

Ann Faraday (1972) reported the case of a gynecologist who discovered in a dream how to tie a surgical knot deep in the pelvis with his left hand. LaBerge (1985) told of a hockey player who improved her skills in a lucid dream, and went on to adapt the new approach to rollerskating and skiing (pp. 171-172).

William Keepin (personal communication, August 19, 1986), a Princeton University researcher, has used lucid dreams to solve mathematics problems. He recalls,

> At times when I am stumped by a particular problem, dream images and ideas develop with the purpose of gaining insight into the problem, or seeing it in a new way . . . . I remember that one problem was in the field of complex analysis, and another was in the field of theoretical fluid mechanics. It is important to note that in one case, I woke myself up (by lifting my eyelids in the dream), and went over to my desk to write out the equations that followed from the idea I had had while sleeping.

A physicist, Elizabeth Rauscher, had a lucid dream in which she claimed to formulate a solution to Einstein's field equations, later publishing the results (Rauscher, 1972). However, Rauscher found that there were limits to her ability to solve problems in lucid dreams.

> It should be noted that I have made algebraic errors in equation manipulations in my dreams. For example, I was solving an equation in which I was substituting the numerical values of certain quantities and divided by zero. I woke up with a mental red error sign . . . . I make the same mistakes when awake as when I'm dreaming because it's the same mind! (Rauscher, personal communication, August 9, 1986)

Lucid dreaming is not for everyone. Some people reject the notion of tampering with the spontaneity of their dream life in any way. Others lack the motivation or the interest to follow through on procedures usually needed to dream lucidly. Others do not recall their dreams frequently enough to know if the suggestions have worked. Even those people who advocate lucid dreaming typically report that relatively few of their dreams are lucid; they often go for months without having one. However, the knowledge that such a phenomenon is possible, and has been demonstrated in the sleep laboratory, should encourage individuals who have chosen this way to facilitate creative problem-solving in their dreams.

In Summary

- Research studies indicate that pre-sleep thoughts and feelings often influence dream content.
- Some experimenters have reported success in having their subjects incubate dreams relevant to their specific waking concerns, but other researchers have been unsuccessful.
- Dream incubation has been used by a number of creative people advantageously.
- Lucid dreaming research indicates that some people can engage in problem-solving while dreaming and utilize the results in their daily lives.

Exercises

1. *Meditation.* Many people find meditation a helpful procedure to enhance dream recall and clarity. In addition, Frances Vaughan (1979) suggests that a regimen of meditation can foster one's intuitive abilities. The self-regulation of attention involved in meditation may also increase one's ability to incubate dreams and/or to dream lucidly. People interested in meditation might read the books by Benson (1975), Bloomfield, Cain, and Jaffe (1975), Carrington (1977), Dillard (1985), and LeShan (1974). Meditators often report other benefits as well, but there are individual differences and the outcomes are not predictable. Nevertheless, meditation is a safe way to alter one's awareness, and learning to meditate, whether through following written instructions or by taking classes, is usually interesting and worthwhile. The book *Dreams and Spiritual Growth* suggests meditating upon a dream image (such as a mandala or other symbol of what Jungians call the Self), trying not to alter, control, or manipulate it (Savary, Berne, & Williams, 1984, pp. 155-156).

2. *Incubation.* One simple way to initiate dream incubation is to review your upcoming schedule just before falling asleep. Even if you do not remember dreaming about the following day's events, reflect on whether the day went unusually well for you. If so, you might want to spend more time on incubation procedures.

3. *Dream Continuation and Lucidity.* To decide whether to attempt lucid dreaming, you might want to begin with the dream continuation technique and attempt to extend your dream until you experience a sense of closure. Sometimes the dream will not continue; it has told you everything it can disclose. In other instances, the continuation will reveal new information and insights. We do not believe that it is beneficial to tamper with the contents of the dream itself. But the continuation procedure can be illustrative and can lead you to attempt lucidity exercises (LaBerge, 1985).

12

Putting The Pieces Together

I can never decide whether my dreams are the result of my thoughts, or my thoughts the result of my dreams . . . . But my dreams make conclusions for me. They decide things finally. I dream a decision.

— D. H. Lawrence

When a dreamworker begins to work with dreams on a professional level, it is not unusual for problem-solving issues to appear in one's dreams. William Dement (1974) recalls:

Some years go I was a heavy cigarette smoker—up to two packs a day. Then one night I had an exceptionally vivid and realistic dream in which I had an inoperable cancer of the lung. I remember as though it were yesterday looking at the ominous shadow in my chest x-ray and realizing that the entire right lung was infiltrated. The subsequent physical examination in which my colleague detected widespread metastases in my . . . lymph nodes was equally vivid. Finally, I experienced the incredible anguish of knowing my life was at an end, that I would never see my children grow up, and that none of this would have happened if I had quit cigarettes when first I learned of their carcinogenic potential. I will never forget the surprise, joy, and exquisite relief of waking up. I felt I was reborn. Needless to say, the experience was sufficient to induce an immediate cessation of my cigarette habit. The dream had both anticipated the problem, and solved it in a way that may be a dream's unique privilege. (p. 102)

Figure 26.

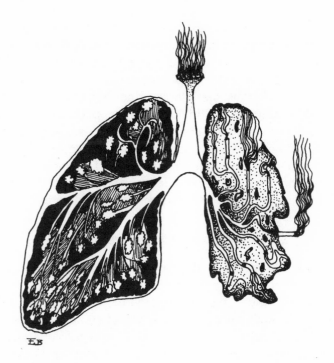

E.B

Dement speculated that a function of REM sleep and dreaming may be to allow dreamers to experience their alternative courses of action and to make a more informed choice.

In September 1947, during the time he was undergoing psychoanalysis, Montague Ullman recalled a dream in which he entered his analyst's waiting room and was immediately aware that the arrangement of the furniture was different than it had been. On September 18, Ullman walked into his analyst's waiting room and found that a large upholstered couch was gone; it had been moved into his analyst's office where it replaced a studio couch. The analyst said he had decided to have his studio couch removed before Ullman's dream occurred, and agreed with

Ullman that the dream might have been anomalous in nature (pp. 43-45).

In 1951, one of Ullman's clients reported a dream in which he took a chromium soap dish and made a remark about "building a house." The previous week, the workers who were building Ullman's house noticed a chromium soap dish which had been shipped to him by mistake (Ullman, Krippner, & Vaughan, 1973, pp. 50-51). Ullman (1986) and other psychoanalysts and psychotherapists have reported that anomalous dreams between client and therapist are not uncommon. Indeed, the more immersed a person becomes in the world of dreams, the more likely it is that they will be provided with a source of instruction, assistance, wonder, and amusement through dreams.

Overemphasis and Underemphasis

Freud built his model of the mind and his hypotheses about dreaming directly on the structure of his biological model of the brain. He recognized the psychodynamic nature of the dream and provided dreamworkers with a way of looking at how information with a bearing on past and present tensions enters a dream. He appreciated the role of recent events, or day residue, as they become the organizing focus for the dream and make connections with older, unresolved issues. The feelings associated with day residue echo through the dreamer's past, mobilizing bits and pieces of earlier life experiences related to a problem needing to be solved. In the course of dreaming, one brings together the relevant data—past and present—and attempts to come to some resolution in a symbolic, disguised form which will not awaken or alarm the dreamer.

Adler recognized the purposeful nature of dreams. He saw the dream as an integral part of one's thought processes and stressed its congruent relationship to the individual's life-style. Dreams reflect unfinished business from the past, as well as the dreamer's view of life at present and in the future. However, the dream permits one to plan without the limitations set by external reality; upon awakening, the individual can accept or reject the dream's solution on the basis of practical constraints. The dream also provides an opportunity for rehearsal, uses analogy and metaphor to intensify its emotional impact, employs feeling to motivate the dreamer to attempt a solution to the problem posed by the dream, and presents symbols which reflect the dreamer's interactions with his or her social and cultural environment.

Jung recognized the growth-enhancing potential of the dream and its confrontational nature. The ability of the dream to confront dreamers can move them to higher levels of personality integration (or individuation) by focusing not only on conflict, but on unrealized potential. The dream's emphasis is not only on two or more sides of the dreamer's personality warring against each other, but also on the need for compensation—the recognition of neglected, ignored, or undeveloped aspects of the psyche. The dream can relate present behavior to early development and provide information about both the dreamer's external and internal reality.

Ullman recognized that sometimes the dreamer is concerned with specific, unresolved problems from the past, and at others with the impact of new experiences and the forward thrust of emotional growth. In either instance, the kind of waking experience which sets up enough tension to influence one's dreams can be said to have the quality of intrusive novelty, hinting at something new and unfamiliar. This intrusive quality stems from the connections a recent event makes with vulnerable areas from the dreamer's past. The dream is then used to explore the significance of this novel experience as measured against the backdrop of earlier experiences and the dreamer's available coping resources.

Hobson and McCarley recognized that synthesis in dreams occurs in much the same way as it does during wakefulness. Their activation-synthesis model of dream formation holds that during sleep, sensory input from the external world is constricted, but parts of the brain's sensory and motor systems are activated internally by neural activity and the organism's affective states. The ensuing sensations play preeminent roles in the construction of the dream experience because they become linked together and compared with information about the dreamer's past experiences. The synthetic aspects of dream formation knits together the physiological and mental domains of the dreamer. Dreams are not the result of an attempt to disguise information, but are a direct expression of this synthetic effort.

In our opinion, all these researchers acknowledged that dreams can provide both a synthesizing and a problem-solving function. They also have recognized the importance of emotion and bodily activity in dream formation, the symbolic nature of much of dream content, and the dream's usefulness in psychotherapy. However, Freud probably underemphasized the impact of cultural factors on dream symbolism, and devalued the dreamer's ability to work with his or her own dreams. Jung probably overemphasized the compensatory nature of dreams and, like Freud, did not fully acknowledge the continuity between waking and dream life. Adler and Jung underemphasized the ability of the dream to incorporate internal and external stimulation. Freud, Adler, Hobson, and McCarley underemphasized the spiritual aspects of the dream, while Adler, Hobson, and McCarley ignored anomalous dreams. It should be observed that Hobson and McCarley had the advantage of laboratory dream research data in formulating their theories; thus, they were better able to relate dreams to the dream-sleep cycle than the other writers.

None of these writers have taken the extreme positions characteristic of some Gestalt psychologists who insist that every aspect of the dream represents some part of the dreamer, or of Crick and Mitchison, who believe dreams should be forgotten because they represent thought patterns the organism is attempting to erase. Psychologist Barbara Brown (1980) noted that dreams can solve many problems the dreamer, while awake, cannot solve (p. 172). Even so, "science knows virtually nothing about . . . how dream logic can solve nondream problems" (p. 10). However, laboratory and clinical research is slowly providing data to unravel the many enigmas of dream phenomena; only time will tell which theory most closely reflects the actual nature of Stage REM and recalled dreams (Krippner & Hughes, 1977).

It is possible, of course, that the dream's psychodynamic function is minimal, dreams being simply the result of a fortuitous choice of subject matter to account for the direction, size, and velocity of eye movements (Dement, 1964), a series of random images produced by an activated brain (Hobson & McCarley, 1977), or the residue of a memory filter disposing of irrelevant information (Evans & Newman, 1964). However, the accumulated evidence makes it seem more plausible that dreams serve an important and useful psychological function. Fiss (1979) points out the universality of dreaming, the insistence with which it occurs, and the obvious thematic coherence of a person's dreams collected over the course of the night. Given these occurrences, it appears likely that dreaming has a function of its own, quite apart from REM sleep. Just because dreaming and REM sleep usually occur at the same time does not mean they are identical. Fiss points out that there exists a certain biological need for certain sleep stages; the content and quality of dreaming seem just as vital for adaptation and functioning as the amount of REM obtained each night (p. 41). Fiss conjectures, "Perhaps we dream in order to concentrate periodically on what troubles and ails us, or work out some kind of solution. Maybe sleep is necessary in order to safeguard our need to dream" (p. 57). Dreams could serve multiple functions affecting how dreamers think, feel, and act—even on a creative basis (p. 64).

Step-by-Step

Discipline and self-control must be learned if a person is to develop and maintain one's creativity. But if they are overlearned, a person will become a technician instead of a creator. Once learned, creative skills and attitudes should be used flexibly, rather than rigidly and compulsively (MacKinnon, 1978, p. 70). Henry Reed's (1985) description of his procedure for stimulating artists serves as a valuable model for other dreamworkers:

> *How I have worked with selected artists to help them*
> *innovate in their dreams is exactly as I have worked with*

anyone who was working on a problem and who was willing to allow dreams to make a statement about their work. What is your goal? What are the perceived obstacles in your reaching your goal? What solutions have you tried? In what ways have these solutions been satisfactory and in what ways have they been unsatisfactory? What will be the consequences of your achieving your goal? Are you afraid of any of the consequences? Are there any rules of procedure that you feel you must abide by in reaching your goal? What assumptions have you made about the nature of your problem that limit your choice of solutions? The answers to these sorts of questions help clarify the nature of the challenge the person has accepted and the meaning it has for the person. (p. 137)

You need to develop an individualized system for dreamwork; perhaps the following step-by-step procedure will help you develop your method for creative problem-solving through dreams. Observe the pre-sleep procedures for facilitating dream recall, and remember that if you awaken with a dream in the middle of the night, write down a few notes about it before going back to sleep.

1. In the morning, take your dream notebook and record anything you remember about your last dream or dreams. If you recall only a feeling or a mood, write it down. If you recall only a hypnopompic image, write it down. If you recall only a random thought, write it down. If you remember only a small detail, write it down. If you recorded some notes in the middle of the night, expand upon them now, adding as much additional material as you can recall. As you begin writing, you may remember additional details. Also, reviewing the list of content items may jog your memory, especially for such dream content as emotions, settings, and modifiers (e.g., colors).

2. Do not interpret the dream as you write it down; it is more important that you record as many details as you can. Your

first priority is to capture as much of the living experience of the dream as you can. Drawings may help; if you draw dream images, be aware that you may be portraying visual symbols to which you will return. Use of the first person, present tense will help (e.g., write "I am in a palace" not "Mary was in a palace"). Remain close to the dream images; if you recall an image of a strange creature, half-human and half-deer, don't call it a "centaur" (half-human, half-horse). Accuracy is important; unusual dream content is probably more significant than commonplace images. As you write, be aware that you are transforming the dream images into metaphors for further study. If there is any item of which you are not sure, immerse yourself in that activity, object, or character in a nonevaluative way to obtain a clearer picture or feeling about it.

3. A series or entire collection of dreams will best illuminate your inner life. If you recall more than one dream on a particular night, compare them to see if they contain common themes. When you are undergoing anxiety or stress, read the dreams for that entire period to determine if they contain collective advice. Some dreams you find especially puzzling may be better understood within the context of other dreams. Some innovative dreamworkers have used their home computers and word processors to store their dreams, to observe the context of frequent symbols, and to develop their own "symbol dictionary." A king may represent a father figure for one dreamer, the world's privileged elite for another, and emotional control for a third. Dreamworkers will often engage in research, looking up material on symbols in dictionaries and other reference books.

4. Develop the proper attitude for dreamwork. When you pay attention to your dreams, they will usually return the compliment and reward you with insights. Using a special notebook (or note cards) for your work is one way to demonstrate the sincerity of your intention. Another is to remain steadfast, attempting to recall a dream virtually every morning and providing sufficient time for its recording and interpretation. Amplification and associ-

ations to dream symbols and metaphors can be written down or worked through mentally. If an occasional dream baffles you, don't be discouraged. Even Jung acknowledged that some dreams are impenetrable. There may not have been a suitable match between your internal neural activation and the memories available to convey the life issue with which you were struggling on that occasion. However, any message that the enigmatic dream needed to convey will usually emerge again.

5. Analyze the structure of the dream. Examine the dream for points where there are changes of activity or emotion; these are usually the most significant parts of a dream. Identify the main character; if it is not you, is it part of you? If it is a stranger, does it represent someone in your social or family circle, or a part of your psyche? Retell the dream as a fairy tale; this will help you identify the beginning, middle, and end. Retell the dream from the vantage of an important content item (e.g., "In this dream, I am a flower blooming in the meadow") and ask if you could identify with that activity, object, or person. Some dreams are chaotic and have little structure. The disorganized nature of the dream might be a clue to its meaning. Engage in dreamwork with each image. You might discover that the lack of organization points to something that is disorganized in your personal or professional activities. Or you might observe that something in your life is in the process of emerging and is so new that it could not possibly display a coherent structure. Use the continuation technique, carrying the dream forward, if you think the dream has something more to tell you.

6. Dialogue with your dream elements. If there is a stranger in the dream, give him or her a posture and a voice. Speak as if you were the stranger, or any other unusual item of dream content. Carry on a conversation with these items. Imagine you are placing one of them in a nearby chair, and speak out loud to it. Write a page or two of dialogue, or draw it and imagine you are creating a scenario for a comic strip. Look at yourself in a mirror while playing the role of a dream character. What changes

do you notice as you shift from the dream character back to yourself? Exaggerate your gestures, emotions, and vocal tone during the dialogue. Ask why it appeared in your dream, what it has to teach you, and what gifts it has for you. Does the dialogue remind you of any life issues or significant people or situations in your past or present?

7. Make a personal connection with the feeling tone in the dream. Allow it to carry you back to an earlier experience when you had the same or similar feeling. Compare the real-life experience with the dream experience. How were they the same? Was something going on in your life then which is emotionally connected with something taking place in the dream? Find a related life issue for all the moods and feelings expressed in your dream. Is there a common theme running through these issues? You might try carrying the feeling forward in time. Where might you feel that way in the future? If there was a bodily feeling in the dream, imagine what it would be like to experience that sensation in your body while awake. Does this remind you of anything from the past or present—or suggest something which may occur in the future? Because emotions are among the most important of all items in a dream be sure you note them as you record your dream.

8. Explore the timing of the dream. Why did the dream occur when it did? Are conflicting personal myths illustrated? Are there undeveloped resources you need to discover to cope with some challenge? Is the dream warning you of some impending illness or crisis? Are there ethics, morals, or values which need to be reexamined, or adhered to more strictly? Is an important event coming up for which the dream was attempting to prepare you? One important clue to the dream's meaning is any uncharacteristic behavior you performed in the dream. This activity may indicate a possible future direction, or it might represent part of you which needs to be acknowledged but, at the same time, kept in check.

9. Be aware of the role played by projection in dreamwork. As they do with the face of a new acquaintance, people easily and naturally read into a dream what is in their own psyche. When they work with a dream report, they project meaning in a similar way. Remember that you usually work not with the dream itself but with the memory of it, its symbols and metaphors. And keep in mind that symbols and metaphors can be intrapersonal, interpersonal, cultural, and/or spiritual. The meaning you discover, to a large extent, is the meaning you project into it. Dreamwork is a powerful tool for creative problem-solving because it stimulates dreamers to look for solutions in novel ways. Dreams, at least in part, are the product of internal activation and have their own function to perform. Thus, projection is necessary because the dream may not be inherently produced to speak to your concerns. You can be assured that your projection accurately reflected inner and outer reality if it felt correct on an emotional basis, made sense on an intellectual basis, and worked out once you put the dream solution into practice.

10. Whenever you feel you have reached a block in dreamwork, ask yourself or one of the dream characters or objects a question such as: "How do I/you like being in this dream?" "How well do I/you like my/your fellow dream characters?" "How would I/you change this dream if it could be altered?" "What changes would I/you recommend for the waking life of this character?" "What advice do I/you have for the problem I/you have been trying to solve?" You might also ask, "What is the central point of this dream?" "Why did the dream appear now?" "What issues in my life is this dream raising?" "Is this dream for me alone or does it also pertain to others?" When you have completed your dreamwork, ask yourself, "What would be the most appropriate title I could give to this dream?" "What sentence best conveys the meaning of this dream?" "What concrete action can I take in my life to carry through on the lesson implicit in this dream?"

If you feel there are gaps in your appreciation of the dream, attempt to incubate another, to answer the unresolved questions.

In addition, examine future dreams to determine whether they are following up on some of the information presented in the current dream.

A few individuals become overwhelmed by dreamwork and decide that they cannot cope with the material that emerges. If you have this feeling, it would be wise to seek professional counseling before you continue. At the very least, find a trusted friend to talk to, or shift from individual dreamwork to working with a partner or group.

Computers and Dreamwork

This age represents a new era in the annals of humanity, and its effects are seen in every aspect of life. Several landmark events have had a transforming effect upon the worldview of human beings—the moon landing, nuclear weaponry, and the development of the computer (Bair, 1981). The computer revolution can be seen as an extension of human language; its effects upon civilization may be similar to those of language in many ways. For example, the silicon memory chip in a computer resembles verbal memory in human beings. In both systems, everything must be done in sequence, one step at a time. A computer is an outward manifestation of the rational and logical thought processes which have been responsible for considerable problem-solving among humans.

The Processor Unit in the computer performs mathematical and logical computations, operating on one or more "old" pieces of information to produce a logical combination or manipulation. In so doing, it parallels logical thought in humans. The Control Unit is analogous to the human discrimination and decision-making which leads from one thought to the next of several alternatives. Computer Storage and Memory correspond to the brain's memory centers while the Input/Output devices (e.g., keyboards, video displays, printers) are the computer's sensory-motor system. The detachment of one computer from another matches ego functioning among humans, except that the separateness of one computer from another is much more obvious than the separation of one person from another (Bair, 1981, pp. 482-483).

However, computers cannot mimic the affective, associative, divergent, intuitive, metaphoric, nonrational, parallel, primary process, or symbolic activity involved in many types of creativity. In job selection, people with these types of abilities may well have an edge when applying for high level positions. They will not necessarily be hired because of their grasp of essential knowledge; much of this type of information can be provided by on-screen library bases. What prospective employers prize may well be creative problem-solving, and the ability to associate dissimilar ideas and arrive at useful solutions. People with practice in dreamwork will find themselves ideally equipped for this type of mental activity.

Industrialized societies find themselves in the midst of a global marriage of human thought processes and machines. This is a polygamous relationship involving computer language, logic, mathematics, pattern recognition, visually-oriented thinking, objective thought, and subjective thought. The marriage is lopsided, however. It favors binary selection at the expense of more flexible cognitive processes. It maintains the type of problem-solving habits which have produced the nuclear and environmental cancers threatening humanity's very existence on the planet.

In his book *Megatrends,* John Naisbitt (1982), pointed out that every "high tech" social movement based on automatization, mechanization, and regimentation, is eventually balanced by a "high touch" social movement. Naisbitt identifies several examples of "high touch," such as the use of "quality circles," meditation, "pop" psychology, sensitivity training, "T-groups," and yoga. What will be the "high touch" counterparts to the computer revolution? Dream groups would be a likely candidate.

Dream groups do not represent an escape from "high tech" so much as a balance to it. The use of dreams in creative problem-solving can actually enhance job performance and, at the same time, put dreamers in touch with their inner world within a supportive social context. Sharing dreams can enhance interpersonal

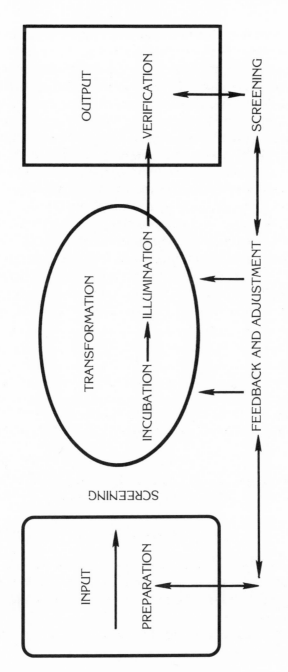

Figure 27. Creativity System.

empathy, sensitivity to others' feelings, and the ability to understand alternative life-styles, personal myths, and worldviews. All these skills are potentially useful in the classroom, factory, hospital, laboratory, or office. Dreamwork integrates intellectual and emotional development in harmonious ways that make it an excellent candidate for consideration by teachers at all levels. Health care providers can obtain an impressive amount of information simply by asking their clients to relate a recent dream. Relationships between family members, friends, and lovers can be enhanced by occasional or regular dream-sharing.

Creative problem-solving is urgently needed in the world today at the intrapersonal, interpersonal, community, and international levels. Dreams, emerging as they do from the deepest part of the psyche, provide an opportunity for creative expression to be given to the most basic murmurings of the human spirit. A world in peril, just as an individual in distress, yearns for healing from whatever source which may be available. Dreams are easily evoked, and are always ready to serve dreamers, their society, and their world.

In Summary

- Although dream theorists and researchers differ in many ways, most agree that dreams serve both integrative and problem-solving functions.
- Dreamwork can yield a supportive structure for interaction in problem-solving which can provide an important balance to the analytic emphasis of modern technology.

Exercises

1. *A Review.* Review your work with dreams. How have dreams assisted your problem-solving ability? How do your waking thought processes solve problems more adroitly? Remember that there are individual differences. Make a tentative decision about which areas of your life are most amenable to insight from your dreams.

2. *Further Reading.* There are a number of practical books you may want to consult for further study. For creative problem-solving in dreams, our favorites are those by Delaney (1979), Faraday (1972, 1974), Garfield (1974), Morris (1985), Taylor (1983), and Thurston (1986). If you are interested in forming a dream group, you will find assistance in books by Shohet (1985), Taylor (1983), and by Ullman and Zimmerman (1979/1985). Lists of books covering various aspects of dreaming have been prepared by Garfield (1984) and by Taylor (1983).

3. *Further Networking.* Henry Reed developed a computer database, the Dream Net Project. If you are online, instruct your modem to dial 1 (303) 722-6210 where you may choose from Menu One (which includes an open forum, a premonitions registry, and intuitive computer games); Menu Two (dream news, lucid dreaming, the dream interpreter, anecdotes about anomalous dreams, and the near-death column); or Menu Three (dream bibliographies, statistical evaluations, a dream newsletter). Reed foresees the day when computers can interview dreamers about their most recent dreams, remind them of previous dream content, help them create animated cartoons of their dreams, and display dream themes and images collected within the past few hours from around the world. Would networking of this type be of value to you? What type of dreamworkers and dreamers would you contact via computer if you had the opportunity?

3. *Further Contact.* How have dreams enhanced creativity in your life? We would be interested in hearing about any instances of dream-inspired, creative problem-solving you might care to share. We would also welcome any interesting experiences you may have had while working with the material in this book. We value your thoughts and experiences. Write to Joseph Dillard and Stanley Krippner, Institute for Creative Problem Solving, 501 East Sage Street, Scottsdale, Arizona 85253.

References

Abrams, M. H. (1970). *The milk of paradise*. New York: Harper & Row.

Adelson, J. (1960). Creativity and the dream. *Merrill-Palmer Quarterly, 6,* 92-97.

Adler, A. (1938). *Social interest: Challenge to mankind.* London: Faber & Faber.

Adler, A. (1958). *What life should mean to you.* New York: Capricorn.

Altshuller, G. S. (1984). *Creativity as an exact science: The theory of the solution of inventive problems* (A. Williams, Trans.). New York: Gordon & Breach.

Anderson, H. A. (1959). Creativity in perspective. In H. A. Anderson (Ed.), *Creativity and its cultivation* (pp. 236-267). New York: Harper & Row.

Anonymous. (1978, Dec. 25). Hard choices in Tehran. *Time,* p. 32.

Ansbacher, H., & Ansbacher, L. (Eds.). (1956). *The individual psychology of Alfred Adler.* New York: Basic Books.

Arieti, S. (1976). *Creativity: The magic synthesis.* New York: Basic Books.

Aristotle. (1951). On dreams. In R. M. Hutchins (Ed.), *The works of Aristotle, Vol. 1* (pp. 702-706). Chicago: Encyclopedia Britannica.

Arnheim, R. (1969). *Visual thinking.* Berkeley: University of California Press.

Aserinsky, E., & Kleitman, N. (1953). Regularly occurring periods of eye motility, and concomitant phenomena, during sleep. *Science, 118,* 273-274.

Austin, M. D. (1971). Dream recall and the bias of intellectual ability. *Nature, 213,* 59-60.

Bair, P. K. (1981). Computer metaphors for consciousness. In R. S. Valle & R. von Eckartsberg, (Eds.), *The metaphors of consciousness* (pp. 473-485). New York: Plenum Press.

Bakan, P. (1977-1978). Dreaming, REM sleep and the right hemisphere: A theoretical integration. *Journal of Altered States of Consciousness, 3,* 285-307.

Barker, R. (1972). The effects of REM sleep on the retention of a visual task. *Psychophysiology, 9,* 107.

Barrios, M. V., & Singer, J. L. (1981-1982). The treatment of creative blocks: A comparison of waking imagery, hypnotic dream, and rational discussion techniques. *Imagination, Cognition and Personality, 1,* 89-109.

Barron, F. X. (1969). *Creative person and creative process.* New York: H. H. Holt.

Bastick, T. (1982). *Intuition: How we think and act.* New York: John Wiley & Sons.

Baylor, G. W., & Deslauriers, D. (1986-1987). Dreams as problem-solving: A method of study – Part I: Background and theory. *Imagination, Cognition and Personality, 6,* 105-118.

Belicky, D., & Belicky, K. (1982). Nightmares in a university population. *Sleep Research, 11,* 116-120.

Benson, H. (1975). *The relaxation response.* New York: William Morrow.

Berger, R. J. (1969). Oculomotor control: A possible function of REM sleep. *Psychological Review, 76,* 144-164.

Bigge, M. L., & Hunt, M. P. (1965). *Psychological foundations of education.* New York: Harper & Row.

Black, A. (1977). *Dream diary.* William Morrow.

Blakeshlee, T. R. (1980). *The right brain.* London: Macmillan.

Bloomfield, H. H., Cain, M. O., & Jaffe, D. T. (1975). *TM: Discovering inner energy and overcoming stress.* New York: Delacorte Press.

Boring, E. G. (1950). Great men and scientific progress. *Proceedings of the American Philosophical Society, 94,* 339-351.

Boss, M. (1958). *The analysis of dreams.* New York: Philosophical Library.

Boss, M., & Kenny, B. (1978). Phenomenological or Daseinsanalytic approach. In J. L. Fosshage & C. A. Loew (Eds.), *Dream interpretation: A comparative study* (pp. 149-189). New York: Spectrum.

Bradford, S. (1981). *Harriet Tubman: The Moses of her people.* Gloucester, MA: Peter Smith. (Original work published 1869)

Breger, L., Hunter, I., & Lane, R. W. (1971). *The effect of stress on dreams.* New York: International University Press.

Bro, H. (1976). *Edgar Cayce on dreams.* New York: Warner Books.

Brook, S. (1983). *The Oxford book of dreams.* Oxford, NY: Oxford University Press.

Brown, B. B. (1980). *Supermind: The ultimate energy.* New York: Harper & Row.

Bruner, J. S. (1960). *The process of education.* Cambridge, MA: Harvard University Press.

Budzynski, T. H. (1976). Some applications of biofeedback-produced twilight states. In T. X. Barber (Ed.), *Advances in altered states of consciousness & human potentialities* (Vol. 1) (pp. 103-112). New York: Psychological Dimensions.

Carrington, P. (1977). *Freedom in meditation.* Garden City, NY: Anchor Books.

Cartwright, M. L. (1955). *The mathematical mind.* New York: Oxford University Press.

Cartwright, R. D. (1974). Problem-solving: Waking and dreaming. *Journal of Experimental Psychology, 83,* 451-455.

Cartwright, R. D. (1983). Rapid eye movement sleep characteristics during and after mood-disturbing events. *Archives of General Psychiatry, 40,* 197-201.

Cartwright, R., Bernick, N., Borowitz, G., & Kling, A. (1969). The effect of an erotic movie on the sleep and dreams of young men. *Archives of General Psychiatry, 20,* 262-271.

Cartwright, R. D., Lloyd, S., Knight, S., & Trenholme, I. (1984). Broken dreams: A study of the effects of divorce and depression on dream content. *Psychiatry, 47,* 251-259.

Cherry, L. (1981, July). Sleep's biggest riddle. *Science Digest,* pp. 62-69.

Coleridge, S. T. (1955). Prefatory note to Kubla Khan. In B. Ghiselin (Ed.), *The creative process* (pp. 84-85). New York: Mentor Books.

Colette. (1971). *Journey for myself.* London: Peter Owen. (Original work published 1936)

Colp, R., Jr. (1986). Charles Darwin's dream of his double execution. *Journal of Psychohistory, 13,* 277-292.

Coxhead, D., & Hiller, S. (1981). *Dreams: Visions of the night.* London: Thames & Hudson.

Crick, F., & Mitchison, G. (1983). The function of dream sleep. *Nature, 304,* 111-114.

Darwin, C. (1871). *The descent of man and selection in relation to sex.* London: Murray.

Davé, R. (1979). Effects of hypnotically induced dreams on creative problem solving. *Journal of Abnormal Psychology, 88,* 293-302.

de Becker, R. (1968). *The understanding of dreams and their influence on the history of man.* New York: Hawthorn Books.

de Bono, E. (1969). *The mechanism of mind.* New York: Simon & Schuster.

Delaney, G. (1979). *Living your dreams.* New York: Harper & Row.

Delaney, G. (1987, January/February). Generating new ideas in your sleep. *New Realities,* pp. 48-49.

Dement, W. (1960). The effect of dream deprivation. *Science, 131,* 1705-1707.

Dement, W. (1964). Experimental dream studies. In J. H. Masserman (Ed.), *Science and psychoanalysis* (pp. 129-162). New York: Grune & Stratton.

Dement, W. (1974). *Some must watch while some must sleep.* San Francisco: W. H. Freeman.

Dement, W., & Kleitman, N. (1957). The relation of eye movements during sleep to dream activity: An objective method for the study of dreaming. *Journal of Experimental Psychology, 55,* 339-346.

Dillard, J. (1985). *Successful meditation: A practical guide.* Phoenix, AZ: Author.

Dlaboha, L. (1985, December). Mhing's the thing. *United Magazine,* p. 11.

Dodds, E. R. (1971). Supernormal phenomena in classical inquiry. *Proceedings of the Society for Psychical Research, 55,* 189-237.

Domhoff, G. W. (1985). *The mystique of dreams: A search for Utopia through Senoi dream theory.* Berkeley, CA: University of California Press.

Domino, G. (1976). Primary process thinking in dream reports as related to creative achievement. *Journal of Consulting and Clinical Psychology, 44,* 929-932.

Domino, G. (1982). Attitudes towards dreams, sex differences and creativity. *Journal of Creative Behavior, 16,* 112-121.

Edel, L. (1982). *Stuff of sleep and dreams: Experiments in literary creativity.* New York: Harper & Row.

Ehrenwald, J. (1966). *Psychotherapy: Myth and method.* New York: Grune & Stratton.

Eindhoven, J. E., & Vinacke, W. E. (1952). Creative processes in painting. *Journal of General Psychology, 47,* 139-164.

Einstein, A. (1952). Letter to Jacques Hadamard. In B. Ghiselin (Ed.), *The creative process* (pp. 43-44). New York: New American Library.

Ellis, H. (1911). *The world of dreams.* Boston: Houghton Mifflin.

Erickson, E. H. (1963). *Childhood and society* (2nd ed.). New York: W. W. Norton.

Evans, C. (1985). *Landscapes of the night.* New York: Washington Square Press.

Evans, C. R., & Newman, E. A. (1964). Dreaming: An analogy from computers. *New Scientist, 419,* 57-579.

Fagen, M. D. (Ed.). (1978). *A history of engineering and science in the Bell system: National service in war and peace (1925-1975).* Murray Hill, NJ: Bell Telephone Laboratories.

Fantz, R. E. (1978). Gestalt approach. In J. L. Fosshage & C. A. Loew (Eds.), *Dream interpretation: A comparative study* (pp. 191-241). New York: Spectrum.

Faraday, A. (1972). *Dream power.* New York: Coward, McCann & Geoghegan.

Faraday, A. (1974). *The dream game.* New York: Harper & Row.

Faraday, A., & Wren-Lewis, J. (1984, March-April). The selling of the Senoi. *Dream Network Bulletin,* pp. 1-3.

Feinberg, I. (1968). Eye movement activity during sleep and intellectual function in mental retardation. *Science, 159,* 1256.

Feinstein, A. D. (1979). Personal mythology as a paradigm for a holistic public psychology. *American Journal of Orthopsychiatry, 19,* 198-217.

Feinstein, A. D. (1987). Myth-making activity through the window of the dream. *Psychotherapy in Private Practice, 4,* 119-135.

Feinstein, A. D., & Krippner, S. (1981). Personal mythology and dreams. *Svensk Tidskrift for Hypnos, 8,* 97-99.

Feinstein, A. D., & Krippner, S. (1987). *Personal mythology.* Basel, Switzerland: Sphinx Verlag. English edition, Los Angeles: J. P. Tarcher.

Fisher, C., Kahn, E., Edwards, A., & Davis, D. M. (1973). A psychophysiological study of nightmares and night terrors. I. Physiological aspects of the stage of night terror. *Journal of Nervous and Mental Disease, 157,* 75-97.

Fiss, H. (1979). Current dream research: A psychobiological perspective. In B. B. Wolman (Ed.), *Handbook of dreams: Research, theories and applications* (pp. 20-75). New York: Van Nostrand Reinhold.

Fiss, H. (1984). Toward a clinically relevant experimental psychology of dreaming. *Association for the Study of Dreams Newsletter, 1* (1), 1-2, 10.

Fordham, F. (1953). *An introduction to Jung's psychology.* New York: Penguin Books.

Fosshage, J. L., & Loew, C. A. (Eds.) (1978). *Dream interpretation: A comparative study.* New York: Spectrum.

Foulkes, D. (1966). *The psychology of sleep.* New York: Scribners.

Foulkes, D. (1982). *Children's dreams: Longitudinal studies.* New York: John Wiley & Sons.

Foulkes, D. (1985). *Dreaming: A cognitive-psychological analysis.* Hillsdale, NJ: Erlbaum.

Foulkes, D., & Griffin, M. L. (1976). An experimental study of creative dreaming. *Sleep Research, 5,* 129.

von Franz, M.-L. (Ed.). (1964). *Man and his symbols.* Garden City, NY: Doubleday.

Freud, S. (1933). *New introductory lectures on psychoanalysis.* New York: W. W. Norton.

Freud, S. (1965). *The interpretation of dreams* (2nd ed.), (J. Strachey, Ed. & Trans.). New York: Avon. (Original work published 1909)

Freud, S. (1966). *Project for a scientific psychology* (J. Strachey, Ed. & Trans.) London: Hogarth Press. (Original work published 1895)

Fromm, E. (1951). *The forgotten language: An introduction to the understanding of dreams, fairy tales and myths.* New York: Grove Press.

Gackenbach, J. I. (1985-1986). A survey of considerations for inducing conscious awareness of dreaming, while dreaming. *Imagination, Cognition and Personality, 5,* 41-55.

Gandhi, M. K. (1957). *An autobiography: The story of my experiments with truth.* Boston: Beacon Press.

Garfield, P. (1974). *Creative dreaming.* New York: Simon & Schuster.

Garfield, P. (1976). Introduction. *Dream notebook* (pp. 6-16). San Francisco: San Francisco Book Company.

Garfield, P. (1979). *Pathway to ecstasy: The way of the dream mandala.* New York: Holt, Rinehart & Winston.

Garfield, P. (1984). *Your child's dreams.* New York: Ballantine.

Garfield, P. (1985, June). Children and dreams. Paper presented at the annual meeting of the Association for the Study of Dreams, Charlottesville, VA.

Gendlin, E. T. (1986). *Let your body interpret your dreams.* Wilmette, IL: Chiron.

Gerard, R. W. (1955). The biological basis of imagination. In B. Ghiselin (Ed.), *The creative process* (pp. 226-251). New York: New American Library.

Ghiselin, B. (Ed.) (1955). *The creative process.* New York: New American Library.

Globus, G. (1986). *Dream life, wake life: The human condition through dreams.* Albany: State University of New York Press.

Goertzel, M. G., Goertzel, V., & Goertzel, T. G. (1978). *Three hundred eminent personalities.* San Francisco: Jossey-Bass.

Gold, L. (1979). Adler's theory of dreams: An holistic approach to interpretation. In B. B. Wolman (Ed.), *Handbook of dreams: Research, theories and applications* (pp. 319-341). New York: Van Nostrand Reinhold.

Goldberg, P. (1983). *The intuitive edge: Understanding and developing intuition.* Los Angeles: J. P. Tarcher.

Green, B. F. (1963). *Digital computers in research.* New York: McGraw-Hill.

Green, E. E., Green, A. M., & Walters, E. D. (1970). Voluntary control of internal states: Psychological and physiological. *Journal of Transpersonal Psychology, 2,* 9-26.

Green, E., & Green, A. (1977). *Beyond biofeedback.* New York: Delacorte Press.

Greenberg, R., & Dewan, E. (1969). Aphasia and rapid eye movement sleep. *Nature, 223,* 183.

Greenberg, R., Pearlman, C., & Gampel, D. (1972). War neuroses and the adaptive function of REM sleep. *British Journal of Medical Psychology, 45,* 27-33.

Greenberg, R., & Pearlman, C. (1975). REM sleep and the analytic process. *Psychoanalytic Quarterly, 44,* 392-403.

Greene, T. A. (1978). C. G. Jung's theory of dreams. In B. B. Wolman (Ed.), *Handbook of dreams: Research, theories and applications* (pp. 298-318). New York: Van Nostrand Reinhold.

Greenwood, P., Wilson, D. H., & Gazzaniga, M. S. (1977). Dream reports following commissurotomy. *Cortex, 13,* 311-316.

Griffin, M. L., & Foulkes, D. (1977). Deliberate pre-sleep control of dream content: An experimental study. *Perceptual and Motor Skills, 45,* 660-662.

Gruber, H. E. (1974). *Darwin on man: A psychological study of scientific creativity.* New York: E. P. Dutton.

Guilford, J. P. (1967). *The nature of human intelligence.* New York: McGraw-Hill.

Guilford, J. P. (1977). *Way beyond the IQ.* Buffalo, NY: Creative Education Foundation.

Gulevitch, G., Dement, W., & Zarcone, V. (1967). All night sleep recordings of chronic schizophrenics in remission. *Comprehensive Psychiatry, 8,* 141-149.

Hadamard, J. (1945). *The psychology of intention in the mathematical field.* Princeton, NJ: Princeton University Press.

Hall, J. A. (1982). The use of dreams and dream interpretation in analysis. In M. Stein (Ed.), *Jungian analysis* (pp. 123-156). La Salle, IL: Open Court.

Hall, C. S., & Nordby, V. J. (1972). *The individual and his dreams.* New York: New American Library.

Hall, C. S., & Nordby, V. J. (1973). *A primer of Jungian psychology.* New York: New American Library.

Hall, C. S., & Van de Castle, R. L. (1966). *The content analysis of dreams.* New York: Appleton-Century-Crofts.

Harman, W., & Rheingold, H. (1984). *Higher creativity: Liberating the unconscious for breakthrough insights.* Los Angeles: Jeremy P. Tarcher.

Hart, J., Corriere, R., Karle, W., & Woldenberg, L. (1980). *Dreaming and waking: The functional approach to using dreams.* Los Angeles, CA: Center Foundation Press.

Hartmann, E. (1983). *The function of sleep.* New Haven, CT: Yale University Press.

Hartmann, E. (1984). *The nightmare: The psychology and biology of terrifying dreams.* New York: Basic Books.

Hathaway, S. R. (1955). Clinical intuition and inferential accuracy. *Journal of Personality, 24,* 223-250.

Hauri, P., & Van de Castle, R. L. (1973). Psychophysiological parallels in dreams. In U. J. Jovanovic (Ed.), *The nature of sleep* (140-143). New York: Gustave Fischer Verlag.

Hobson, J. A. (1983). Sleep mechanisms and pathology: Some clinical implications of the reciprocal interaction hypothesis of sleep cycle control. *Psychosomatic Medicine, 45,* 123-139.

Hobson, J. A., & McCarley, R. W. (1977). The brain as a dream state generator. *American Journal of Psychiatry, 134,* 1335-1348.

Hobson, J. A., Lydic, R., & Baghdoyan, H. A. (1986). Evolving concepts of sleep cycle generation: From brain centers to neuronal populations. *Behavioral and Brain Sciences, 9,* 371-448.

Hock, A. (1960). *Reason and genius.* New York: Philosophical Library.

Howell, J. (1985, March). Just plain Bill. *High Times,* pp. 33-34, 36.

Hughes, J. D. (1984). The dreams of Alexander the Great. *Journal of Psychohistory, 12,* 168-192.

Izard, C. E. (1972). *Patterns of emotion.* New York: Academic Press.

Jacobsen, E. (1938). *You can sleep well. The ABC's of restful sleep for the average person.* New York: Whittlesey House.

Jones, R. M. (1970). *The new psychology of dreaming.* New York: Grune & Stratton.

Jones, R. M. (1979). Freudian and post-Freudian theories of dreams. In B. B. Wolman (Ed.), *Handbook of dreams: Research, theories and applications* (pp. 271-297). New York: Van Nostrand Reinhold.

Jung, C. G. (1933). *Psychological types.* New York: Harcourt, Brace & World.

Jung, C. G. (1961). *Memories, dreams, reflections.* New York: Random House.

Jung, C. G. (1974). *Dreams.* Princeton, NJ: Princeton University Press.

Kaempffert, W. A. (1924). *A popular history of American invention* (Vol. 2). New York: Scribners.

Kant, I. (1900). *Dreams of a spirit seer* (E. F. Georwitz, Trans.). New York: Macmillan.

Kasatkin, V. (1984). Diagnosis by dreams. *International Journal of Paraphysics, 18,* 104-106.

Kedrov, B. M. (1957). [On the question of the psychology of scientific creativity on the occasion of the discovery by D. I. Mendeleev of the Periodic Table of the Elements.] *Voprosy Psikhologii, 3,* 111-113.

Klein, G. S., Fiss, H., Scholar, E., Dalbeck, R., Warga, C., & Gwozdz, F. (1971). Recurrent dream fragments and fantasies elicited in interrupted and completed REM periods. *Psychophysiology, 7,* 331-332.

Knapp, S. (1979). Dreaming: Horney, Kelman, and Shainberg. In B. B. Wolman (Ed.), *Handbook of dreams: Research, theories and applications* (pp. 342-360). New York: Van Nostrand Reinhold.

Koch-Sheras, P. R., Hollier, E. A., & Jones, B. (1983). *Dream on: A dream interpretation and exploration guide for women.* Englewood Cliffs, NJ: Prentice-Hall.

Koestler, A. (1967). *The act of creation.* New York: Macmillan.

Koulack, D., Prevost, F., & De Koninck, J. (1985). Sleep, dreaming, and adaptation to a stressful intellectual activity. *Sleep, 8,* 244-253.

Krippner, S. (1980a). Access to hidden reserves of the unconscious through dreams in creative problem solving. *Journal of Creative Behavior, 15,* 11-23.

Krippner, S. (1980b). *Human Possibilities: Mind research in the USSR and Eastern Europe.* Garden City, NY: Anchor Books.

Krippner, S. (1985). Psychedelic drugs and creativity. *Journal of Psychoactive Drugs, 17,* 235-245.

Krippner, S. (1986). Dreams and the development of a personal mythology. *Journal of Mind and Behavior, 7,* 449-462.

Krippner, S., Dreistadt, R., & Hubbard, C. C. (1979). The creative person and non-ordinary reality. In J. C. Gowan, J. Khatena, & E. P. Torrance (Eds.), *Educating the ablest: A book of readings* (2nd ed.) (pp. 445-470). Itasca, IL: F. E. Peacock.

Krippner, S., & Hooper, J. (1984, March-April). Shamanism and dreams. *Dream Network Bulletin,* pp. 14-17.

Krippner, S., & Hughes, W. (1977). Dreams and human potential. In H.-M. Chiang & A. H. Maslow (Eds.), *The healthy personality: Readings* (2nd ed.) (pp. 106-126). New York: D. Van Nostrand.

Krippner, S., Posner, N., Pomerance, W., & Fischer, S. (1974). An investigation of dream content during pregnancy. *Journal of the American Society of Psychosomatic Dentistry and Medicine, 21,* 111-123.

Krippner, S., & Stoller, L. (1973). Sleeptalking and creativity: A case study. *Journal of the American Society of Psychosomatic Dentistry and Medicine, 20,* 107-114.

Krippner, S., Ullman, M., & Honorton, C. (1971). A precognitive dream study with a single subject. *Journal of the American Society for Psychical Research, 65,* 195-203.

Krippner, S., Honorton, C., & Ullman, M. (1972). A second precognitive dream study with Malcolm Bessent. *Journal of the American Society for Psychical Research, 66,* 269-279.

Kris, E. (1956). The personal myth: A problem in psychoanalytic technique. *Journal of the American Psychoanalytic Association, 4,* 653-681.

Kupfer, D., Wyatt, R., Scott, J., & Snyder, F. (1970). Sleep disturbance in acute schizophrenic patients. *American Journal of Psychiatry, 126,* 1213-1223.

LaBerge, S. (1985). *Lucid dreaming: The power of being awake and aware in your dreams.* Los Angeles: Jeremy P. Tarcher.

Ladd, G. T. (1892). Contribution to the psychology of visual dreams. *Mind, 1,* 299-304.

Lawren, B. (1986, March). Dreamless sleep. *Omni,* p. 34.

LeShan, L. (1974). *How to meditate: A guide to self-discovery.* Boston: Little, Brown.

LeVine, R. (1966). *Dreams and deeds: Achievement motivation in Nigeria.* Chicago: University of Chicago Press.

Levinson, D. J. (1978). *The seasons of a man's life.* New York: Ballantine.

Loewi, O. (1960, Autumn). An autobiographical sketch. *Perspectives in Biology and Medicine*, pp. 3-25.

Lowy, S. (1942). *Foundations of dream interpretation.* London: Kegan Paul, Trench, & Trubner.

Luce, G. G., & Segal, J. (1967). *Sleep.* New York: Lancer Books.

MacKinnon, D. W. (1978). *In search of human effectiveness: Identifying and developing creativity.* Buffalo, NY: Creative Education Foundation.

Mahoney, M. (1966). *The meaning of dreams and dreaming.* New York: Citadel Press.

Maslow, A. H. (1971). *The farther reaches of human nature.* New York: Viking Press.

Maslow, A. H. (1976). Creativity in self-actualizing people. In A. Rothenberg & R. Hausman (Eds.), *The creativity question* (pp. 86-92). Durham, NC: Duke University Press.

May, R. (1959). The nature of creativity. In H. H. Anderson (Ed.), *Creativity and its cultivation* (pp. 55-68). New York: Harper & Brothers.

McCarley, R. W., & Hobson, J. A. (1977). The neurobiological origins of psychoanalytic dream theory. *American Journal of Psychiatry, 134,* 1211-1221.

McCarley, R. W., & Hobson, J. A. (1979). The form of dreams and the biology of sleep. In B. B. Wolman (Ed.), *Handbook of dreams: Research, theories and applications* (pp. 76-130). New York: Van Nostrand Reinhold.

McLeester, D. (1976). *Welcome to the magic theater: A handbook for exploring dreams.* Worcester, MA: Saltus Press.

Mindell, A. (1985). *Working with the dreaming body.* Boston: Routledge & Kegan Paul.

Megroz, R. L. (1939). *The dream world.* London: Bodley Head.

Monroe, R., Nerlove, S., & Daniels, R. (1969). Effects of population density on food concerns in three East African societies. *Journal of Health and Social Behavior, 10,* 161-171.

Morris, J. (1985). *The dream workbook.* Boston: Little, Brown.

Moss, C. S. (1967). *The hypnotic investigation of dreams.* New York: John Wiley & Sons.

Murphy, G. (1958). *Human potentialities.* New York: Basic Books.

Naisbitt, J. (1982). *Megatrends.* New York: Warner Books.

Newman, J. R. (1948). Sriniwasa Ramaujan. *Scientific American, 178,* 544-557.

O'Flaherty, W. D. (1982). Hard and soft reality. *Parabola, 7*(2), 55-65.

O'Nell, C. W. (1976). *Dreams, culture, and the individual.* Novato, CA: Chandler & Sharp.

Parnes, S. J. (1981). *The magic of your mind.* Buffalo, NY: Creative Educational Foundation.

Partington, J. R. (1972). *A history of chemistry* (Vol. 4). London: Macmillan.

Patrick, C. (1935). Creative thought in poets. *Archives of Psychology, 26,* 1-74.

Patrick, C. (1937). Creative thought in artists. *Journal of Psychology, 4,* 35-73.

Paupst, J. (1975). *The sleep book.* New York: Collier Books.

Perls, F. C. (1969). *Gestalt therapy verbatim.* Lafayette, CA: Real People Press.

Poincaré, H. (1955). Mathematical creation. In B. Ghiselin (Ed.), *The creative process* (pp. 33-42). New York: Mentor Books. (Original work published 1913)

Porte, H. S., & Hobson, J. A. (1986). Bizarreness in REM and NREM sleep research. *Sleep Research, 15,* 81.

Price, G. W. (1937). *I knew these dictators.* London: Harrap.

Prince, R. (1963). *Noted witnesses for psychic occurrences.* Hyde Park, NY: University Books.

Progoff, I. (1973). *Jung's psychology and its social meaning.* Garden City, NY: Anchor Books.

Quinn, A. (1981). *Dreams: Secret messages from your mind.* Tacoma, WA: Dream Research.

Raine, K. (1971). *William Blake.* New York: Praeger.

Rallo, J. (1974). A discussion of the paper by G. H. Allison and J. C. Ullman on "The intuitive psychoanalytic perspective of galdos in fortunata and jacinta." *International Journal of Psychoanalysis, 55,* 345-347.

Rauscher, E. (1972). Closed cosmological solutions to Einstein's field equations. *Lettre al Nuovo Cimento, 3,* 661-664.

Rechtschaffen, A., Verdone, P., & Wheaton, J. (1963). Reports of mental activity during sleep. *Canadian Psychiatric Association Journal, 8,* 403-414.

Reed, H. (1976). Dream incubation: A reconstruction of a ritual in contemporary form. *Journal of Humanistic Psychology, 16,* 52-70.

Reed, H. (1985). *Getting help from your dreams.* Virginia Beach, VA: Inner Vision.

Rogers, C. R. (1970). Towards a theory of creativity. In P. E. Vernon (Ed.), *Creativity* (pp. 137-151). Baltimore: Penguin Books.

Rogers, S. L. (1982). *The shaman: His symbols and his healing power.* Springfield, IL: Charles C Thomas.

Roheim, G. (1952). *The gates of the dream.* New York: International University Press.

Rosen, G. M. (1981). Guidelines for the review of do-it-yourself treatment books. *Contemporary Psychology, 26,* 189-191.

Rossi, E. (1972). *Dreams and the growth of personality: Expanding awareness in psychotherapy.* New York: Pergamon Press.

Rothenberg, A. (1979). *The emerging goddess: The creative process in art, science, and other fields.* Chicago: University of Chicago Press.

Rowan, R. (1979, April 23). Those business hunches are more than blind faith. *Fortune,* pp. 110-114.

Rowan, R. (1986). *The intuitive manager.* Boston: Little, Brown.

Rycroft, C. (1979). *The innocence of dreams.* New York: Pantheon.

Savary, L. M., Perne, P. H., & Williams, S. K. (1984). *Dreams and spiritual growth: A Christian approach to dreamwork.* Ramsey, NJ: Paulist Press.

Schlipp, P. A. (Ed.). (1949). *Albert Einstein: Philosopher-scientist.* Evanston, IL: Library of Living Philosophers.

Schechter, N., Schmeidler, G. R., & Staal, M. (1965). Dream reports and creative tendencies in students of the arts, sciences, and engineering. *Journal of Consulting Psychology, 29,* 415-421.

Schneider, E. (1953). *Coleridge, opium, and "Kubla Khan."* Chicago: University of Chicago Press.

Sechrist, E. (1968). *Dreams: Your magic mirror.* New York: Cowles.

Segal, J. (1974, January). Cited in: Recurring nightmares: Examination dreams. *Time,* p. 78.

Shapero, H. (1955). The musical mind. In B. Ghiselin (Ed.), *The creative process* (pp. 49-54). New York: Mentor Books.

Shohet, R. (1985). *Dream sharing.* Wellingborough, Northamptonshire, England: Turnstone Press.

Singer, J. (1973). *Boundaries of the soul.* Garden City, NY: Anchor Books.

Singer, J. (1976). *Androgyny: Toward a new theory of sexuality.* Garden City, NY: Anchor Books.

Singer, J. L. (1975). *The inner world of daydreaming.* New York: Harper/ Colophon.

Sladeczek, I., & Domino, G. (1985). Creativity, sleep and primary process thinking in dreams. *Journal of Creative Behavior, 19,* 38-55.

Smith, C. I., Kitahama, K., Valtax, J. L., & Jouvet, M. (1974). Increased paradoxical sleep in mice during acquisition of a shock avoidance task. *Brain Research, 77,* 221-230.

Snyder, F. (1970). The phenomenology of dreaming. In L. Madow & L. H. Snow (Eds.), *The psychodynamic implications of the physiological studies on dreams* (pp. 124-151). Springfield, IL: Charles C Thomas.

Springer, A. (1983, December). It came to Harlem. *American Film,* p. 13.

Stein, M. I. (1963). Creativity in a free society. *Educational Horizons, 41,* 115-130.

Stein, M. I. (1974). *Stimulating creativity* (Vol. 1). New York: Academic Press.

Stevens, A. (1982). *Archetypes: A natural history of the self.* New York: William Morrow.

Stevenson, R. L. (1925). *Memories and portraits, random memories, memories of himself.* New York: Scribner.

Stoney, B. (1974). *Enid Blyton: A biography.* London: Hodder.

Stukane, E. (1985). *The dream worlds of pregnancy.* New York: Quill.

Talamonte, L. (1975). *Forbidden universe.* New York: Stein & Day.

Tart, C. T. (1979). From spontaneous event to lucidity: A review of attempts to consciously control nocturnal dreaming. In B. B. Wolman (Ed.), *Handbook of dreams: Research, theories and applications* (pp. 226-268). New York: Van Nostrand Reinhold.

Taub-Bynum, E. B. (1984). *The family unconscious.* Wheaton, IL: Quest Books.

Taylor, D. W. (1963). Variables related to creativity and productivity among men in two research laboratories. In C. Taylor & F. Barron (Eds.), *Scientific creativity: Its recognition and development* (pp. 228-250). New York: John Wiley & Sons.

Taylor, J. (1983). *Dream work: Techniques for discovering the creative power in dreams.* Ramsey, NJ: Paulist Press.

Thurston, M. (1978). *How to interpret your dreams—practical techniques based on the Edgar Cayce Readings.* Virginia Beach, VA: A. R. E. Press.

Thurston, M. (1986). *Dream interpretation made easy.* Virginia Beach, VA: A. R. E. Press.

Tolaas, J., & Ullman, M. (1979). Extrasensory communication and dreams. In B. B. Wolman (Ed.), *Handbook of dreams: Research, theories and applications* (pp. 168-201). New York: Van Nostrand Reinhold.

Tooker, E. (Ed.). (1979). *Native North American spirituality of the Eastern woodlands: Sacred myths, dreams, visions, speeches, healing formulas, rituals and ceremonies.* New York: Paulist Press.

Torrance, E. P. (1962). *Guiding creative talent.* Englewood Cliffs, NJ: Prentice-Hall.

Torrance, E. P. (1979). *The search for satori and creativity.* Buffalo, NY: Creative Education Foundation.

Ullman, M. (1958). Hypotheses on the biological roots of the dream. *Journal of Clinical and Experimental Psychopathology, 19,* 128-133.

Ullman, M. (1961). Dreaming, altered states of consciousness and the problem of vigilance. *Journal of Nervous and Mental Disease, 133,* 519-535.·

Ullman, M. (1965). Discussion: Dreaming—a creative process. *American Journal of Psychoanalysis, 24,* 10-12.

Ullman, M. (1969). Dreaming as metaphor in motion. *Archives of General Psychiatry, 21,* 696-703.

Ullman, M. (1972). Vigilance, dreaming and the paranormal. In C. Muses & A. Young (Eds.), *Consciousness and reality* (pp. 35-36). New York: Outerbridge & Lazard.

Ullman, M. (1973). Societal factors in dreaming. *Contemporary Psychoanalysis, 9,* 282-293.

Ullman, M. (1978). Foreword. In J. L. Fosshage & C. A. Loew (Eds.), *Dream interpretation: A comparative study.* New York: Spectrum.

Ullman, M. (1979). The experiential dream group. In B. B. Wolman (Ed.), *Handbook of dreams: Research, theories and applications* (pp. 406-423). New York: Van Nostrand Reinhold.

Ullman, M. (1980). Dream workshops and healing. In S. Boorstein (Ed.), *Explorations in transpersonal psychology* (pp. 150-161). New York: Science and Behavior Books.

Ullman, M. (1983). Dreams: An under appreciated natural resource. In J. Taylor, K. Taylor, & J. Van Damm (Eds.), *Coat of many colors* (pp. 24-26). San Rafael, CA: Dream Tree Press.

Ullman, M. (1984). Group dream work and healing. *Contemporary Psychoanalysis, 20,* 120-130.

Ullman, M. (1986). Vigilance theory and psi. Part II: Physiological, psychological, and parapsychological aspects. *Journal of the American Society for Psychical Research, 80,* 375-391.

Ullman, M., Krippner, S., & Vaughan, A. (1973). *Dream telepathy.* London: Turnstone Books.

Ullman, M., & Zimmerman, N. (1985). *Working with dreams.* Los Angeles: J. P. Tarcher. (Original work published 1979)

Van de Castle, R. L. (1971). *The psychology of dreaming.* Morristown, NJ: General Learning Press.

Vaughan, A. (1973). *Patterns of prophecy.* New York: Hawthorn Books.

Vaughan, F. (1979). *Awakening intuition.* Garden City, NY: Anchor Books.

Vogel, V. W. (1975). REM sleep reduction effects on depression syndromes. *Archives of General Psychiatry, 33,* 96-97.

Vogel, V. W. (1983). Evidence for REM sleep deprivation as the mechanism of action of anti-depressant drugs. *Progress in Neuropsychopharmacology and Biological Psychiatry, 7,* 343-349.

Wasserman, I., & Ballif, B. L. (1984). Perceived interactions between the dream and the waking division of consciousness. *Imagination, Cognition and Personality, 4,* 3-13.

Watkins, M. (1976). *Waking dreams.* New York: Harper & Row.

Webb, W. W. (1979). A historical perspective of dreams. In B. B. Wolman (Ed.), *Handbook of dreams: Research, theories and applications* (pp. 3-19). New York: Van Nostrand Reinhold.

Weisberg, R. W. (1986). *Creativity: Genius and other myths.* New York: W. H. Freeman.

White, R. (Trans. & Ed.). (1975). *The interpretation of dreams—the oneirocritics of Artemidorus.* Park Ridge, NJ: Noyes Classical Studies.

Whitmont, E. O. (1978). Jungian approach. In J. L. Fosshage & C. A. Loew (Eds.), *Dream interpretation: A comparative study* (pp. 53-77). New York: Spectrum.

Wilber, K. (1983). *Eye to eye.* Garden City, NY: Anchor Books.

Williams, S. (1980). *Jungian-Senoi dreamwork manual.* Berkeley: Journey Press.

Winson, J. (1985). *Brain and psyche: The biology of the unconscious.* Garden City, NY: Anchor Press.

Witty, P., & Kopel, D. (1938). Studies of the activities and preferences of school children. *Educational Administration and Supervision, 24,* 429-441.

Woods, R., & Greenhouse, H. (1974). *The new world of dreams.* New York: Macmillan.

Appendix

Identifying and Using Your Personal Myths

Because your personal mythology, like your dreams, is rooted initially in your biological nature, your psychological history, and your cultural environment, the challenge of unearthing its deeper aspects and intentionally bringing about changes may seem formidable. Yet, there is a propensity in human nature which encourages us to develop ourselves in this direction, even though it may demand substantial effort and concentration (Feinstein & Krippner, in press). Jung believed it was inherent in the nature of the psyche to be motivated toward self-realization–toward integrating into our personalities aspects of ourselves of which we might previously have been unaware. He presented evidence for this assertion from both his clinical observations and from prehistoric and ancient myths which portrayed primordial psychological insights into the nature of personality integration (Progoff, 1973). Of course, the wisdom and maturation coming with age to some extent do make us more capable of being deliberate in shaping our destinies, but the degree to which this occurs is largely in our hands. Psychological maturation depends on many factors, and participants in our workshops have found that actively cultivating skills in self-development increases the speed and extent to which such abilities grow. By gaining control and understanding of the underlying influences upon your personal mythology, you will become a more conscious and purposeful participant in the processes at the foundation of your perceptions, feelings, thoughts, and actions.

Gaining access to these processes, however, is not a simple endeavor. In the play *Troilus and Cressida,* one of William Shakespeare's characters complains, "My mind is troubled, like a fountain stirred, and I myself see not the bottom of it." Other literary figures have been more successful in enhancing awareness. In Fyodor Dostoyevsky's *The Idiot*, one character comments, "It's as though something new, prophetic, that you were awaiting, has been told you in your dream." Dostoyevsky also observed that the dream reveals "something belonging to your actual life, something that exists and always has existed in your heart."

Daydreams and other spontaneous imagery can also provide access to personal myths which may underlie our daily problems and concerns. Like dreams, fantasies and daydreams contain important material. Jerome Singer (1973), a leading researcher in this field, reported that children who daydream frequently are less likely to develop schizophrenia than those who do not, and that adult daydreams prepare people to accept their inner processes and more precisely to differentiate fantasy from reality.

Emotions, feelings, and body tensions are also clearly connected to personal myths. C. E. Izard (1972) identified the major emotions as anger, contempt, disgust, distress, enjoyment, fear, interest, shame, and surprise. Other psychologists would add or subtract from this list, but all would agree that each emotion has a variety of neurological, muscular, and psychological aspects. As a result, an inner conflict can be experienced as both distress and a headache, as both a sharp pain in the chest and a sense of fear. Physical symptoms such as backaches, constipation or loss of appetite frequently indicate the presence of internal struggles.

The most productive starting point for exploring personal myths is typically the area of conflict in one's life—anxieties, phobias, physical symptoms, puzzling dreams, self-contradictions, and areas of confusion, ambivalence, and dissatisfaction. By using various means for tapping into the workings of the psyche, you may discover that beneath these contentions are personal myths guiding you in opposing directions. If you are always complaining about how busy you are but are also over-scheduling every opportunity for free time, your behavior may be following a deeper myth which is conflicting with the view you are aware of holding. Bringing such conflicting myths to your attention makes a constructive resolution possible. In fact, the cutting edge of personal growth usually follows the points of conflict in one's mythology. Your dreams can be used to initiate a process for focusing on conflicts in your life and productively working with their underlying myths.

Justin's Journey: Chapter One

Before suggesting specific techniques you can use in the first stage of this five-stage process of uncovering mythic conflicts, we want to present the experiences of a typical participant from one of our workshops. His story illustrates the use of these techniques for consciously entering the mythic underworld through one's dreams.

Justin is a high school counselor who was 29 when he participated in a personal mythology workshop. In the first session, each member was asked to identify an unpleasant feeling in a recent dream. They were also asked to sense that feeling in their body, by focusing upon it, and to find a word to describe it. Justin recalled a dream in which he had the sensation of nausea. The leader helped the group go back in time to remember an early experience which had evoked the same feeling. Justin recalled an incident that had taken place when he was about nine years old. He told his partner:

> *What came to me was a time when I got sick and stayed home from school. I told my mother I would feel better if I could just lie in bed and read Aquaman comic books. But my mother responded that nobody can be cured by reading comic books. She telephoned a physician. By the time the doctor came, I had read two Aquaman comic books and was feeling fine. I had really felt quite ill before, but after the physician examined me, he said that there was nothing wrong. In fact, he suggested that I may have been faking illness to get out of school. I felt very embarrassed, angry, and ashamed that neither he*

nor my mother would believe I had been sick. In retrospect, I see that I had healed myself by reading and relaxing.

The members were then told to reflect on that early experience to see what attitudes, beliefs, or rules of conduct might have emerged from it. Justin reflected:

It occurs to me that one of the results of this experience, and those like it, was not to trust my own abilities. For instance, yesterday I felt ill but didn't know what to do about it. Maybe the reason was that I feared I would be embarrassed again if I tried to heal myself. If I were to have healed myself someone would criticize me and say that I hadn't really been sick. I have never made this connection before. I have been interested in unorthodox forms of healing, but I find it easier to give advice to other people than to attempt healing myself. It's as if it feels too difficult. But perhaps one of the reasons I don't try healing myself is that this early experience has evolved into a personal myth. The myth is: if I heal myself, nobody will believe I was sick in the first place, and I will end up feeling ashamed and humiliated. So it is better to depend on someone else to look after me.

At this point, the leader asked if someone would share a dream with the group. Justin volunteered and went to the front of the room where he related his dream:

I was driving a huge truck, an 18-wheeler. It might have been down a road known as Brush Creek. I ran it off the side of the road into a puddle of water. I had not been hurt by the accident and felt relieved. But at the same time I felt somewhat guilty about all the baggage I had been carrying that I was leaving on the side of the road. I'm not sure that I got out of the cab of the truck, but that was my intention. The only uncomfortable aspect about my accident was the feeling of guilt, but even that

*wasn't too strong. For some reason, there was more of
a feeling of relief.*

The group leader then asked each member to retell his or
her dream as a fairy tale, augmenting it with the feeling from the
dream and the early memory which it triggered. As an example,
he used Justin's dream, creating it in this form:

*Once upon a time there was a young prince named
Justin who lived with his father, the King, and his mother,
the Queen. His parents were very powerful and, of course,
very wise. They owned many splendid possessions. One
of their most valued objects was the chariot they used
to visit other villages for festivals and fairs. Prince Justin
was eager to drive the chariot. When he asked permission, the King and Queen replied, "Yes, when you are
old enough we will let you take out the chariot. But you
must not drive it alone until you learn how to manage
the horses, and you need to be especially careful of the
country roads that curve and wind around the castle."
The young prince answered, "Oh yes, I will do all of that.
You will not have to worry about the chariot being in
foolish hands when I drive it."*

Justin told his partner he was fascinated by this recasting
of his dream, as it captured much of the dream's emotional tone,
combining it with his recollections of childhood. The leader continued:

*The day arrived for Prince Justin to take the chariot and
its 18 horses out by himself. Off they went down the
road. But the surging power was somewhat stronger
than Justin had expected. Further, the coach seemed
larger than he had imagined, and the road was bumpier
than he recalled. Just for a second, Justin lost control
of the reins and some of the horses ran off into a ditch,
taking the coach with them. There was no great damage.
The horses were in disarray, but they easily climbed out
of the ditch. However, the coach was stuck in the mud.*

Prince Justin felt nauseous. What would he do? What would he tell the King and Queen? He was given great responsibility and had assured his parents that he would not abuse it. Then, on thinking the matter over, Justin felt somewhat relieved. "Because of my accident, it will be a while before my parents let me take out the coach again. It is just as well. Perhaps I am not ready for such a responsibility. Maybe I should take a little longer to grow up and to observe how other people drive their coaches. In the meantime, I can let my parents take the responsibility and I can continue to enjoy being a child." So even though the young prince felt some guilt, he also felt a sense of relief.

Justin shared with his partner his irritation at being portrayed as an immature young prince. However, after some thought, he recalled his recent ambivalence about being given new responsibilities at work, describing them as both an opportunity and a burden. "Come to think of it," he told his partner, "I've been trying to keep the truck on the road and it's a big job. Sometimes I'm tempted to goof up and drop the whole thing, and since my boss could be a stand-in for my father, in a way it's my parental truck after all."

Justin started to think of alternatives to running his truck off the road. He told his partner, "I could get the truck down the highway and let somebody else take it over. Or I could take the damn thing all the way to its destination and get whatever praise comes from having done the job well. But in the dream, I actually felt relieved when I ran the truck off the road. It was too tough to deal with all that power, all that responsibility. It's a heavy truck. When you turn it, the momentum is such that it doesn't respond too well. I've never driven an 18-wheeler before I did it in my dream. And I've never worked in association with someone as "heavy" in the metaphorical sense of the word, as my current boss."

The leader allowed time for members to tell their dreams to their partners as if they were fairy tales, and to discuss their reactions. He suggested that this story could be viewed as Chapter

One of their personal myth. Later they would have a chance to develop "Chapter Two."

Justin and his group were given paper plates with the instructions to divide the center into four equal parts. They were then invited to find or create a symbol from Chapter One that they could draw on this "personal shield." Justin remarked:

The symbol that best captures the flavor of Chapter One is the stalled truck in the puddle of water. It represents my tendency to procrastinate, to avoid responsibility, and to delay getting on with my life.

Justin's Journey: Chapter Two

After a lunch break, the leader introduced a new set of exercises to lead to the construction of "Chapter Two." The group was asked to relax and focus upon the unpleasant feeling from the morning. Justin easily recalled his sensations of nausea which originated in the disturbing dream about the truck accident.

The leader asked the group to imagine a feeling just the opposite of the emotion from their dream. The group was then to allow their body sensations to match that emotion. Again, they were requested to find a word for the feeling, and to go back and forth between the word and the feeling to determine if they matched. Once the match was made, members were asked to immerse themselves in the feeling.

Justin's sensations of nausea evoked a sense of weakness. When he turned the feeling around, sensations of strength emerged. He could feel the strength in his muscles. His mind was clear, he felt competent—able to perform well on any challenging task.

The group was guided back to early experiences brought to mind by the feeling. Justin remembered a minor incident which had occurred when he was about four. Yet, it made an important impression on him and was associated with the feeling of strength. Justin's mother was carrying two bags of groceries into the house and was having trouble negotiating the door. Justin opened the door and held it while his mother entered and deposited the groceries in the kitchen. She was very complimentary and referred to him as "my strong little man." Justin saw himself beaming with pride following the remark. He felt competent and quite proud of himself.

The leader asked Justin's permission to use him and his experience in front of the group to demonstrate how Chapter Two could be constructed. Justin responded favorably, and the leader continued the story of the young prince.

Prince Justin returned to the palace following his accident with the chariot. His expectations were confirmed: the King and Queen revoked his driving privileges indefinitely. He was rather relieved and started to play with his toy chariot again, something he had not done for many months. As he was unable to travel too far from the palace, he decided that he could spend more time allowing his parents to guide and direct him. But soon this pattern of life proved to be unsatisfactory. Justin realized that he was destined to become a king, so he would simply have to grow up.

Justin began to rehearse with his toy chariot, pretending that it was driven by a team of 18 horses. He thought of himself driving and coordinating the horses so the chariot would provide a smooth ride and not fall into gulleys and ditches. Eventually, he returned to his parents with a request to take out the chariot again. At first they refused to consider the request, but later the King decided that they might go driving together. The King started to drive, then turned the reins over to Prince Justin. Much to the delight of them both, Justin performed impeccably.

The horses raced down the narrow, winding road. The chariot remained on course and did not jostle to the right or to the left. After they returned to the castle, the King said, "My son, I am proud of you. Not only can you use my chariot from time to time, but next year I will have the royal charioteer prepare you a chariot of your own." As a result, Prince Justin later was able to

*travel about the realm—a kingdom which he would some-
day rule.*

Justin told his partner this interpretation rang true on several counts. He had been born into a wealthy family. But, he had been burdened by the awareness that other people were less well off. He felt privileged but without reason: his wealth was an accident of birth. As a result, he lived in a $27-per-month room in a low income area of New York when he graduated from college. At the same time, some of his friends who had been born in the slums lived in expensive apartments. Justin told his partner, "My parents were the ones who owned the chariot. I felt like I didn't deserve it because I had not done anything to earn it. Everything was given to me but I felt burdened by material possessions. In a sense, what I did in my early years was to run the chariot not only into a ditch but off a cliff."

The other workshop participants developed the second chapter of their fairy tale, and discussed it in terms of their personal lives. Many could see two conflicting myths beginning to take form. In some cases, people's myths emerged out of two conflicting emotions such as distress and calmness, or apathy and interest. In other cases, the conflict was between generalized feelings, such as anxiety and tranquility, or insecurity and confidence. In other cases, the conflict was between bodily sensations—pain and euphoria, or heaviness and lightness. In each case, however, the conflict could be felt in the body and could be translated into a word by the matching process taught by the leader.

When the leader asked the members to place another image in their shields, Justin selected the elegant toy chariot. He said:

*It is something of beauty and something I can manage,
yet no long-term substitute for the real thing. It may
symbolize my ideals and my aspirations which may or
may not ever be actualized.*

As a participant in the personal mythology workshop, Justin had taken an active interest in Chapter One and Chapter Two of his real-life drama. The leader now asked the participants to stand and use insights from these imaginative creations in another way. Each was requested to assume the voice, posture, and gestures characteristic of each chapter, and to have each confront the other. To demonstrate, he acted out Justin's first "chapter" by speaking in a whine, by becoming stooped and rigid, and by taking on the expression of someone quite withdrawn, fearful, and on the verge of nausea. The workshop leader whined:

> I'm really afraid to take that chariot out by myself. In fact, I'm glad that I had the accident. Now I get to stay home—close to mommy and daddy—and don't have to make any big decisions on my own. I can stay in the castle where it is safe and comfortable.

The leader then became the hero from Chapter Two, adopting a firm, demanding voice and an erect, powerful posture:

> What do you mean, "stay at home?" You'll never let go of mother's apron strings if you are not pushed and prodded, and you'll obey each of father's rules without giving them any critical attention. I just can't sit by and watch all of this. I want to grow up and get on with my life. But I can't do it while you are blocking progress. And until you change, I can't get out and explore the world.

Chapter One retorted:

> But it's dangerous out there! It's really scary away from home. I just don't think I can make it on my own. If I go out and try to be independent, I'll just run another chariot into the ditch. I'd rather play it safe. I'm just afraid to grow up and leave my mommy and daddy.

The protagonist of Chapter Two fought back:

> I've been waiting all my life to grow up and get away

from home. After all, mother and father will not be around forever. Someday I'll have a kingdom of my own. In the meantime, I have to start preparing to deal with the world. Otherwise, the kingdom will fall apart when I become king. I should say, when we become king, because I can't get away from you—much as I would welcome the opportunity!

Justin recognized the conflict. It pitted dependence against independence, passivity against activity. These were issues which had always disturbed him. He portrayed the two chapters in his own way while his partner observed him, then discussed several childhood experiences he recalled during his dramatization. Then the members were asked to close their eyes and allow an image to emerge which would represent Chapter One, and later Chapter Two. Justin's symbols were a radiant sun for Chapter One and a dismal "X" for Chapter Two. Justin's next exercise required him to explore the conflict between his myths in another manner. Participants were told to close their eyes, hold forth their hands, and imagine that Chapter One had been placed on one hand and Chapter Two in the other. The leader suggested they explore the differences between the two, using tactile and kinesthetic imagery, asking themselves:

1. Which myth is harder to hold? Which is easier to hold?

2. Which myth has a more pleasant feeling to it?

3. Does one have jagged edges? Is one smoother? Is one rougher?

4. Are there differences in weight? Is one heavier? Is one more buoyant?

The participants were asked to reflect upon these experiences asking themselves:

1. If the myth is harder to hold, does it mean it is too difficult to manage, or could it be that it is so new it will take a while to get accustomed to it?

2. If one myth is rougher, does that mean that it is causing you trouble, or that it is trying to get you to abandon old ways of experiencing your world?

3. If one myth is heavier, does it mean it involves more problems or is more important?

4. If one myth is more buoyant, does that mean it is more inspirational or is it impossible to achieve?

Justin observed that Chapter One, his old myth, felt like a jagged piece of metal. He also sensed he had to hold it because it would be deadly if stepped on or thrown at someone. He then experienced the new myth, Chapter Two as a 16-pound round ball. These tactile, or touch, and kinesthetic, or muscular, feelings were associated with irresponsibility (the jagged piece of metal) and responsibility (the round ball).

The group leader continued the exercise, stating, "Slowly begin to bring your hands together. Feel what happens when the two myths begin to approach and touch each other. In some cases, there will be so much of a repulsion between the two that they will not touch. In other cases, one will overwhelm the other with its weight and power. In still other instances, you will be able to clasp your hands as the two myths merge in either a compromise or a synthesis. When there is a conflict between myths, sometimes the old seems to be too powerful to eliminate. Sometimes the new myth appears to have so much weight it simply overwhelms the old. There may also be continued conflict as the two refuse to touch each other. Or, there could be a compromise as some type of contact is made between the two as you bring your hands together. In other instances, the hands will clasp and a synthesis will occur. In these cases, the best of the old remains and combines with the best of the new."

As Justin attempted this he found the two myths in conflict: his hands simply would not touch. He felt a conflict between the myths, just as when one holds two magnets together with similar poles pointing to each other, hence repelling the magnetic fields of both. However, Justin observed a subtle change. The repulsion gradually subsided and the hand holding the new myth began to approach the hand holding the old. The two hands touched and eventually clasped. Justin sensed great relief and relaxation. He felt as if the jagged metal was melting in his hands and was coating the ball.

In discussing this experience with his partner, Justin stated that driving the chariot off the road to keep from driving it at all was simply not necessary. Just because he now perceived himself as a responsible person did not mean he had to be responsible for everyone all the time. The coating of the ball symbolized to him the fact that it was possible for him to say "no" if he was asked to do something which he did not want to undertake. It also symbolized the fact that he could choose when to allow someone to take care of him, and to assume responsibility in some aspect of their relationship. Nevertheless, the inner core of the sphere was the round ball, suggesting the inner strength and responsibility which he could carry into his daily life.

Why was the ball described as weighing 16 pounds? Justin's partner recalled that his original dream had concerned an 18-wheel tractor. Justin, who had a flair for mathematics, observed that 16 is a more manageable number than 18, being the square root of four—a symbol of completeness and unity in the mandala and other mythic traditions. Perhaps he had dropped two wheels to reflect the valuable residue of the old myth—the two exceptions to assuming total responsibility. It was foolish of him to assume responsibility all the time, especially when he wanted to reject a task or when it felt right to allow someone else to assume the responsibility.

Justin had originally rejected the old myth completely, telling his partner about the many times in his life when immaturity and the avoidance of responsibility had held him back. Now, however, he was pleased that there was something in Chapter One which could be integrated into his current life, and that the synthesis of two myths was pleasing to him.

Justin's Journey: Chapter Three

Justin's next activity began with a simple relaxation exercise as group members rested on the matted floor. The leader requested participants to recall the image of their younger selves from earlier in the day. They were then invited to bring that younger self into the room so the two of them would be lying side by side. The leader said, "Introduce yourself to your younger selves and offer them your assistance. Imagine that they are at a point in time where a destructive personal myth is taking shape. They have just experienced a rejection, a disappointment, or an abusive act which will affect them for years. From the perspective of your current age, and with the wisdom you now possess, what would you do to heal the child you once were? What advice would you give? What emotional support could you offer?"

The participants followed these suggestions in silence, while classical music played softly in the background. Occasionally, someone could be heard sobbing or crying as the emotional impact of the exercise produced its effect. Finally, the leader suggested that each person embrace the younger self. "Bring the younger version of yourself into unity with yourself as you are now. Be sure you incorporate all the positive traits of that age so these can become an important part of you again."

In the subsequent discussion, Justin remarked, "I went back to the nine-year-old boy who remained in bed after his mother and the doctor left the room. They expressed their doubts about my sincerity and honesty, strongly suspecting I was pretending to be sick so I would not have to attend school. It just was not true, and I reassured my younger self that the two adults did not know any better. When I brought the younger self into my current psyche, I tried to incorporate the spontaneity, the joy, and the originality I felt at that age—and which I could use right now."

Justin continued his discussion with his partner. "I realize I have taken on too much of the physician's attitude, playing the sophisticated scientist who looks down his nose at all the possibilities in the world which I have been told cannot happen. I

know that the doctor part of me is alien to my feelings. Nevertheless, I can use this part of me to be sure I remain critical, and to
appear intelligent to the outside world. But I now know that I do
not have to direct the doctor's voice to myself ever again. If I feel
something very strongly, I am going to give those feelings a
chance to be acknowledged and even acted upon, and I am
going to remain more open-minded than I have been for some
time when faced with unusual and controversial alternatives. I
feel much more whole as a result of getting back in touch with
that nine-year-old body. I also feel grateful for the opportunity to
have experienced this process."

You can attempt the same exercise. Find a comfortable spot
to lay down or to sit. Play some appropriate music in the
background, if you prefer. Imagine that you have just come
through the distressing experience brought to mind by the feeling
associated with your dream. Then think back to your previous
image of the younger version of yourself: imagine what you
looked like, what your facial expression may have been, how your
hair may have been cut, what clothes you might have been
wearing, and any other details which come to mind.

Now bring that self into your room. Place the younger self
by you on the bed or near your chair. Now be of what help you
can. What would you have liked some adult to have done for
you then? What advice would have benefitted you? What expression of concern would have assisted you? What type of affection
would have helped you move through the negative feelings
brought by this experience? What words and actions would have
made this a learning experience for you rather than an event
which initiated or reinforced a dysfunctional personal myth?

Once you have counseled your younger self, reach out to
embrace the child, adolescent, or infant you once were. Bring
that younger version of yourself into your present mind and body.
Do this slowly so you can feel all the positive assets of that child
becoming part of you. You have given your younger self the best
advice and love you could offer. Now imagine that your younger
self is giving you some gifts—childish glee, enthusiasm, creativity,
hope—that you can put to good use as an adult.

After a break, the participants recalled the images they evoked in portraying these chapters of their fairy tale. Justin's images were a round smiling sun and a dark, foreboding "X." The leader asked everyone to discuss these images again with their partners, in light of the day's exercises.

Justin explained that the sun was a symbol of what he wanted to be; the "X" represented the force preventing him from attaining his goals. Now, Justin added, the sun reminded him of his aunt who placed confidence in him to assist his cousin's healing. The "X" suggested his mother who had ridiculed him when he had apparently healed himself by resting in bed, reading comic books.

The leader asked the members to close their eyes and to imagine the two images coming closer and closer together, meeting, and transforming into a different image. He indicated this new image would reflect what happened during the day, and would indicate how each participant might work with his or her obstacle to growth. Group members were invited to draw the image on their personal shield.

Justin drew his new symbol on another sheet of paper. It was a palm tree, in roughly the same shape as the "X" but with the sun behind it, bringing it life and growth. He told his partner he was amazed by the depth of the imagery and the way it accurately reflected his central concerns. The warmth of the sun had taken the "X" and had given it life, just as the love he experienced through his life was strong enough to resurrect part of himself which had been stultified and which he had given up as dead.

The group was now ready for Chapter Three. The leader gave a brief introduction by telling how Justin's fairy tale insight ended:

Eventually, Prince Justin received a chariot of his own. He enjoyed driving the vehicle but soon learned it was not all fun and glory. The horses had to be fed and cared for. Sometimes, one would rebel and have to be disciplined. Sometimes the chariot wheel would become loose and would have to be repaired. Prince Justin also had

*to take chariot lessons before he could travel about the
kingdom. Nevertheless, he gradually was able to accomplish these tasks.*

Justin told his version of the story to his partner. The final
space upon his shield was filled by a golden wheel. Justin said
it represented the cycles of trial and error, defeat and success,
challenge and mastery which were part of his quest.

Justin's day at the workshop was drawing to an end. He had
finished a morning and an afternoon session, and started the
evening program: The group leader observed,

*You have been learning a process for intervening in the
development of your own personal mythology. Ordinarily, it develops without your help but today you have
learned how to take more conscious control.*

> *Psychotherapists have their own models of develop-
ment and change. If you see a behavioral therapist, the
prevalent model will be that people help themselves by
learning how to control their behavior. In psychoanalysis,
the predominant model is that understanding your behavior will lead to change. Until the 1950's, control and
understanding were the two basic therapeutic orientations, often in conflict with each other. When humanistic
psychologists began to influence psychotherapy, the
growth perspective became popular. It was felt that a
seed can grow in one's psyche toward self-actualization;
hence conscious nurturance by self and others can help
one's development. A decade later, transpersonal
psychology emerged. In the transpersonal model, the
context is one-ness of humanity and one-ness of the
universe; from that context we can understand our inter-
connectedness with all life and existence. A word expressing this connectedness is love, and it is love that can
assist development and change behavior.*

> *I am going to suggest that we use the personal
model of love at this point in our workshop. Sometimes,*

participants will see that an old myth is destructive and will want to kill it. What we will attempt instead is to find tools and techniques based on love to change our behavior, in a less violent, less narrow context. A clear example of this is the exercise in which we reclaimed our younger self, and extended love towards him or her to that part of us which became directed toward an unhealthy myth.

Justin responded strongly to this idea, mentioning to his partner that the workshop might be summarized by the phrase, "The broadest context is love."

The workshop leader continued:

Relax, close your eyes, and remember a time when you felt loved. If you can not recall such a time, simply construct or invent such a time. Now open your eyes, and sit facing your partner, allowing that love to emanate from you. Take your partner's hands and squeeze them, allowing that squeeze to intensify the love you feel. Be aware of your power to take the love you feel internally and direct it to your partner externally.

Justin described coming out of the exercise as if he were emerging from a deep sleep. He told his partner that, for him, the "loving context" he remembered took place when he was about twelve. He recalled, "My mother's sister asked me to heal her daughter who was ill with a cold. My aunt asked me to take a copy of *Science and Health*, the textbook of Christian Science by Mary Baker Eddy, to my cousin's bedroom. Just for good measure, I was instructed to take the *Bible* along as well, to heal her. I do not recall if my efforts aided my cousin's recovery, but I felt truly loved because my aunt relied on me so strongly to be of service." Justin was surprised when he considered how much of an impact that experience had upon him.

The leader led a final exercise. He suggested that each participant condense their myth into one sentence, then think of the first available opportunity to put it into practice, fantasizing the activity. When Justin finished this exercise, he told his partner:

I'm going to let my light shine. And I'm going to let the sun shine in. I will take obstacles like the dark "X" and shine on them. I will transform them into beautiful palm trees and will enjoy watching them grow. I will shine as much as I can, as often as I can, and not worry about how being an alchemist looks on my resume. If my light can turn base metals into gold, I don't care who knows about it. I'll be very proud of the fact myself.

Tomorrow I will be seeing the parents of one of my clients in school. Their son is overly active—hyperkinetic—and the physicians have been giving him drugs over the years. Sometimes the drugs don't seem to help at all. At other times, the drugs slow him down, but more often than not they put him to sleep or make him so drowsy he can't learn very well in the classroom. His parents want to take him to a therapist who specializes in vitamin supplements and in changing his diet. Ordinarily, I would advise against this, more to protect my own reputation than to aid the child. I know the literature on hyperkinetic children, and nutrition is no panacea. But sometimes it seems to help, and this may be one of those times. At least it will give the parents a choice for which they show some enthusiasm, and perhaps the enthusiasm will be contagious. So, in my fantasy I resolved not to let the voice of my childhood physician drown out my intuitive hunches when I talk with the parents. On the other hand, I remained reasonably skeptical in my fantasy and asked the parents to keep me posted on any changes, one way or the other, they notice in their son's behavior once he goes on the new diet and takes the vitamins.

This week I am going to be extra sensitive to the responsibility issue. If someone asks me to do something which I really do not want to do, and which is not my responsibility, I am going to feel free to say "no." I'm not going to agree, and then mess up as a way to get out of it—or to do the job so poorly that I'll never be asked again. I must realize that the choice is mine. Just because somebody else wants me to take charge doesn't mean it's right for me.

When I choose a role to play as me, I'm going to live it whole-heartedly, openly, and honestly. In other words, I'm going to keep the chariot on the right track. If I decide I don't want to be a chariot driver eight hours a day, I'll just take it back—in one piece—and tell them to find someone else to drive it. But I won't run the chariot off the road and let myself evade responsibility in that matter.

Justin and his partner decided to keep in touch with each other. A week later, they spoke on the telephone to compare notes about their resolutions. And five months after the workshop, Justin's partner received a letter from him. He wrote about how the young prince had started to grow up. He described his latest dream, "I drove a city bus through town, around curves, and even up and down a hill. I got safely back to the main street again, and woke up with the feeling that I could do anything. Well, just about anything!" This account summarizes Justin's exploration of his personal myths—and the beginning of your own series of exercises.

Your Personal Shield

Studies of how people develop as adults provide a map for understanding the mythological conflicts likely to emerge throughout life. Erik Erikson's (1963, chapter 7) classic formulation of the stages of human development and more recent empirical studies of the patterns of psychosocial growth (e.g., Levinson, 1978) both point toward the tasks which characterize each developmental stage. The underlying personal myths and the counter-myths emerging within each period set the stage for the individual's developmental drama.

You might ask how to initiate a journey similar to Justin's. The number of dream seminars, personal mythology workshops, and ongoing personal development groups are increasing. Not all are of equal quality and some can be dangerous if the leader is not well-trained and well-qualified. Do not hesitate to inspect the leader's credentials before you enroll. It is also wise to speak to someone who has worked previously with the leader.

One important resource is the *Dream Network Bulletin.* It lists dream courses and workshops given by its subscribers as well as articles, book reviews, and pertinent information. Another resource is the Association for the Study of Dreams, which has several publications and an annual convention. Information about both the bulletin and the association is available from Dr. R. L. Van de Castle, 6 East, Blue Ridge Hospital, Charlottesville, Virginia 22901. Another set of resources are the books about dreams we have described which contain suggested exercises. The book *Personal Mythology* (Feinstein & Krippner, 1987) takes readers through a step-by-step process, helping them contact their personal myths and change those which have become dysfunctional. The exercises in *Personal Mythology,* as is true of the exercises in this book, follow guidelines for self-help books described by G. M. Rosen (1981) in *Contemporary Psychology.* For example, in addition to extensive experience in testing the book's exercises in face-to-face settings, Rosen suggests that several people serve as subjects for refining and validating the self-guided format. It is also important to balance one's statements of what is believed to be possible with appropriate cautions about the limitations of a self-help format and the dilemmas involved in working with deep levels of the human psyche.

One of the valuable exercises attempted by Justin involved creating a personal shield. This was inspired by practices in Native American cultures and their use of personal shields, totem poles, medicine wheels, and sand paintings. All depict images which have profound meaning for the individual or tribe. Many times these images occur in dreams, on vision quests, during purification ceremonies in sweat lodges, or during periods of fasting. This shield also serves some functions similar to those of the Coat of Arms which has been used for centuries by European nobility. Each Coat of Arms symbolically represents family heritage as well as important events in their history.

Perhaps the simplest way to construct your personal shield is to take a large paper plate or other symmetrical form on which you can write. Select a variety of crayons or felt-tipped pens. Whatever your choice, the artistic material should allow you to express yourself in color because you may discover that certain colors allow you to convey feelings of which you may not be consciously aware. Divide your shield into four sections with your marker or in your imagination. Place a symbol for Chapter One on one section, a symbol for Chapter Two on the second, a symbol for the conflict between them on the third, and a symbol for Chapter Three on the fourth.

Drawing the symbols on a shield is only one way to conduct this exercise. Some people would rather mold the symbols from clay, preferring more direct contact between the feelings in their body and the medium of expression. Others have played with music or sung into a tape recorder, portraying the four aspects of their life through sound. As is true throughout the book, we urge you to adapt, change, and revise the exercises in any way which will make them more useful to you in uncovering your personal mythology.

When you begin placing designs on your shield, try not to be overly critical of your talent. Allow the design to flow through the crayon, pen, or marker with a minimum of effort. We know that sometimes people become self-conscious about their artwork by overlaying their efforts with a myth which is characterized by certain judgements about what is esthetic or "correct." Sometimes it is an advantage *not* to be especially artistic when performing this exercise. Concentrating on the style or technique of the drawing may interfere with your ability to allow the unconscious to express itself through your fingers.

Your shield is a map symbolizing many aspects of your personal mythology. You may wish to display your shield in a special place so you can have an ongoing dialogue with this representation of your mythology. You may also, from time to time, wish to add a new symbol to it. You may reach a point where the shield seems outdated. We encourage you to draw a new shield at that time to replace the old shield.

Riding a Feeling Back in Time

You have witnessed how Justin began to uncover areas of mythic conflict. Your journey could begin with a dream. Look through your dream notebook and locate a dream that involved conflict or an unpleasant feeling. The exercise you will undertake with this dream (from Feinstein & Krippner, in press) involves directions you can read to yourself, have someone read for you, or tape record so you can turn the instructions off if you want to proceed in a more leisurely manner. You can undertake these activities alone, with a partner, or in a small group.

This exercise begins with laying down on the floor, propping your back up on a bed, or sitting in a comfortable chair. Some people have learned relaxation techniques, meditation, or self-hypnosis and already know how to reach such states. But even without this preparation, you will find it easy to turn inward and relax deeply simply by finding a comfortable position and following the instructions.

Some people prefer to have soft inspirational music in the background during an exercise of this nature. Participants in our workshops have particularly enjoyed various tapes of classical music as well as the more contemporary flute music of Paul Horn, the harp of Georgia Kelley, the works of Michael Jones or Steven Halpern, and various other recordings, e.g., "Tibetan Bells" and "Golden Voyage." While background music is not necessary, you might wish to experiment with it. If you are making a tape with the words that begin in the following paragraph, you might also find it useful to experiment a bit to get the right tone and tempo for you.

> Now that you have identified a dream, fantasy, evocative picture, or area of conflict associated with an unpleasant emotion, allow yourself to turn inward. Take a deep breath and as you exhale allow yourself to sink more comfortably into the place where you are sitting or lying. Permit yourself to go deeper into relaxation with each breath.

Now point your toes and feet toward your head and hold with some pressure at the toes and ankle. Hold ONE, TWO, THREE, FOUR, FIVE, and RELEASE. Allow any tension or "stale energy" to drain from the lower part of your body and out your toes as if your toes were spigots. See and feel the tension draining out of your toes. Again, point your toes and feet toward your head and hold ONE, TWO, THREE, FOUR, FIVE, and RE-LEASE. Pull your fingers and wrists backward and hold ONE, TWO, THREE, FOUR, FIVE, and RELEASE. Allow any tension or stale energy to drain from the upper part of your body and out your fingers as if they were spigots. See and feel the tension draining out of your fingers. Again, pull your fingers and wrists backward and hold ONE, TWO, THREE, FOUR, FIVE, and RELEASE. As you continue to breathe deeply, be aware that with each inhalation you are taking in the fresh soothing energy of oxygen in the air, and with each exhalation, you allow any remaining tensions to drain from your body.

Bring the dream fantasy picture or conflict to mind and concentrate upon the feeling it brings to you. If there is more than one feeling, concentrate on the one that is the most uncomfortable, the one you experience as being the most negative. Focus upon this feeling and notice in which part of your body you experience it. Does the negative emotion affect your stomach? Your back? Your heartbeat? As you allow the feeling to permeate your consciousness, observe the way that your body reacts to it.

What name could you give to this emotion? Is it loneliness? Despair? Frustration? Rage? Confusion? Irri-tation? Hostility? Jealousy? Find a word that applies to the feeling. Does this name adequately describe the feel-ing? Allow the word and the emotion to meet and see if they "fit" together. If not, try another word. Match the word with the body sensations. Reflect on how they do or do not match each other. Keep doing this until you have a word expressing the emotional feeling fairly accurately.

Take this feeling back in time. Where have you had it before? Maybe you recall having had it very recently. That's a starting point. Now take it back to your adolescence, to your childhood; you may even be able to take it back to your infancy. Take it back to the first time you had this feeling or the first time you might have had the feeling. If you're not sure, go along in your imagination. Imagine what you might have been doing when you first had the feeling. How old were you? What did you look like? What were you wearing? Who, if anyone, was with you? Where were you? What were the surroundings? What sights, sounds, tastes, or smells do you associate with the event? What brought about the feeling? You are putting the emotion into an earlier context. Recall or imagine as many details of that earlier time as you can.

Now reflect on some decisions you might have made as a result of this experience and others like it. What conclusions did you come to about yourself and your world? What rules of conduct did you adopt? Do they still work for you? What attitudes toward other people began to emerge? What views of the world? What philosophy of life? Of this, what has proven to be valuable? What has not worked for you?

Now imagine yourself speaking to this younger version of yourself. Tell that earlier self something that might have been valuable for you to know back then. You might find a conversation developing between yourself and this younger person. Often people will find themselves spontaneously embracing this image of their younger self. Allow whatever emerges to happen during the following pause. (Leave 30 seconds of silence here.)

Now it is time to return to your ordinary state of consciousness. You will be able to recall all you need of this experience. Count to five along with the tape. When you reach five you will be alert and refreshed as if awakening from a wonderful nap. ONE, starting to come up now. TWO, wiggling your toes and feet. THREE, moving your fingers and hands. FOUR, stretching your body comfortably. And FIVE, opening your eyes, wide awake.

Having completed this process, open your notebook and write down a summary of the experience: 1) What was your initial dream, fantasy, picture, or conflict? 2) What was the negative emotion or unpleasant feeling it evoked? 3) Describe the scene you went back to in as much detail as you can recall. 4) What rules of behavior and codes of conduct did you adopt based on experiences such as the one to which you returned? 5) What attitudes toward people, what views of the world, what philosophy of life began to emerge with such experiences? 6) Are these rules, codes, attitudes, views, and philosophy related to your initial dream, fantasy, picture, or conflict? 7) How do they affect your present life, are there ways they have become out of date? If you are working with a partner or a group, you may share as much of this as you wish.

The answers will reveal many qualities of a personal myth you might have developed early in life. For example, some people recall unpleasant experiences with one or both of their parents which are associated with their emotion. As a result of those experiences they might realize they decided never to attempt anything which could possibly risk losing their parents' love and approval. Or, they might have decided that they would never do anything again which would require them to trust their parents. Or, perhaps as a result of that experience they decided they had to remain dependent on someone. Or perhaps they adopted the opposite posture, that they would never be dependent on anyone again. Some people in our workshops have expressed these attitudes and values with such phrases as: "People cannot be trusted." "I am a weak and dependent person." "The world is a jungle." "I am not worthy of love or attention."

In some cases, the myth you adopted long ago may still be serving you well. In other instances, the old myth may no longer be influencing you, even though it was quite powerful at one time. More frequently, however, the myth identified in this exercise has in some way become dysfunctional and is interfering with your further development though it may have at one time solved real problems. One woman we worked with had at an early age developed the belief that people are undependable. The overall effect of this position, was, for her, a positive one. She became very self-reliant and confident in her abilities to attain her goals. As the years went by, she also amassed a backlog of experience, suggesting that some people are quite dependable, despite her reluctance to trust them. But she had not completely revised her belief until the self-contradiction was plainly laid out for her during an exercise similar to the one you just completed. As a result, she was able to begin to receive far more from those in her life than she ever had, and her relationships improved substantially. At the same time she was able to maintain the self-reliance which sustained her as she was growing up.

We have noticed some common patterns from observing the individuals who have used this exercise. People quite reliably go back to an experience which leads them to identify an area of their personal mythology that is in some way out of date and in conflict with a new myth emerging for them. They may not, however, be aware of the new myth. Of course, each person will in some respects respond differently to every exercise in this book. By monitoring your reactions, thinking through any new realizations or discoveries, and adapting our comments to your individual needs, you will be able to identify an old myth that will be of value for you to know about because it is in conflict with some of your current needs and growth directions.

You may also conduct this exercise with other areas of dream content. You can ride a dream character back in time, or a setting, or a color, or an activity. This exercise is a helpful one to attempt the understanding of any puzzling image you can not seem to fathom in any other way.

We have found this exercise to be extremely potent, and while you may use it over and over in different situations, many other methods also exist for uncovering mythic conflict. Sometimes mythic conflicts outside your awareness may be somaticized; that is, they may become physical illnesses ranging from colds or rashes to more serious conditions. Shifting the burden of awareness from the physical level to the conscious level sometimes frees the body from needing to symbolize a mythic conflict at its own expense.

As your understanding grows of how conflicting myths operate in your life, you will be able to devise other approaches for identifying underlying conflicts that may need to be resolved. For instance, after some practice with the imagery technique presented in this chapter, you will find that by simply attending to areas of discomfort and confusion in your life, you will sometimes gain an immediate intuitive grasp of the mythic dimensions of the conflict. You may extend that awareness by developing ways to connect present feelings to past experiences as in the technique emphasized above. You might also want to attempt some of the other exercises Justin and his group used in creating their three chapter fairy tales. But even without this type of extension, riding a dream image back into time can be a useful procedure.

Aurora and Marcel

Aurora and Marcel were two members of Justin's workshop. Both rode their dreams back in time with surprising results. Aurora, a teacher, recalled her dream:

I dreamed about the lumps in my left breast. I entered the breast, attempting to clean away the tumors. They were large stones and I lifted them up and over the rim of a chute, getting help from someone as the lifting distance became greater. I was finally able to clear out the bottom. There I found a small tunnel which, upon inspection, led around and up into my heart. My heart was filled with black blood clots, and was tightly clenched with angry energy.

Aurora told her partner she actually did have benign growths in her breast, but had been ignoring them and their possible significance. She focused upon her feeling from the dream; they seemed localized across her right hip and her buttocks as well as in her chest. She found that the word "rage" best expressed these feelings. After she went into time, she reported:

I have a sense of being very young and being slapped around. My throat is contracting and I feel myself wanting to vomit even though I feel no nausea. I am very angry at whoever is slapping me. It is not my parents but it might be the baby sitter. I keep thinking "No one can help me. I have to put up with it. I have to do it. I have to make it all alone. Just me."

For many years, Aurora suspected she had been a physically abused child. This exercise reinforced that belief and led her to explore the possible association between her pent-up rage and the lumps in her breast. She resolved to work through this issue before the lumps grew larger or became malignant. She also suspected that this rage prevented her from allowing herself to receive care, since a person from whom she was supposed to have received care quite possibly abused her. Aurora entered psychotherapy to work with these issues in greater depth, realizing that ignoring them might be physically as well as emotionally hazardous.

Marcel, a psychotherapist, related his dream:

I see a snake coiled on a rock under a rain cloud. It moves through large round boulders as I try to climb them. When I go the wrong way or don't know which way to go, the snake jumps up and bites my shirt sleeve, pulling me along. I ask the snake where we are going. The snake says, "I am calling you to heal." I am apprehensive about the snake's message, suspecting the snake is correct but being afraid of the risks involved.

Marcel focused upon his feeling from the dream, observing it constricted his breathing and increased his bodily tension. The word "fear" seemed the most appropriate description. Riding it back in time, he had an unusual experience:

> *I was five or six years of age, playing in a yard down the block and across the street from our house. I was supposed to be home at 5:00 P.M. but was so engrossed in enjoying my activities that I lost track of time. So I walked to the street and rush hour traffic had already started. There is a long procession of cars and I instantly became frightened and scared. I thought that I would never get home and began to cry. Then a tramp appeared. He was scraggly-faced with a battered and a long, funny-smelling coat. He asked me if I wanted to cross the street. I had always been told that tramps were no good—that they would hurt me or even steal me, and that under all circumstances I must stay away from them. So when the tramp appeared, my fear increased. I thought to myself, "If I tell the tramp to go away, I will never get across the street and he will steal me. But if I ask him for help he will steal me anyway!" So I nodded my head in assent and the tramp took my hand and slowly led me across the street. He held up his other hand to stop the cars and we made it safely to the other side. When we reached the other side, I was sure he would take me with him. But he let my hand go and waved goodbye. I ran home still crying and full of fear, but now the fear felt different.*

Marcel told his partner, "When I went through this exercise, I realized my feelings changed from fear to anger. My parents had lied to me! That experience with the tramp had cracked my reality. What should I trust, my training or my experience? I knew that *some* tramps were bad people because I had seen them kick animals, but I realized that one cannot judge a book by its cover."

Marcel engaged in dreamwork, equating his parents with the powerful social institutions that scorned non-traditional healers, and the snake with the tramp who had demonstrated the fallacy of conventional stereotypes. Marcel had always disliked snakes, so was suspicious of the snake's call in his dream. Nevertheless, he began to read widely on the topic of unconventional healing, and to take courses on the topic led by psychotherapists and nurses who engaged in laying-on of hands, visualization, prayer, and meditation. Eventually he began to incorporate some of these approaches into his psychotherapeutic practice.

Both Aurora and Marcel went through the entire series of exercises Justin had experienced, and in both instances, decisions were made that initiated new developments in Aurora's personal life and in Marcel's professional life. As you work with your dreams, you will become aware of many new capacities and opportunities. By using your dreams for creative problem solving you may also be able to increase your options and encounter new ways of thinking, feeling, and behaving that will enrich your life and actualize your potentials.